Building Findable Websites

Web Standards, SEO, and Beyond

Building Findable Websites: Web Standards, SEO, and Beyond

Aarron Walter

New Riders
1249 Eighth Street
Berkeley, CA 94710
510/524-2178
510/524-2221 (fax)

Find us on the Web at: www.newriders.com
To report errors, please send a note to errata@peachpit.com

New Riders is an imprint of Peachpit, a division of Pearson Education

Project Editor: Michael J. Nolan
Development Editor: Box Twelve Communications, Inc.
Production Editor: Kate Reber
Technical Editor: Jonathan Snook
Proofreader: Doug Adrianson
Indexer: FireCrystal Communications
Interior design: Charlene Charles-Will, Bumpy Design
Cover design: Charlene Charles-Will
Compositor: Bumpy Design

ISBN 13: 978-0-321-52628-1
ISBN 10: 0-321-52628-7

9 8 7 6 5 4 3 2

Printed and bound in the United States of America

For Jamie

Acknowledgments

It's good to have people on your side, especially when you're facing big challenges. I had some wonderful people helping me out and cheering me on before, during, and after this process to whom I owe my humble thanks.

Many thanks to acquisitions editor Michael Nolan for giving me the opportunity to share my thoughts on this subject and convincing the great folks at Peachpit Press to give this book a shot.

Thanks to my development editor Jeff Riley for helpful writing advice, entertaining email exchanges, and helping me beat the comma into submission. Thanks also to my technical editor Jonathan Snook for expert advice on all the code and techy stuff within this book. You're a master of your craft, and I'm grateful to have had your guidance.

Thanks to Glenn Bisignani for pointing me towards a title for this book that best communicates the contents within, and for wisely persuading me away from the one that didn't.

Thanks to production editor Kate Reber for her sharp eye, and to designer Charlene Will for her aesthetic talents.

Many thanks to my brilliant colleagues and students at The Art Institute of Atlanta who have always kept me on my toes, curious, and inspired. Dr. Ameeta Jadav, my department chair, mentor, and friend, gave me guidance as I prepared to write this book, and much support along the way for which I am grateful. My Senior Project class gave me valuable feedback on the table of contents before a single page was written. Thanks guys.

On an almost daily basis my mother and father-in-law kept me fed with home cooked meals that were a delight and a much needed, kind gesture of support. Thanks Jim and Linda for your unparalleled catering skills.

My mom and dad have given me constant support and encouragement all my life and have always made me feel confident, capable, and loved. These gifts are the most valuable a person can give, and I'm grateful.

My wife Jamie is an amazing person. As I wrote this book she tolerated my distracted mind, put up with my neglected domestic duties, and excused my frequent absences. Through it all she never stopped cheering me on like a dedicated track coach, always making me feel like the finish line was reachable if only I put one foot in front of the other. What a lucky guy I am! I love you, Jamie, and I wrote this book for you. Maybe I'll read it to you at night when you're having trouble sleeping.

Finally, I'd like to give a big shout out to my little chipmunk friend outside my office window that has kept me company while writing this book. I sure hope Toots and Colonel Sanders don't eat you for lunch.

Contents

Preface xiii
The Companion Website xiv

Chapter 1 Introducing Findability 1

What Is Findability? 2
The Development Side of Findability 3
The Deepest Desires of Search Engines 4
Beyond Search Engine Optimization 6
Get Your Team on Board from the Start 6
Using Your Moral Compass To Guide Your Way 8

Chapter 2 Markup Strategies 11

A Web Standards Primer 12
Getting Started with Web Standards 13
The Benefits of Web Standards 15
Web Standards and Findability Sitting in a Tree... 16
An Issue of Semantics 17
Will Search Engines Really Reward Adherence to Web Standards? 19
Essential Tags that Promote Findability 20
The Myth of Meta: The Good, the Bad, and the Ugly. 24
Preventing Content Indexing 26
Let Go of the Past To Embrace a Findable Future. 28
Accessible Content Is Findable Content. 29
Making Images Visible 30
Clearing the Roadblocks Caused by Image Maps 32
Image Replacement: Accessibility, Findability, and Beauty Converge 33
The Right and Wrong Way To Use Tables 35
More Keyword Opportunities in Accessibility Related Elements 36
Accessibility Pitfalls that Hinder Indexing 37
The Findability Benefits of Microformats. 37
Making Event Data Portable with hCalendar and hCard. . . . 38
Marking Up Your Contact Information with hCard 42
Tagging Content with rel-tag 43
More Microformats Worth Investigating 44
Using Icons To Point Out Microformat Content 45
Do Search Engines Recognize Microformat Content? 46

Chapter 3 **Server-Side Strategies** 49

File and Folders: The Power of a Name 50

Choosing and Managing Domain Names 51
Solving the Google Canonical Problem 52

Building Search Engine Friendly URLs 54
A Simple Solution 55

Moving Pages and Domains with 301 Redirects 58

Getting Users Back on Track with Custom 404 Pages 60
The Elements of a Successful 404 Page 61

Optimizing Performance for Efficient Indexing 64
Cache and Dash: Getting Clients To Cache Files 64
Managing File Size 69
Compressing Files with Gzip 71
Reducing HTTP Requests 74
Diagnosing Performance Problems with YSlow 75

Controlling Search Engine Indexing with Robots.txt 76

Chapter 4 **Creating Content that Drives Traffic** 79

Content that Sucks (Users In) 80
The Story of Tom 80

Content Karma 82
Blueprint CSS Framework 82
Open Content Generates Attribution 83

The Mark of Quality Content 84
Stay on Topic 85
Fill a Niche 85
Be Passionate and Authoritative 86
Be Trustworthy 86
Appeal to Your Audience's Interests 88
Be Original 89
Use an Appropriate Voice 90
Keep It Coming 90

All Roads Lead to Content 91

Content of Many Flavors 93
Blogs 93
Articles, Case Studies, and White Papers 94
Link Libraries 96
Document Templates, Code Examples, and Other Tools . . . 96
Reviews and Recommendations 96
Syndicated Content (RSS) 98
User-Generated Content (UGC) 98

Targeting Keywords in Your Content 100
Researching and Selecting Keywords 100
Placing Keywords in Your Content 105
Evaluating Keyword Density. 106
Content Development Strategies 107
Displaying RSS Content on Your Site 107
More RSS Parsing Opportunities 115
Using the RSS Parsing System To Create a Link Library . . .117

Chapter 5 Building a Findable Blog **123**

Blogging Best Practices To Improve Findability 124
Write Regularly on a Focused Topic 125
Link Often, and Link to Other Blog Posts To Generate Trackbacks 125
Create Your Own Blog Template 125
Put Keywords in Your Post Titles 126
Archive by Topics 127
Summarize Posts To Direct Traffic Better 128
Add a Popular Posts Section 129
Add a Recent Posts Section 129
Tell People Who You Are and What Your Blog Is About . . 130
Promote Your RSS Feed. 130
Cross Link To Circulate Traffic 131
Encourage Users To Share Your Content With Others . . . 131
Direct Users to Related Posts 132
About Duplicate Content Indexing 132
Working with WordPress 134
Installing WordPress Plugins 135
Creating Your Own Themes 135
Making Your WordPress Blog More Findable 136
Defining Update Services 136
Remapping Your Permalink URLs 138
Using Categories To Archive by Topic 140
Summarizing Posts To Direct Traffic Better. 140
Displaying Your Most Popular Posts 141
Displaying Your Most Recent Posts 143
Promoting and Tracking RSS Subscriptions with FeedBurner 144
Encouraging Social Exchanges of Your Content 144
Displaying Related Posts 145
Automatically Generating an XML Sitemap. 146
Other Handy SEO Plugins for WordPress 146
Tagging Your Posts 147
Optimizing Content Delivery with Caching 149

Chapter 6 Adding Search to Your Site 151

Using Free Search Systems. . . . 153
Using Google Custom Search Engine (CSE) . . . 153
Using Google's Ajax Search API . . . 159
Using Rollyo. . . . 165
Using Atomz. . . . 167
Using Yahoo! Search Builder . . . 168

Purchasing Search Systems . . . 170
Using FastFind . . . 170
Using Zoom Search Engine. . . . 171

Building Your Own Simple Product Search System . . . 173
Creating a Custom Product Search Tool . . . 173
Logging Local Searches To Understand Your Site's Shortcomings . . . 176

Adding OpenSearch To Your Site . . . 176
Setting Up OpenSearch on Your Site . . . 177

Chapter 7 Preventing Findability Roadblocks 179

Avoiding JavaScript Pitfalls . . . 180

Progressive Enhancement . . . 181
Solving JavaScript Navigation Problems. . . . 182
Solving Scripted Style Problems . . . 183
Solving Ajax Problems . . . 189

Findable Flash . . . 198
Using SWFObject for Flash Progressive Enhancement . . 201

Findable Audio and Video . . . 207
Creating Text Transcripts . . . 208

Chapter 8 Bring Traffic Back With a Mailing List 213

Encouraging Subscriptions . . . 214
Earn Their Trust . . . 214
Make It Obvious . . . 215
Make It Quick . . . 216
Tell Them What To Expect and Make It Valuable . . . 216

Using a Mailing List Management System . . . 218
Why Use a Mailing List Management System?. . . . 218

Building an Ajax-Powered Subscription System . . . 220
Monkeying Around with MailChimp . . . 220
Sign Me Up! The Big Picture of the System . . . 222
Creating the Subscription Form . . . 223
Building the storeAddress() Function . . . 225
The Ajax Layer . . . 229

Chapter 9 Putting Findability Into Practice **233**

A Prioritized Approach 234
Priority 1 234
Priority 2 235
Priority 3 235

Discovering Problems on Your Site 235
Sitening SEO Tools 236
Spam Detector 236
Semantics Extractor 236
Keyword Priority and Density Evaluation. 236
Watch Your Stats 236

When Will You See Results? 237

Final Notes: The Day Findability Saved the World. 238

Index 240

Preface

Is this the right book for you?

Although this book is written with developers in mind, it's really a guide for all who plan, design, and build websites. The Web is a vast wilderness in which a message runs the great risk of fading into obscurity. Your creative ideas, and talent deserve more.

The findability strategies outlined in this book are designed to help you deliver your message more intelligently so that you might reach your intended audience and beyond. Each chapter introduces core principles and best practices, which are accompanied by practical code examples that can be applied to any project to overcome findability pitfalls.

Web standards are the foundation of the concepts and examples in this book, but you'll find that findability extends beyond code. Findability is as much about what we say as it is how we say it. As you'll soon discover, search engine optimization via web standards will attract traffic, but it's quality content that captivates and captures an audience.

If you're a web standards guru often struggling to help colleagues and clients see the light, you'll find the concepts and examples in this book of interest. Search engine optimization and general findability are the most compelling arguments for web standards best practices, as they speak to the bottom line.

web standards = improved search traffic = more successful sites

If you're just getting started in the world of standards development you'll find a primer that will introduce you to the core principles and how it fits into your professional practice.

As the title of this book suggests, you'll find plenty of discussion of search engine optimization here, but findability is a multifaceted subject in which SEO is but a piece. Upon reading this book you'll have a complete picture of how a holistic approach to building websites using web standards will not only make your sites more search engine friendly, but they'll be more successful!

The Companion Website

The companion website (**http://buildingfindablewebsites.com**) contains all of the code examples included in this book, useful resources, tools that will help you in your findability endeavors, and bonus chapters on the following five topics:

- Free Search Engine Tools and Services
- Building Viral Marketing Tools
- Places to Promote Your Site
- Analyzing Your Traffic
- Black Hat SEO Techniques to Avoid

As technology and concepts evolve in the world of findability, I'll be sure to share with you any new developments I discover via the companion site's blog.

Your feedback on this book and unique knowledge of the subjects within are gratefully welcomed. You may get in touch with me via the companion website.

1

Introducing Findability

You've heard of SEO, but have you heard of findability?

You may have designed an exceptionally creative website, written compelling content, or developed a useful Web application. But if your work cannot be located by your target audience, it's all for naught. After all, we can't appreciate what we can't find.

What Is Findability?

Search engine optimization, also known as *SEO*, can help people find that brilliant website you've created. Although you can certainly manipulate your code and your content to increase your chances of receiving traffic from search engines, there are other ways to direct traffic to a site. With millions of pages on the Web, contemporary websites need to help users find content using as many methods as possible. *Findability* is the broader discipline that unites all strategies to help your audience find what they seek.

In his 2005 book *Ambient Findability: What We Find Changes Who We Become*, Peter Morville popularized the term *findability*, defining it as:

> *"The quality of being located or navigated, the degree to which an object or piece of data can be located, and the degree to which a system supports navigation and retrieval."*

Morville's definition may spark associations with information architecture, usability, and search engine optimization. Although all of these disciplines play important roles, findability can actually be found throughout the Web project lifecycle, creating a common thread that can unite every facet of the Web planning, design, and development process and all team members involved.

As shown in **FIGURE 1.1**, findability is present in

- Information architecture
- Development
- Marketing
- Copywriting
- Design
- Search engine optimization (SEO)
- Accessibility
- Usability

FIGURE 1.1 *Findability bleeds into all sub-disciplines of the Web industry.*

We discover findability in all of the major disciplines that make up the Web. So often freelancers and members of smaller Web teams end up wearing a number of different hats–doing the work of an information architect, designer, developer, and more. Whether you find yourself handling strictly Web development or being the jack-of-all-trades on projects, it's important to think about findability at every step of the way so you can ensure the success of your site for both users and the client.

The Development Side of Findability

As developers, we have three primary goals in making websites findable:

1. Help people find your website.
2. Help people find what they are looking for once they arrive at your site.
3. Bring your audience back to your website.

Developers can make a tremendous impact on the findability of a website. The way a site is built is one of the most significant factors in how it draws search engine traffic, and keeps people browsing longer. How we write our markup, set up the server, and integrate content–and the plethora of powerful tools we are able to leverage or build–can bring in volumes of traffic and help users find exactly what they're looking for once they've arrived at the site.

Traditionally, findability has been the domain of marketing experts and information architects, both of whom have a lot to contribute to the initiative. But, if developers are not informed and involved in the findability process, many opportunities to make the site successful can and will be overlooked. Simple missteps in coding alone make a site less visible or completely invisible to search engines.

It's the developer's job to keep his team aware of best practices and emerging technologies that could help make a site more findable. Accessibility, Web standards, microformats, search systems, RSS feeds, XML sitemaps, and APIs are all powerful tools that only a developer is likely to be aware of and understand their benefits to a project. The goal of this book is to provide a broad range of strategies, tools, and examples that will get you up to speed on how you can make sure that any site you build will be findable.

The Deepest Desires of Search Engines

SEO is an important part of the many strategies we'll explore in this book to promote findability. The success of SEO depends on your understanding of what search engines like. In no particular order, here are a few important things to keep in mind as you develop sites.

Search engines like

- Content that is naturally keyword rich (not stuffed) and valuable to readers
- Content that is visible to search engine spiders with no barriers that may prevent a full indexing of pages
- Content that communicates a clear information hierarchy so spiders can understand what the page is about
- Content that loads quickly so spiders can index it efficiently
- Links to your site from reputable sources so they can determine the reputation of your site
- Honest content that isn't trying to trick the search engine

- More content than code to mark up the page
- Clean, meaningful URLs with keywords in them if possible
- Domains that have been around for a while

There's a lot of logic in what the search engines are asking of us. They just want us to give them plenty of honest, high quality content in a format that they can read. As we move towards this goal, we are going to reap additional benefits, too.

For example, following accessibility standards not only broadens your audience to include users with disabilities and those on alternate devices (such as handhelds), it will also promote search engine optimization. Content in `alt` and `title` attributes—to name just a couple of elements that promote accessibility—provides more context and relevance for a search engine to understand what a page is about and can more accurately connect searchers with your page. Best practices for findability and accessibility often overlap.

People and search engines both appreciate great content. When people find useful content on a website, they tend to evangelize—creating links on their blog, links on user-generated news sites, and even discussing your content on discussion boards. Those inbound links to your site not only bring other people to your site, they boost your reputation with search engines. Search engines evaluate the reputation of a site based upon how many other reputable sites link to it. This means that when you provide your users with good content, you are also improving the findability of your site.

In his book *Designing with Web Standards*, Jeffrey Zeldman brilliantly outlines the many benefits users, businesses, and developers enjoy by following Web standards. Web standards development practices also provide great findability benefits by improving search engine optimization:

- They help you avoid code errors that could prevent search engines from understanding your content.
- They promote the practice of marking up your content in a semantically meaningful way (which search engines will better understand).
- They help reduce the volume of code required to deliver your content, creating a better content-to-code ratio and faster indexing.
- They foster best practices in coding that allow external code files to cache in the browser, speeding up the load time.

As we will see, Web standards—though not a silver bullet—are a great ally in our findability endeavors.

Accessibility, great content, and Web standards are just a fraction of the findability strategies we'll explore in this book. The common theme we'll discover along the way is that findability serves people as much as it serves search engines. When you improve findability, you improve the user experience.

Beyond Search Engine Optimization

Though SEO is essential to any findable site, there is still a lot more that is required in order to achieve the three primary goals previously mentioned. You can use viral marketing tools and mailing lists to drive traffic to the site. You can promote your site on popular design gallery sites, social networking platforms, and directories. Aside from driving traffic to a website, you can use search systems, sitemaps, and custom 404 pages to help your users find what they are looking for within your site. It's also important to analyze user behavior on the site so you can identify findability pitfalls. Many strategies must work in concert to make a site more findable.

It's important to note that findability is iterative. Vigilance and regular changes are required to dial in each piece of the puzzle to serve the common goals.

Get Your Team on Board from the Start

As we've seen already, there's a lot that you can do as a developer to make your site findable, but it doesn't rest entirely on your shoulders. It's important to make sure all of your team understands the value of findability and how they can contribute. If you are an independent freelancer doing the work of all or most of the members of a Web team, you probably don't have to lobby anyone to do their part. If you work in a firm, however, chances are you'll need to rally the troops. Here's how you might outline each team member's role in the findability initiative:

A **Project Manager** should speak to the client about the benefits of findability. It will make the client's site more successful and could potentially be a value-added service offered, which could make projects more profitable. Make sure findability is a priority for all team members.

An **Information Architect** should research user search behaviors and keywords relevant to the site's content. Be sure to name sections of the site with these keywords in order to drive search traffic. Create and share a keyword master list with the marketing specialist and copywriter so online advertisements and the site's content can feature the targeted terms. Consider including a site-wide search to assist users in finding what they want. What additional content could be added to the site (such as link libraries, case studies, or articles) that will drive more traffic? A *folksonomy*, or user-based tagging system of content, could be a powerful way of organizing site content that better matches users' search behaviors. The tags that users create might also serve as a tool to identify valuable target keywords that might have been overlooked by initial research.

A **Designer** should design pages that highlight search fields and mailing-list signup fields. High-quality design establishes credibility and increases the chances that users will stay once they've found the site. Great design can be showcased in popular online design galleries and competitions, which can drive thousands of visits daily. Make sure your designs show people where to look so they don't miss important content that is provided.

A **Copywriter** should ensure content includes target keywords that flow naturally. In other words, if keywords show up too often, search engines will think that the copy has been stuffed with terms in a dishonest effort to improve page rankings. *Keyword density* is the frequency of a keyword in a page. It's considered natural if the keyword density is seven percent or lower. Keywords should be included in the copy, but only where they would naturally fit. Search engine penalties are simply too great to risk stuffing content with keywords.

Usability Experts test and improve the usability of the site, which helps ensure users will find what they are looking for–which is a huge boon to findability. They should also evaluate how easy it is to find the site via search engines and check page rankings on target keywords. Traffic analysis tools can also provide very detailed information about user behavior on the website. Usability experts should use these tools to identify where people are getting lost, how long they are staying on particular pages, and how well the site design supports findability. Traffic analysis tools can provide valuable information that helps improve findability long after the launch of a site.

It's important that you share with your peers what you can do as a developer to build the site to be as findable as possible.

In short, findability should be on your mind throughout the planning, design, and development processes. Attempting to retrofit a completed site to be more findable is challenging and often yields poor results.

A common approach many large organizations take when building a major website is to plan and build the project, then have a search engine optimization company come in at the end and try to address a single aspect of making the site findable—often with little control over code, design, copywriting, usability, or content organization. Although certain things can be done to improve a site's findability after it has been built, you will find the job much easier and more effective if it is integrated into your process from the beginning. You'll likely find it considerably more cost effective, too, because you'll be leveraging in-house resources and talent rather than farming out the job to an expensive SEO company.

Once your team becomes educated on what they can do to help make the project more findable for your target audience, they will probably be very motivated to implement strategies. Everyone wants their work to be recognized and found to be useful, so they are likely to jump on board and do what they can to make the site successful.

Of course, clients will love you all the more if you have implemented a findability strategy into your process that helps them reach more people. By tracking the success of your findability plan, you can offer your clients concrete information about how broadly their message is being received and what kind of return they are getting on their investment. Selling your clients on findability is as simple as speaking to their bottom line!

Using Your Moral Compass To Guide Your Way

One central point that is hopefully crystal clear in this book is that findability should never be implemented at the detriment to the trust, privacy, or comfort of your audience. As you are implementing your findability strategy in your projects, always ask yourself:

> *"How would I feel if I were on the receiving end of this message?"*

If your answer is anything but 100 percent positive, then you should rethink what you are doing.

What Color Hat Do You Wear?

In old cowboy films you can always tell the good guys from the bad guys by the color of the hats they wear. The bad guys always wear black hats and the good guys sport white ones.

In the world of SEO, things aren't much different. *Black hat* describes dishonest SEO techniques used to dupe search engines. Best practices that respect the way search engines view Web pages are called *white hat*.

Search engines are privy to most black hat techniques these days. If your site is caught using black hat tricks, you'll be banned from all search listings. Needless to say, it's a good idea to stick with the white hat stuff that we'll be covering in this book rather than delving into the dark side. Otherwise, you may end up the loser in a search engine showdown. (Cue rolling tumbleweeds and distant whistling.) Check out the bonus chapter entitled "Black Hat SEO Techniques To Avoid" on this book's companion website at **http://buildingfindablewebsites.com** for more discussion on this topic.

If you've ever run or read a blog, chances are you've seen a lot of comment spam. SEO spammers often pollute blog comments with unrelated text simply so they can create a link from your site to theirs in order to boost their traffic and page ranking. In the process, they do a good job of annoying readers and the person running the blog. How would these spammers feel if we all went to their blogs and returned the favor? In their frenzy to improve the findability of their site, spammers compromise their reputation and the trust of users.

Treating your audience respectfully will help you stand out from the crowd every time. It will bring your audience back to your website as well as create evangelists who will pass on your message for you. This is far too powerful an asset to your organization to jeopardize your audience's trust by incessantly emailing them, tricking them into visiting your site using black hat SEO tricks, causing elements on a page to blink to solicit attention, or implementing any other technique that is less than honest.

Don't forget that search engines are an important part of your audience as well. They too will not appreciate being duped. If you are caught using black hat techniques like stuffing your pages with keywords, or cloaking text by setting it in the same color as the background, you could be banned from search results indefinitely. A notable example is the German BMW site, which was blacklisted by Google in February 2006 for using black hat SEO techniques. Being banned from a major search engine can crush online businesses.

NOTE For more information about the BMW blacklisting, see **http://news.bbc.co.uk/1/hi/technology/4685750.stm**.

2

Markup Strategies

Web standards, accessibility, and microformats work together to construct findable content that search engines and humans will love.

As we explore the many techniques and strategies in this book that can make your website more findable, we'll see a lot of overlap with best practices that make building sites more efficient while serving the needs of users. These best practices are called Web standards.

A Web Standards Primer

When Sir Tim Berners-Lee created the World Wide Web he recognized that, in order to survive, the Web needed publishing standards to protect the interoperability of its documents and ensure equal access to content for all users. In 1994 Berners-Lee established the *Word Wide Web Consortium* (*W3C*), an international contingency of experts on Web technologies that advocate the best practices for creating Web content. Specialized working groups within the W3C define standards for essential Web languages such as HTML, CSS, JavaScript, and XML, to name just a few.

The standards that the W3C creates help establish consistency in the way that Web documents are authored and how they are rendered in the browser. In the early years of the Web, browsers rendered pages in drastically different ways because they rarely followed any of the W3C's web standards for HTML, CSS, and JavaScript.

Frustrated Web developers spent countless hours building multiple versions of their sites to separately support the rendering quirks of Netscape and Internet Explorer. Many developers gave up on cross-browser support and instead chose to release their site optimized for just one browser. Single-browser support undermined the W3C's goal of universal access for all Web users. It was a very frustrating experience for Web users to encounter a site that would only work in Netscape when browsing with Internet Explorer.

Web developers also contributed to the chaos on the Web by building sites with standards-ignorant methods. Proprietary code and generally sloppy markup made page display a crapshoot.

In 1998 a group of talented Web gurus banded together to form the Web Standards Project (**http://webstandards.org**), whose mandate was to affect real change on the Web by educating browser developers and Web designers about the benefits of adopting Web standards. Jeffrey Zeldman, one of the co-founders of the Web Standards Project, authored an industry-changing book in 2002 entitled *Designing with Web Standards* (**http://www.zeldman.com/dwws/**) that introduced many in the industry to Web standards for the first time. Dave Shea's CSS Zen Garden (**http://csszengarden.com**) project further fueled the adoption of Web standards, debunking misconceptions that accessible, standards-based design was inevitably unattractive.

NOTE If you'd like to learn more about the history of the Web standards movement and how the W3C defines standards, read the Web Standards Project's detailed summaries in its Web standards frequently asked questions at **http://webstandards.org/learn/faq/**.

Browsers and Web developers have come a long way since the dark days of the early Web. Sites developed with Web standards now render much more consistently across multiple browsers and devices.

Web standards have become an essential mark of quality in the Web development community today. Top designers, developers, and the companies they work for have adopted Web standards development practices because of the many practical benefits they offer.

Though there's still a large part of the Web that remains resistive to or ignorant of Web standards, there's been a sea change in recent years towards following W3C recommendations. As we'll see in this chapter, there are far too many advantages to adopting Web standards to continue the bad practices of the past.

Getting Started with Web Standards

The World Wide Web was created as a tool for scientific researchers to publish their findings, but its rapid growth brought demand for websites to deliver different types of content that required more sophisticated formatting than research documents. Formatting was not initially part of the plan for HTML, but tags for styling fonts colors and layout got tacked on anyway. At the end of the 1990s the W3C recognized that HTML had become a Frankenstein language of elements that needed a serious revamp. The result was XHTML.

XHTML is still HTML but it's rebuilt using XML (Extensible Markup Language) to define its structure. Because XML is a language that can be extended when needed, XHTML will easily accommodate future tags and attributes that the W3C can add as need arises.

If you're new to XHTML but are proficient with HTML you'll find the transition relatively easy. Here are a few of the major changes you should be aware of in order to build XHTML documents that meet the W3C's Web standards:

- Separate your page structure (XHTML) from the formatting (CSS) and behavior (JavaScript) by placing each in a separate file. Your XHTML documents can link to and share common external CSS and JavaScript files.
- Discontinue use of deprecated elements that the W3C no longer supports. For a full listing of deprecated elements visit **http://webdesign.about.com/od/htmltags/a/bltags_deprctag.htm**.
- XHTML code needs to be written in lowercase letters.
- All tags need to be closed (example: close `<p>` with `</p>`). Tags that don't have a closing element need to close themselves with a space and a forward slash (example: `<br />`).
- All documents need to start with a document type definition (DTD) to tell the browser what rules should be followed when rendering the page. Visit **http://w3schools.com/xhtml/xhtml_dtd.asp** for examples of XHTML DTDs.
- All image tags must include the `alt` attribute.
- All special characters must be encoded. For a full listing visit **http://w3schools.com/tags/ref_entities.asp**.
- All tag attributes must be written within quotes. Some attributes like `checked`—used in `<input>` to check a radio button or checkbox by default—were not originally designed to have a value. The XHTML way to write this type of attribute is by setting the value to be the same as the attribute (example: `checked="checked"`).

There are some more subtle changes with XHTML but for the most part it looks similar to HTML. You can test your documents to ensure that you are correctly following the W3C's guidelines using the handy validation tool located at **http://validator.w3.org/**.

NOTE To learn more about how to build XHTML documents visit **http://w3schools.com/xhtml/default.asp**

The Benefits of Web Standards

There are plenty of reasons why you should follow Web standards when you build your sites. Businesses, developers, and users all stand to gain from standards-compliant practices. Here are a few of the most compelling reasons why all of the websites you build should be standards-compliant:

Web standards help developers by

- Decreasing development time. You'll avoid redundant code such as `<font>` by controlling the entire design with external CSS files.
- Decreasing maintenance time. Changes in one external CSS file can affect the entire site.
- Increasing design capabilities. There are a number of advanced design features that CSS is capable of but old school HTML formatting is not.
- Creating cleaner code. XHTML that separates formatting, structure, and behavior is much easier to read and maintain.
- Empowering delivery of the same XHTML content in many formats by using separate style sheets. One XHTML document can be styled for screen, handheld, and print display.
- Creating more stable code. Standards-compliant code is likely to work in future version of browsers, and will actually work in legacy browsers as well.

Web standards help businesses by

- Saving money on development costs. Website development costs can be cut dramatically by decreasing the amount of time it takes developers to build a site.
- Saving money on server bandwidth costs. Because structure, formatting, and behavior are kept separate on standards-compliant sites, the CSS and JavaScript will only need to be downloaded once when the user loads the first page that links to them.
- Helping developers meet deadlines. When developers can build and maintain sites efficiently they are more likely to meet tight deadlines.

Web standards help users by

- Speeding up the load times. Externalized CSS and JavaScript only load once rather than every time a page is loaded.
- Improving accessibility. Disabled users and users on alternate devices will appreciate equal access to Web content.

Developers, businesses, and users all reap the benefits of Web standards, but there is one even more compelling reason to make the change: Web standards can help optimize your site for search engines and can generate more traffic on your site. Poorly constructed legacy code can cause problems for search engines when indexing your site.

As we'll see in this chapter, Web standards and findability are an inseparable pair.

Web Standards and Findability Sitting in a Tree...

Web standards and findability are a complementary duo. By following Web standards you can improve findability by making your content more meaningful and legible for search engines. Web standards provide the structure and hierarchy of information that search engines need to discern what a page is about and what's most important in the content.

There are a number of ways that Web standards development practices can serve our goal of building more findable websites. Here are some of the most significant ones:

- Ensures search engine spiders can parse your code without stumbling on errors such as missing close tags or syntax errors
- Often decreases the ratio of markup to content, which can help improve search engine rankings
- Improves page load times so search engines can quickly index your entire site
- Improves the communication of the information hierarchy of your pages so search engines can discern what content is important

- Accessibility standards provide a number of opportunities to include descriptive keywords in your markup that will help disabled users and search engines better understand the contents of your page.

Web standards can put you on the right path to building documents that are search engine friendly. However, it's important to note that following standards is not an SEO silver bullet. If only it were that simple!

When marking up a document, you still need to use your head when considering the most appropriate tag for your content. What the content of your pages says is important to search engines–but *how* you say it is equally important.

An Issue of Semantics

Although computers possess great computational power, they still can't evaluate the context of a message (like the human brain does). When a search engine scans the content of an HTML page, it cannot identify the most important pieces of content unless it's marked up properly. When search engines look at documents, they see words but they don't know which words or topics are most important. One critical goal when marking up a document is to choose tags that communicate the hierarchy of information on the page. This is called *semantic markup*.

Let's start with a very common example. When we consider a typical Web page, the logo and the name of an organization are at the top of the information hierarchy in our message. We could simply show the logo on the page using an image tag like this:

```
<img src="i/logo.gif" alt="Espresso Impresso Logo" width="200"
height="200" />
```

The problem with this approach is that there is no way for search engines–which can't "see" the design of the page–to discern the importance of this information. A search engine can read the text in the `alt` attribute but assigns a lower rank to the content than it really deserves. A better approach would be to use the <h1> tag, which assigns the highest importance to this content:

```
<h1>Espresso Impresso: Makers of commercial Italian espresso
machines and equipment</h1>
```

Notice I've added a more detailed description of the company rather than the relatively meaningless text in the `alt` attribute of the first example. The <h1> tag allows us to deliver relevant content to search engines while assigning the keywords in the tag the highest rank in the information hierarchy of the page. There's no need to overstuff the tag–just make your text relevant and meaningful.

Now that we have keyword-rich content at the top of the information hierarchy, we need to use some CSS to show the logo, creating the same visual result as using a less meaningful `<img />` tag:

```
h1 {
  text-indent: -9999px;
  background: url(i/espresso-impresso-logo.gif) no-repeat center;
  width: 200px;
  height: 200px;
}
```

I've used a general element selector to pinpoint the logo <h1> tag since, logically, we would have only one piece of content that is the most important on the page and deserving of the tag. The `text-indent` style property places the text of the tag 9999 pixels to the left, far out of view for sighted users, but still visible to search engines. With the text out of the way the `background` property displays the image in place of the text, centering it in the 200px by 200px display area defined by the `width` and `height` properties.

TIP Notice that I have renamed the logo image file to include the name of the organization. Search engines can detect keywords in file names, so it's a good idea to briefly include such relevant words that may provide more context to the content of the page.

This technique is called *image replacement*. We'll be investigating it in more detail later in this chapter in the section entitled "Image Replacement: Accessibility, Findability, and Beauty Converge."

How To Use Heading Tags

When using heading tags, think of them like a pyramid. There is just one point at the top of a pyramid that occupies the highest location. The same is true for the <h1> tag. Use it only once to identify the top of your information hierarchy. An <h2> tag might also have limited use, perhaps only for the title of the page. The lower heading tags such as <h3> and <h4> can be used many times, creating the base of the information hierarchy pyramid, yet still more important to search engines than regular copy.

Will Search Engines Really Reward Adherence to Web Standards?

For some time there has been great speculation as to how much of an advantage a website actually gains by following Web standards. Unfortunately, the answer to this question is not so black and white. In order to arrive at the answer, we need to know a bit about how search engines "think."

When evaluating a page to assign rank, search engines look at a host of *signals of quality* that might provide clues to what a page is about and the value of its content. One such signal of quality that we can safely identify is the number of inbound links to a page from reputable sources. If a page has a number of good inbound links to it, then it is likely that it has high quality content and therefore should be ranked high when displaying relevant search returns. This particular signal of quality is what allowed Google to rise to the top in the business of search engines while other search algorithms were looking at less reliable signals of quality. Obviously, looking at the right signals of quality is of utmost importance in the multi-billion-dollar search industry.

So if we can discern that links are a signal of quality, logic would imply that we should be able to get a straight answer about the relevance of Web standards to SEO. There is a problem, though, in arriving at the answer. Because search engine companies make their livelihood from their exclusive algorithms, they are very protective of the details about the way they rank pages. They don't want to reveal their trade secrets to competitors or to those who would try to undermine their system.

How much do search engines value standards compliance? Mike Davidson has run some simple yet interesting experiments that have provided insight into the answer to that question. He's posted the results on his blog (**http://www.mikeindustries.com/blog/archive/2006/01/the-roundabout-seo-test/**). Davidson created a series of pages that featured the term *lodefizzle*, a word he created and then marked up in various ways. By creating a nonsensical word that was used only on his pages, Davidson would gain a clearer picture of the critical signals of quality used to determine search engine rankings.

The results confirmed some common assumptions and, surprisingly enough, challenged others. Here are a few things he discovered:

- Using semantic markup like the <h1> tag with keywords within it does indeed boost page rankings and beats other methods (such as <b>) of marking up the same text.

- Using complex nested tables for layout does, in fact, penalize your search engine rankings to some degree—probably because of the increased ratio of code to content, which makes the page seem less valuable.
- Invalid code can significantly impact your search engine rankings and, in some cases, even prevent your page from being listed!
- Semantically correct markup does certainly help improve search engine ranking, but other techniques are sometimes better—such as listing a keyword a number of times naturally in a document (surrounded by other words), naming files with keywords, placing keywords in the labels of inbound links to the page, and placing keywords in the title tag.
- It is possible in some situations for pages that don't follow Web standards to rank higher than those that do.

SXSW 2006 Podcast
"Web Standards and SEO: Searching for Common Ground"
http://player.sxsw.com/2006/podcasts/SXSW06.INT.20060313.WebStandardsAndSEO.mp3

What we ultimately learn from Davidson's research is that Web standards foster the right practices that will allow search engines to successfully read and rank pages in a meaningful way, making your pages more likely to receive higher rankings and be found. The fact that your pages do validate, however, is not necessarily an important signal of quality to the major search engines. To further complicate the issue, search engine algorithms undergo changes regularly to adapt to new SEO development methods, both white hat (*honest*) and black hat (*dishonest*). Performing your own tests following Mike Davidson's methodology is a good idea because it's perhaps the best way to stay abreast of the changes to the algorithms of top search engines.

SXSW 2006 Podcast
"Web Standards and Search Engines: Searching for Common Ground"
http://player.sxsw.com/2006/podcasts/SXSW06.INT.20060313.WebStandardsAndSearchEngines.mp3

The last point should be carefully noted. Poorly coded sites with compelling, keyword-rich content and a number of inbound links from reputable sites can outrank a standards-compliant page. Code alone will not win the SEO war, but when combined with the right content, it *can* be the factor that pushes you to the top.

The final answer to our original question of the value of Web standards to search engine ranking is that Web standards *are not* a 100 percent guarantee of top page rankings, but they *are* an important piece on the path to SEO success, and therefore should be followed as closely as possible.

Essential Tags that Promote Findability

We've seen how heading tags can be a powerful way to promote findability in your markup, but what other tags are highly valued by search engines?

The <title> Tag

The <title> tag is one of the most important places to position your keywords and phrases. There are a few factors to keep in mind when creating an effective title tag:

- It should not be a wholesale dumping ground for your keywords and phrases. Keep it concise (less than 12 words) and natural rather than an everything-plus-the-kitchen-sink listing.
- Make sure your title tag is written to serve humans too, as it is still a critical component of navigation and usability on a website.
- The title tag text is the main heading and link to a site when shown on search results pages, and often determines whether or not a user decides to visit your site.
- Write your title tags in such a way that they can be easily read in stats applications like Google Analytics and Mint (you can learn more about these applications in the bonus chapter entitled "Analyzing Your Traffic" on the companion website at **http://buildingfindablewebsites.com**).

Here's an effective approach to building <title> tags to satisfy each of the above goals:

```
<title>page title | organization or site name | short keyword-rich
phrase</title>
```

Listing the page title and organization/site name first gives visitors a quick way to identify the page and site they are on even when they have their browser minimized. The way you write your <title> tags will affect the legibility of your website traffic statistics. Typically, Web statistics packages will list the pages visitors have been viewing by showing the <title> tag text. If you place your keywords first in the <title> tag, you will have a rough time discerning which pages your visitors are viewing. See **FIGURE 2.1**.

A Note About Keywords in Your Markup

The keywords in your content play a big role in directing search traffic to your site. In this chapter we'll discover the best places to position your keywords inside your XHTML documents in order to optimize your pages for search engine indexing.

Before marking up your documents, it's generally a good idea to research the keywords and phrases you should try to position in prominent places in your pages. In Chapter 4 we'll learn about some research techniques and tools that shed light on how to go about finding the terms people are searching for, and with which you can be most competitive.

FIGURE 2.1 *This is how an optimal title tag might display in the popular Web analytics package Mint, making it easy to see which pages have been recently visited. If you list keywords first, the truncated title may totally clip the page name, rendering this data meaningless.*

Pages

Most Popular **Most Recent** Watched

Page	When
Espresso Machines | Espresso Impresso | Commercial I ... From /	× 6 mins ago
Home | Espresso Impresso | Commercial Italian Espres ... From a search for commercial espresso machines	+ 2 hours ago
About Us | Espresso Impresso | Commercial Italian Esp ... From a search for italian espresso	+ 3 hours ago

Poorly written <title> tags can cause problems for your users too. When <title> tags are stuffed with keywords, browsers will awkwardly clip your text if the window is not wide enough to accommodate all of the text. Users may not be able to view the name of the page they are on or the name of the site, which can be a usability annoyance.

When users bookmark your site in their browser or in social bookmarking systems like Delicious (**http://del.icio.us**) the <title> tag text is used as the label for the bookmark. If you've overstuffed your <title> tag with keywords positioned at the front of text, the important information like the name of your site will be clipped off the end. A bookmark label that makes no sense is not likely to generate repeat traffic.

A short phrase at the end of your <title> tag can provide visitors and search engines a quick summary of what the site is about. Just make sure you keep it brief and descriptive. This <title> tag efficiently educates visitors and search engines alike about the page they are viewing, on which site, and briefly what it's about.

```
<title>About Us | Espresso Impresso | Commercial Espresso Machines
and Equipment</title>
```

<strong> and <em> Tags

There are a number of other advantageous places within your markup to position keywords and phrases. The <strong> and <em> tags emphasize small portions of your content, elevating their ranking within the information hierarchy of the page, and are subsequently seen as important content by search engines. Here's an example of how you might use them in your copy:

```
<p>
At Espresso Impresso, we strive to produce the finest
<strong>commercial espresso machines</strong> on the planet, so
you can enjoy the best cup of <em>coffee</em> every day.
</p>
```

Anchor Tags

The text labels for links are perceived as one of the most critical places to position relevant keywords. Make your link labels keyword-rich where possible, but without compromising usability. The title attribute of links is also a valuable place to include your target keywords, and can provide further context for the link label, improving usability.

```
<a href="espresso-machines.php" title="Shop for commercial
espresso machines">Espresso Machines</a>
```

Keep the title attribute and label text in links concise and relevant. The name of the file linked to in this example also includes target keywords so that search engines can direct those searching for "espresso machines" to the page.

Keywords inside of link labels are especially important when linking to an external site, as this is considered by search engines to be a reliable way to find out what a page is really about. Keep this in mind when doing a *link exchange* with friends, colleagues, and affiliates, as an inbound link with the same keywords in the label as your site targets is extremely effective in driving search traffic to your site and boosting your reputation with search engines.

Using Link Exchanges

A link exchange is simply the act of making a reciprocal link to a site that links to yours in an effort to build the number of inbound links, which is one of the top determiners of page rank. Google specifically looks at the number and quality of sites that link to yours in order to determine the reputation of your site. It's a bit like being in high school where your reputation is determined by the people you hang out with. If you have friends, colleagues, affiliates, or acquaintances from the Web that you would feel comfortable soliciting for an inbound link, by all means take advantage of the opportunity, as this can help you boost your page rank.

Watch out for disreputable link exchanges, though. There are plenty of companies of questionable reputation that send thousands of emails to strangers asking to exchange links. If you begin linking to disreputable sites you could hurt your site's page rank. Stick to exchanging links with sites that you know and trust. Providing great content is one of the most effective ways to generate inbound links to your site without having to ask for them. We'll explore some content strategies that will drive traffic, and bring visitors back again and again, in Chapter 4.

The Myth of Meta: The Good, the Bad, and the Ugly

There is a myth about the keyword's meta tag that needs to be dispelled in the Web development community. For some time it has been seen as an important part of any SEO initiative, but none of the major search engines see the keyword's meta tag as a reliable means of determining the content of a page, and don't even look at it. In the mid to late 1990s the keyword meta tag was highly abused by many sites on the Web by stuffing the keyword tag with popular but irrelevant terms in an effort to trick search engines into directing traffic their way. Search engines started to address this problem in 1998 by looking to the actual content of the page rather than the keyword meta tag for clues about a page's relevance to a search term. Today, all of the major search engines have followed suit, making the keyword's meta tag obsolete. You can safely omit it from your pages without worry of missing out on ranking benefits.

Other meta tags, like description, are still quite valuable. The description of a site shown on search results pages often comes directly from your meta description tag if it exists, so it is important to write this content effectively. When writing your description, keep it concise and attractive to visitors, avoiding hard-sell marketing-speak. A description like *"Espresso Impresso is an amazing site you have to visit!"* is aggressive and sounds like a bad infomercial. Speak to your visitors with respect and relevance to their needs rather than as a marketer making demands, and you'll get better results. If appropriate for your site, consider using a more informal voice, as so many organizations use frumpy corporate-speak, and it can be the factor that distinguishes you from your competitors on the search results pages.

Long meta descriptions get truncated when displayed on search result pages, so try to keep them between 150 and 200 characters long (maximum is 1024). Of course, including your keywords and phrases in your description is important, as they will be highlighted for the user on search results pages. See **FIGURE 2.2**.

Using the lang Attribute

If you manage a multilingual site, you may want to provide your meta description in more than one language using the `lang` attribute. Google can pull the appropriate description based on the user's location, which is determined by their IP address, or when a specific language is defined in their search preferences. Here's how to deliver a multilingual description:

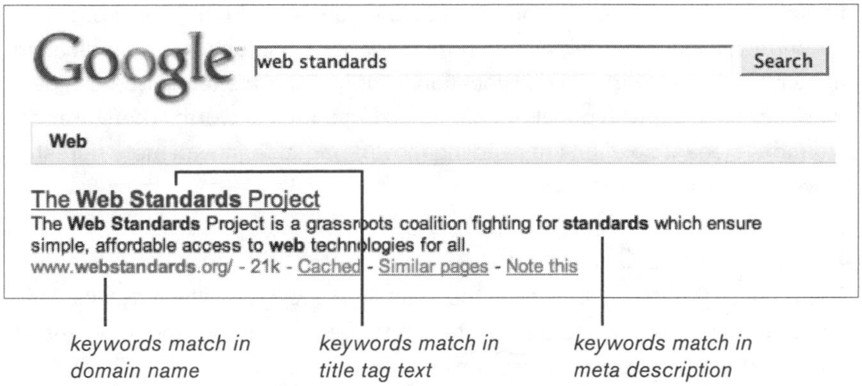

FIGURE 2.2 *Google identifies search term matches in a number of places when displaying results. The bold text on the search results page clues you in to where it is important to position keywords.*

```
<meta name="description" lang="en-us" content="Aarron Walter is an
Interactive Designer living in Athens, Georgia, and faculty member
in the Interactive Media Design department at The Art Institute of
Atlanta." />

<meta name="description" lang="de" content="Aarron Walter ist
ein interaktiver Entwerfer, der Athen, Georgia, und Lehrkörperim
bauteil in der interaktiven Media-Konstruktionsabteilung am kunst-
Institut von Atlanta lebt." />
```

Avoid Using robots

The `robots` meta tag is typically used unnecessarily. Often you will see the following in the `<head>` of a page requesting search engine spiders to crawl all of the content on the site:

```
<meta name="robots" content="all" />
```

It would seem to be a good idea to tell search engines to index everything, but in actuality, it's not necessary. By default search engines will crawl all of the pages on your site they can reach unless you tell them otherwise. You can save yourself the time and energy of including it because it won't provide any real returns.

Avoid Using refresh

One meta tag to be avoided at all cost is `refresh`. A meta refresh simply refreshes or redirects the browser to a different location at a specified interval. It is perceived as a potentially black hat SEO practice because many people have used meta refresh to deliver a bait-and-switch strategy to search engines by showing a page filled with keywords, then automatically refreshing to a different location where the content has nothing to do with the initial page. Although you may be using a meta refresh for honest intentions like indicating that a page has moved to a new location, simply using the technique can generate more trouble with penalized page ranking than it is worth. There are safer and more elegant solutions to handling moved pages than with meta refresh, as we will see in Chapter 3.

Always Include Content-Type

One meta tag to always include is the meta Content-Type, which defines the character set to be used to display the content. Failure to include it can result in some strange rendering of your text.

```
<meta http-equiv="Content-Type" content="text/html;
charset=utf-8" />
```

Optional Meta Tags To Consider

Here are some optional meta tags to include that are nice, but won't make any significant impact on the findability of your site:

Author author is not used by Google, Yahoo! or MSN:

```
<meta name="author" content="Aarron Walter" />
```

Content-Language Content-Language assists search engine spiders in cataloging the language of the page:

```
<meta http-equiv="Content-Language" content="en-us" />
```

copyright copyright declares the copyright of the content:

```
<meta name="copyright" content="Copyright 2007 Aarron Walter. All
rights reserved." />
```

Geo Tags Geo tags identify the location of the author of the site. Generate geo tags for your location at **http://www.geo-tag.de/generator/en.html**:

```
<meta name="ICBM" content="33.928205, -83.391906" />
<meta name="geo.position" content="33.928205; -83.391906" />
<meta name="geo.placename" content="Athens, Ga, USA">
<meta name="geo.region" content="usa-ga" />
```

Preventing Content Indexing

There are some situations where you may want to actually prevent search engines from indexing portions of your site such as with student exercises.

There are two markup strategies that can help you control what content gets indexed, and what content remains hidden:

- `nofollow, noindex` meta tag
- `robots-nocontent`

NOTE We'll see another technique that can prevent search engines from indexing certain content on your site in Chapter 3 in the section entitled "Controlling Search Engine Indexing with robots.txt."

nofollow, noindex meta tag

To prevent any search engine from indexing a page, simply use the `robots` meta tag:

```
<meta name="robots" value="noindex, nofollow" />
```

robots-nocontent

In May 2007, Yahoo! introduced a standard to remove small portions of content in a page from its search engine index. At the time of publishing this book, the standard had not yet been adopted by other search engines, and had received criticism from some in the developer community who argued that search engines should be able to determine what content in a page is important, and what content should be ignored without unnecessary additions to the code. Others argued that all search engine-specific communication should be kept in an external file called "robots.txt" in the Web root, as is already the standard. Like it or not, the standard is in the wild and may prove useful in some situations like when you want to hide ads that could distort the perception of your page's content. In order to implement Yahoo!'s selective cloaking standard, simply add `class="robots-nocontent"` to any tag you wish to hide.

```
<div class="robots-nocontent">excluded content</div>
```

The Misleading rel="nofollow"

The `rel="nofollow"` attribute that is often added to anchor tags is very misleading. The code suggests that this attribute prevents search engines from crawling any links to pages that contain this attribute. In fact, `rel="nofollow"` just prevents search engines from assigning any page rank weight to the recipient site because of the inbound link. It's simply a way for a site to indicate that it does not endorse the site it is linking to. Search engines will still crawl these links.

Here's an example of how `rel="nofollow"` is used:

```
<a href="http://example.com" rel="nofollow">An un-vetted site</a>
```

If your site displays user-generated content, the `rel="nofollow"` attribute may be a good idea, as the quality and appropriateness of content you have not reviewed could potentially impact your search engine rankings.

Let Go of the Past To Embrace a Findable Future

There are a number of antiquated development techniques that we can safely let go of in order to create more findable content:

- Frames
- Deprecated elements
- Pop-up windows

Frames

Hindered findability is just one of the many reasons why frames should be officially laid to rest. The individual pages that make up framesets divide content, adversely affecting keyword density when viewed by search engines. Each page of the frameset runs the risk of being discovered by itself via a search engine query, resulting in the awkward display of content without branding/ site identity, navigation, or other important information as originally intended. For users, the result is a dead end. Individual pages are cumbersome to bookmark making return visits less likely.

Deprecated Elements

Formatting tags and other deprecated elements such as `<font>`, `<b>`, and `<i>`, to name just a few, should be eliminated from all code in favor of contemporary Web standards. Formatting tags redundantly mark up the design of a page without communicating a meaningful hierarchy of the information. Search engines look for semantic markup with a high ratio of content to code. The `<font>` tag alone can create an exponentially negative effect to this ratio.

Standards-compliant sites use external CSS files to handle their formatting. Moving the formatting to an external file greatly improves the content-to-code ratio of a page while making the site easier to maintain. It also speeds up the load time of your pages for users and search engines because the CSS formatting code will download once and then be stored in the browser's temporary memory for all subsequent page requests.

Pop-up Windows

Pop-up windows can be problematic for some of the same reasons as frames. Often pop-up window documents have no site identity or navigation, so when they are indexed and viewed individually the user is provided no clue to their location or how to navigate. The JavaScript often used to spawn pop-up windows is not executable by search engine spiders, creating a roadblock to indexing. We'll take a look at some solutions to working with JavaScript in Chapter 7, but in general, pop-up windows should be avoided.

Accessible Content Is Findable Content

As the Web has matured into a sophisticated communication medium, the demand for accessible content that can be consumed by users with disabilities or on alternate platforms has grown.

In February 2006, the National Federation of the Blind filed a class action lawsuit against Target.com alleging that the site was not accessible to users with disabilities, violating a California law that requires businesses to offer equal access to their services to consumers with disabilities. Missing alternate text for images, inaccessible image maps, and a host of other accessibility guideline violations made it impossible for blind patrons on Target.com to navigate the site and complete transactions.

So what does this have to do with making findable websites? The accessibility violations that prevented blind users from navigating Target.com would also prevent search engine spiders from indexing the site, making large portions invisible to search queries. Many have observed that the wealthiest, most influential blind users on the Web are the indexing spiders of Google, Yahoo!, and MSN Live Search, who suffer from the same limitations as many disabled human users. Search engine spiders cannot see the content within images, and get tripped up by such things as JavaScript, image maps, and poorly constructed pages just like many screen-reader browsers used by blind users.

Google actually requests in its Webmaster Help Center that developers build their sites to follow accessibility guidelines (**http://www.google.com/support/webmasters/bin/answer.py?answer=40349**). It's a task that's not as daunting as it may initially seem, and the return on investment can be significant. Increasing the audience for a site, avoiding reputation-destroying and expensive litigation, and optimizing for search engine queries are all

High Accessibility Is Effective Search Engine Optimization

http://www.alistapart.com/articles/accessibilityseo

compelling reasons why accessibility should not be thought of as an optional feature of a site, but rather as essential to its success.

Accessibility techniques often introduce more content into a page that is fodder for search engine indexing. Let's take a look at some best practices that are easy to implement, and can ensure your content is accessible to search engines and disabled users alike.

Making Images Visible

The `alt` attribute, which provides a short text description for images, is perhaps the best known accessibility technique yet is too often overlooked. Under the W3C specifications for XHTML, the `alt` attribute is required in all image tags. It is read to screen-reader users when an image is encountered, is displayed when image display is disabled or unavailable, and is incorrectly displayed in a tool tip box on image rollover in Internet Explorer.

NOTE The W3C XHTML spec states that tool tip text should only be generated by the `title` attribute, not `alt`.

Search engines actively index `alt` text for both image and text searches, factoring in this text when evaluating the density of keywords in a page.

Keep your `alt` text short (less than 100 characters), and descriptive, avoiding text like "photo of ..." or "image of ..." as they unnecessarily clutter keyword density, and are redundant since the user/search engine will already be aware that the element is an image.

If you find yourself unsure of what text description to place in the `alt` attribute because the image is not informative, but is simply decorative, then you should consider if the image is necessary or could be presented in another way that would not affect accessibility. Meaningless images like pixel shims (an outdated technique where 1 pixel square, transparent GIFs are used to position elements on a page) should be avoided at all costs as superior layout control can be achieved with CSS without garbling up the page with meaningless image tags. Decorative images that have no information can instead be presented as background images in a `<div>` tag or other block level tag using CSS.

Imagine you want to show a decorative flourish next to a page heading (see **FIGURE 2.3**). Rather than marking up this heading with an image tag like the following:

```
<h2><img src="i/flourish.gif" alt="decorative flourish" />About
Us</h2>
```

The image should be applied with a CSS background image and some padding to push the text out of the way of the decorative element:

FIGURE 2.3 *A simple page heading with a decorative flourish.*

XHTML

```
<h2>About Us</h2>
```

CSS

```
h2 {padding-left:25px; background:url(../i/flourish.gif) no-repeat
left; }
```

The rule of thumb is if the visual content is not informational, all imagery should be presented via CSS.

When `alt` is not enough to accurately describe the content within an image, use the `longdesc` attribute as well to create a link to a more complete description. Traditionally, `longdesc` has been used to link to an external HTML file that contains the detailed description:

```
<img src="client-logos.gif" alt="Logos of our top clients"
longdesc="logo-description.html" />
```

This approach has a number of shortcomings:

- Requires the user to navigate away from the page they are on, which can be annoying
- Moves important, keyword-rich content to another page that could be individually indexed by a search engine, rather than keeping it with the rest of the page with which it is associated
- Creates yet another file to manage in the site, which can be cumbersome when many images require `longdesc` content

Instead of placing `longdesc` text in another page, you can simply create a footnote area in your markup and place an anchor link in your `longdesc`:

```
<img src="client-logos.gif" alt="Logos of our top clients"
longdesc="#footnote1" />
```

In the footer of your page ...

```
<ul id="footnotes">
<li id="footnote1"><a name="footnote1"></a>
Some of our top clients include The Chipmunk Saddle Factory, Quick
E Mart, Dewy Cheatum Poker Chips, the Springfield Nuclear Plant,
and the Fisher and Sons Funeral Home.
</li>
</ul>
```

Using an unordered list as a container for your footnotes you can easily add more as needed, keeping them organized in a single structure. Optionally, you can choose to hide the footnote from sighted users who would get the same information by viewing the image. To do so, simply position the content off the page –9999px:

```
#footnotes {text-indent:-9999px; position:absolute;}
```

Because a stack of footnotes can create a seemingly unnecessary scrolling blank area at the bottom of the page you'll want to remove it from the document flow. Elements that are absolutely positioned with CSS are removed from the document flow, which means the page will behave as if it's not there. With the footnote in place, we now have a search engine friendly image.

NOTE If you'd like to learn more about CSS positioning and the document flow read "Web Design 101: Positioning" on Digital Web (**http://www.digital-web.com/articles/web_design_101_positioning/**).

Clearing the Roadblocks Caused by Image Maps

Image maps are used infrequently these days, but when they are they can pose significant problems to the indexing of a site. If you have to use an image map, be sure to create a text link navigation system equivalent to ensure search engines can navigate and index all pages:

```
<img src="i/us-map.gif" alt="Map of Espresso Impresso store
locations in the United States" longdesc="#mapnavigation"
usemap="#map" />
<map name="map" id="map">
    <area shape="poly" coords="322,126,311,130,305,134,305,137,
297" href="store-locater.html#alabama" />
    <area shape="poly" coords="283,163,273,163,263,168"
href="store-locater.html#alaska"/>
```

```
    ...
</map>

<ul id="map-navigation">
    <li><a href="store-locater.html#alabama">Alabama</a></li>
    <li><a href="store-locater.html#alaska">Alaska</a></li>
    ...
</ul>
```

Using the same `longdesc` technique we saw earlier, we can link the image map to an unordered list containing a text link navigation alternative.

There are nice alternatives to old-school image maps that provide users with more features, and deliver content in a way that is naturally search engine friendly. Seth Duffy offers a CSS and JavaScript-based alternative at A List Apart (**http://www.alistapart.com/articles/cssmaps**) that includes text descriptions of each active area on the map, which creates more content indexing opportunities for search engines.

Image Replacement: Accessibility, Findability, and Beauty Converge

Image replacement is an essential staple in the Web designer/developer's toolbox. The goal of image replacement is to present content as a graphic without sacrificing accessibility or search engine visibility. Graphical headings give a designer a wider rage of aesthetic possibilities than XHTML and CSS alone. We saw a simple example of image replacement already at the beginning of this chapter (see the section entitled "An Issue of Semantics"), which used Mike Rundle's Phark technique (**http://phark.typepad.com/phark/2003/08/accessible_imag.html**) to position the text of a heading tag off the page, replacing it with a background image instead. The content in this example remains readable to search engines and screen readers, while providing a great deal of design freedom.

Since image replacement was introduced in 1999, a number of analogs have followed, the breadth of which can't be fully discussed here. A nice catalog of the most popular techniques can be found at Dave Shea's website (**http://www.mezzoblue.com/tests/revised-image-replacement/**). Shea himself provides a worthy option to the Phark method, which displays the heading text when images are disabled where Phark does not, making it more accessible but equally search engine friendly.

XHTML

```
<h3 id="header" title="Revised Image Replacement">
    <span></span>Revised Image Replacement
</h3>
```

CSS

```
#header {
    width: 329px;
    height: 25px;
    position: relative;
    }
#header span {
    background: url(sample-opaque.gif) no-repeat;
    position: absolute;
    width: 100%;
    height: 100%;
    }
```

The Shea method scales the heading tag to the size of the image to be displayed then covers the text behind it with an opaque GIF. The drawbacks to the Shea method are the additional, empty <span> required within the heading tag to cover the text, and the slightly increased complexity of CSS required.

SIFR (or Scalable Inman Flash Replacement) is a related but quite different solution to accessibly displaying graphical text using Flash and JavaScript rather than CSS. Initially, this may sound like an ironic option to choose to deliver content that can be seen by search engines, but because it only displays the styled text when JavaScript and Flash support are detected, and gracefully degrades to HTML text when not supported, it is a perfectly search engine friendly option. The general idea behind it is that as an HTML page loads, some JavaScript searches the document for tags, classes, and ids defined by the developer, and overlaps them with a SWF file of the same size. The text of the original element is fed into the SWF file where ActionScript dynamically draws your text in the font and to the typographic specifications you declare. SIFR provides exceptional typographic control over small portions of content, which is perfect under very specific design constraints. It does, however, require more development time than CSS-driven alternatives, and can require more time to wrap your head around. The documentation is good, however, providing detailed explanations, examples, a wiki, and a forum to get help if needed. All of the gritty details can be found at **http://www.mikeindustries.com/sifr/**.

Regardless of which image replacement technique you opt for, be sure to avoid the old-school, original approach (called *FIR* or *Fahrner Image Replacement*), which uses `display:none` to hide the heading text. Using `display:none` makes content inaccessible to screen readers, and can be mistaken by search engines as a dishonest, black hat SEO technique. Black hat techniques can cause your site to rank lower in search engines. Keep this in mind when styling any content on your pages!

The Right and Wrong Way To Use Tables

Table-based layouts, as you may already be aware, cause significant accessibility issues for users with disabilities. As we saw earlier in Mike Davidson's research on the relationship between Web standards and SEO, table-based layouts can also negatively impact your search engine rankings. The best we can do is speculate as to why this is, but there are two likely reasons: Perhaps the increased ratio of code to content leads search engines to downgrade the ranking, or maybe the sheer complexity of the nested table structure is more difficult or time consuming for the spiders crawl. Whatever the reason, a table-based layout is not worth the risk of a downgraded ranking. Stick to CSS-based layout systems for better results.

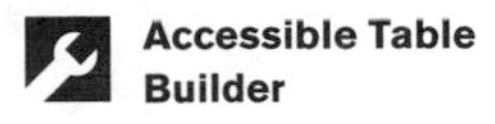

Accessible Table Builder

http://www.accessify.com/tools-and-wizards/accessibility-tools/table-builder/

Just because table-based layouts are a bad idea does not mean tables are obsolete relics of the past. When you need to present tabular data, there's no better tool than a well-built table. If written correctly, tables can also offer great opportunities to include more search engine friendly content that can help build the keyword density of a page. Let's take a look at a simple example of an accessible table used to display tabular data:

```
<table summary="Top-selling espresso machines">
    <caption>Espresso Impresso's top-selling commercial espresso
machines</caption>
    <thead>
        <tr>
            <th id="model">Model</th>
            <th id="price">Price</th>
            <th id="num-sold">Number Sold</th>
        </tr>
</thead>

<tbody>
        <tr>
            <td headers="model">AZ-500</td>
            <td headers="price">$500.00</td>
```

```
            <td headers="num-sold">200</td>
        </tr>

        <tr>
            <td headers="model">AX-1200</td>
            <td headers="price">$1000.00</td>
            <td headers="num-sold">100</td>
        </tr>
</tbody>
</table>
```

Notice the summary attribute in the <table> tag, and the <caption> tag present two valuable opportunities to tell search engines and users alike what the content within the table is communicating. The <th> tag also communicates an elevated information hierarchy to search engines, and can be a good place to position keywords where relevant. By building the table following accessibility standards, we've naturally increased the keyword density of the page, which can boost its ranking in searches for these terms.

More Keyword Opportunities in Accessibility Related Elements

The title attribute, which can be added to a variety of tags, can provide further description of content on the page and more opportunities for inclusion of keywords. The title attribute displays a small tool tip box when the user mouses over an element such as a link:

```
<a href="about-us.html" title="About Espresso Impresso's coffee
experts">About Us</a>
```

Although the link label is short to facilitate usability, the title attribute provides users with a more detailed description of the page, and adds relevant keywords for search engines to index.

Acronyms and abbreviations in content pose a findability problem. Users searching for information on the W3C's WCAG standards may search with the acronym, or the full phrase "Web Content Accessibility Guidelines." If your content displays only the acronym, searches for the full phrase will not point users to your page even though it may contain just what they are looking for. Using the acronym tag and the title attribute you can deliver the content in both forms simultaneously.

```
<acronym title="Web Content Accessibility Guidelines">WCAG
</acronym>
```

Abbreviations can be handled in a similar fashion.

```
<abbr title="Georgia">GA</abbr>
```

In standards-compliant browsers like Firefox users will see a dotted line under these tags, tipping them off to further information available by mousing over the text. Internet Explorer, however, does not style the text, so you'll need to use some CSS to provide visual distinction to users.

Accessibility Pitfalls that Hinder Indexing

Technologies like Flash, JavaScript, audio, and video all create SEO headaches if not used properly. Many of the same methods used to make these technologies more accessible can also be employed to ensure search engines can crawl every bit of your site. We'll take a look at each of these technologies in detail in Chapter 7.

The Findability Benefits of Microformats

If you regularly keep tabs on hot topics in the Web industry, chances are you've run across microformats, which seem to be on the tip of every Web designer/developer's tongue these days. Because of their amazing power and simplicity, microformats have been the subject of countless articles in online and print publications, conference presentations, panel discussions, and a book by John Allsopp, *Microformats: Empowering Your Markup for Web 2.0* (**http://microformatique.com/book/**), published by Friends of Ed. Although we'll get a brief primer on the subject, if you are absolutely new to microformats you may want to get yourself up to speed quickly by reading Allsopp's informative article called "Add Microformats Magic to Your Site" (**http://www.thinkvitamin.com/features/design/how-to-use-microformats**) on the popular Web design ezine Vitamin. Brian Suda, a microformats guru, has written another great introductory article on the subject called "Microformats: More Meaning from Your Markup" (**http://www.sitepoint.com/article/microformats-meaning-markup**) published on Sitepoint.

In a nutshell, microformats can be defined as a series of standardized methods for marking up common content using simple, semantic HTML and CSS class names in order to allow machines to read and understand data that might otherwise be intelligible only to humans. Though the heart of microformats is really nothing more than the HTML and CSS that you probably already know, they deliver great potential power and convenience for users and Web applications. Microformats allow content on a website to be ported to other applications with ease, resulting in increased use of the information they describe.

To better understand the value of microformats, consider this scenario. Imagine you've built a site to promote a popular band, and have created a page with the complete touring schedule. Thousands of fans visit the site, read the schedule, and write down on paper the time, date, location, and other relevant info for later reference. Many fans misplace the paper or simply forget about the show they were so excited about earlier, they don't go to the show, and the band misses out on ticket sales.

If the schedule information had been built to be portable, it could have been quickly downloaded to a PDA, mobile phone, MP3 player, or ported to an online calendar system with the click of a button. This is the magic of microformats, which serves as the API (Application Programming Interface) to the content of your site, providing unprecedented interoperability between platforms. When data like a band's tour schedule is marked up in a standardized format, it's a piece of cake to make it portable, as computers can then recognize specific types of content that would otherwise be indistinguishable from any other text. Applications could send it to other applications knowing which text is the date, and which text is the event name. When information is packaged in a way that is portable, users can move it to a location where it won't be lost. This is a perfect illustration of how findability is more than just search engine optimization; it's about finding the information you want *when* you want it.

Microformats Cheat Sheets

http://suda.co.uk/projects/microformats/cheatsheet/

http://www.ilovejackdaniels.com/cheat-sheets/microformats-cheat-sheet/

TIP To get started with microformats, you may want to download a cheat sheet for quick reference, or if you are a Dreamweaver user, you can grab the free microformat extension, which makes the markup process even easier.

Dreamweaver Microformats Extension

http://www.webstandards.org/action/dwtf/microformats/

Making Event Data Portable with hCalendar and hCard

Let's take a look at the markup to create a microformat called hCalendar, which describes event data, to make the band's tour schedule portable and more findable:

```
<div class="vevent">
   <h3 class="summary">Wilco</h3>
   <p class="description">Wilco live at the 40 Watt Club</p>
```

```
  <p>
    <abbr class="dtstart" title="2007-08-12T21:00:00-05:00">12
August 2007 from 9:00pm EST</abbr>
     until <abbr class="dtend" title="2007-08-12T23:00:00-05:00">
11:00pm EST</abbr>
  </p>
</div>
```

Notice that all of this markup uses typical HTML. What makes this content a microformat is the standardized series of tags and class names, which create a recognizable pattern of data containers that applications can easily recognize. Once common content such as events are delivered in a pattern, applications can quickly gather and manage them for us, making the content more findable when we need it.

In the above example, the date and time of the event is delivered to users in a human-intelligible fashion as "12 August 2007 from 9:00pm EST", and in a format legible to applications within the `title` attribute of the *abbr* tag as "2007-08-12T21:00:00-05:00". With this dual listing approach, both machines and humans can identify and use the same information.

hCalendar Creator
http://microformats.org/code/hcalendar/creator.html

There is a conspicuously absent piece of information in our hCalendar listing that would make attendence impossible: the location of the venue. We'll use yet another microformat for the venue location called hCard, combining it with the hCalendar content.

```
<div class="vevent">
  <h3 class="summary">Wilco</h3>
  <p class="description">Wilco live at the 40 Watt Club</p>
  <p>
    <abbr class="dtstart" title="2007-08-12T21:00:00-05:00">12
August 2007 from 9:00pm EST</abbr>
     until <abbr class="dtend" title="2007-08-12T23:00:00-05:00">
11:00pm EST</abbr>
  </p>

  <!-- Venue -->
  <div class="venue location vcard">
    <span class="fn org">40 Watt Club</span><br />
    <div class="address adr">
    <span class="street-address">285 W Washington St</span><br />
    <span class="locality">Athens</span>,
    <span class="region">Georgia</span>
    <span class="postal-code">30601</span>
  </div>
```

```
  <span class="geo">
    <span class="latitude">33.9584</span>,
    <span class="longitude">-83.3801</span>
  </span>
  </div><!-- /Venue -->

</div><!-- /Event -->
```

With the venue address and geographic coordinates included in the event listing, users now have all information they need to attend the event. The last thing we need to do to make the content portable is provide users with a method for moving the data from the Web page to their calendar or address book. We can do this by adding links to Technorati's (**http://technorati.com**) microformat translation services that will convert our XHTML into a universal format that will download to the user's preferred calendar and contact application for syncing with portable devices:

```
<p>
  <a href="http://technorati.com/contacts/http://site.com/
events.html ">Download this event</a> |
  <a href="http://technorati.com/events/http://site.com/
events.html">Download venue information</a>
</p>
```

Using Technorati's microformat conversion service is quite simple. Just by linking to the service with the URL to your page trailing, Technorati has all it needs to convert your data into the appropriate, universal format.

The Operator Firefox add-on (**https://addons.mozilla.org/en-US/firefox/addon/4106**) provides users further options for consuming microformat content. Operator adds a toolbar to Firefox with a series of buttons that become active when different microformats are detected on a page. These buttons allow you to send hCalendar event data to your Google Calendar, export hCard contact info to your address book, and map the addresses or coordinates in Google Maps. See **FIGURE 2.4**.

A single click of the Google Calendar button in Operator will take you to your online calendar, and fill in all of the info listed on the page in the hCalendar format. With the info ported over, you can set alarms to remind you of the event, or even invite friends. Users enjoy the convenience of not forgetting an important date, and the developer helps ensure a good turnout at the event. See **FIGURE 2.5**.

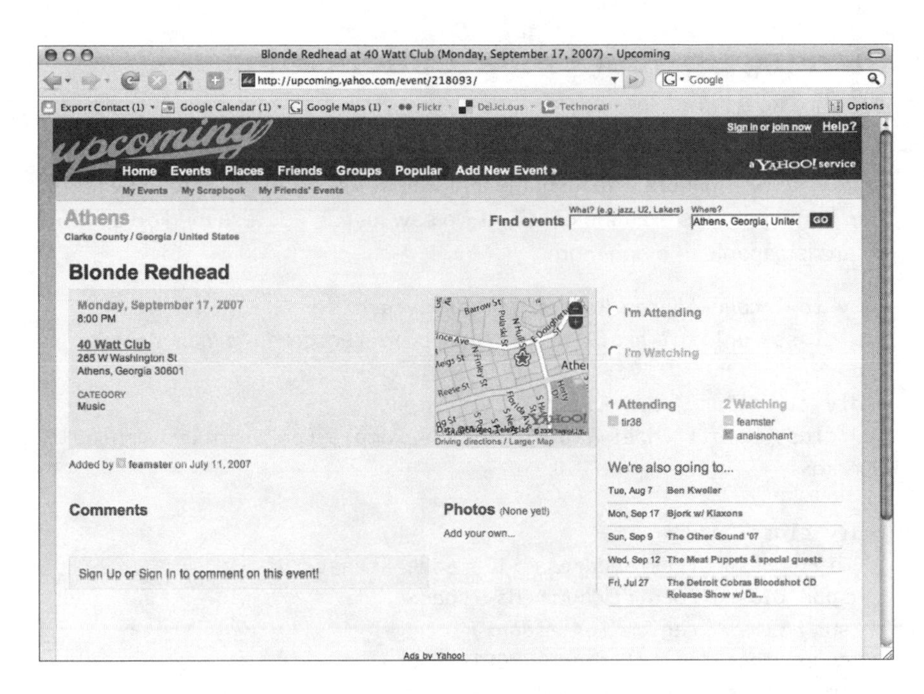

FIGURE 2.4 *Upcoming.org, a social networking website, lists events around the world and serves them up in microformats.*

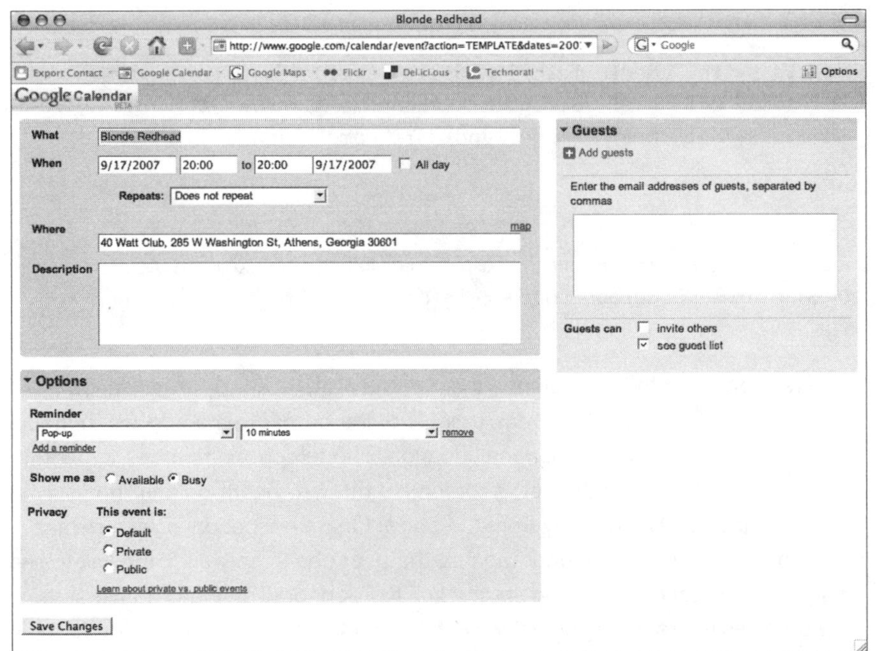

FIGURE 2.5 *All hCalendar content is seemlessly ported to Google Calendar via Operator.*

Marking Up Your Contact Information with hCard

A contact page is a staple of most any website, and it's generally a good idea to provide your visitors with all of the info they will need to get in touch with you. In the previous example of hCard we saw just an address marked up, but hCard is capable of much more.

```
<div id="hcard-Aarron-Walter" class="vcard">
 <a class="url fn" href="http://aarronwalter.com">Aarron Walter
</a>
 <div class="org">New Riders</div>
 <a class="email" href="mailto:email@example.com">email@example.
com</a>

 <div class="adr">
  <div class="street-address">123 Some Street</div>
  <span class="locality">Athens</span>,
  <span class="region">GA</span>,
  <span class="postal-code">30601</span>
  <span class="country-name">USA</span>
 </div>

 <a class="tel" href="tel:1115551212">(111) 555-1212</a><br />
 <a class="url" href="aim:goim?screenname=AIMname">AIM</a>
 <a class="url" href="ymsgr:sendIM?YIMname">YIM</a>
</div>

<p>
 <a href="http://technorati.com/contact/http://example.com/
contact.html">Download contact information</a>
</p>
```

The first portion of hCard includes the name (`fn`), URL (`url`), organization affiliation (`org`), and email address (`email`) of the contact. The address markup can accommodate any international location. The telephone number is marked up in an anchor tag with the `tel:` protocol so that any users on an iPhone could dial the number directly from the page. Chat application screen names are also marked up with anchor tags so the user can simply click the link to begin a conversation. Once again, the link to Technorati's hCard conversion service gives users a convenient way of adding the contact information to their address book, increasing the likelihood that they will get in touch.

All of these class names that serve as the identifiers of the content they mark up can also serve as hooks to style your content with great precision.

John Allsopp has written a brief but informative article called "Styling hCards with CS" (**http://24ways.org/2006/styling-hcards-with-css**) on 24 Ways that provides some useful styling examples that will make your contact information look as great as it functions.

hCard Creator

http://microformats.org/code/hcard/creator.html

Tagging Content with rel-tag

If you have used any of the popular Web application services such as Flickr, Last.fm, Delicious, or Magnolia then you are probably very familiar with the concept of tagging. A tag is simply visible meta data about a page, or a portion of content within it. By tagging our content, we provide humans and applications more detailed information about it, making finding what we are searching for much easier. See **FIGURE 2.6**.

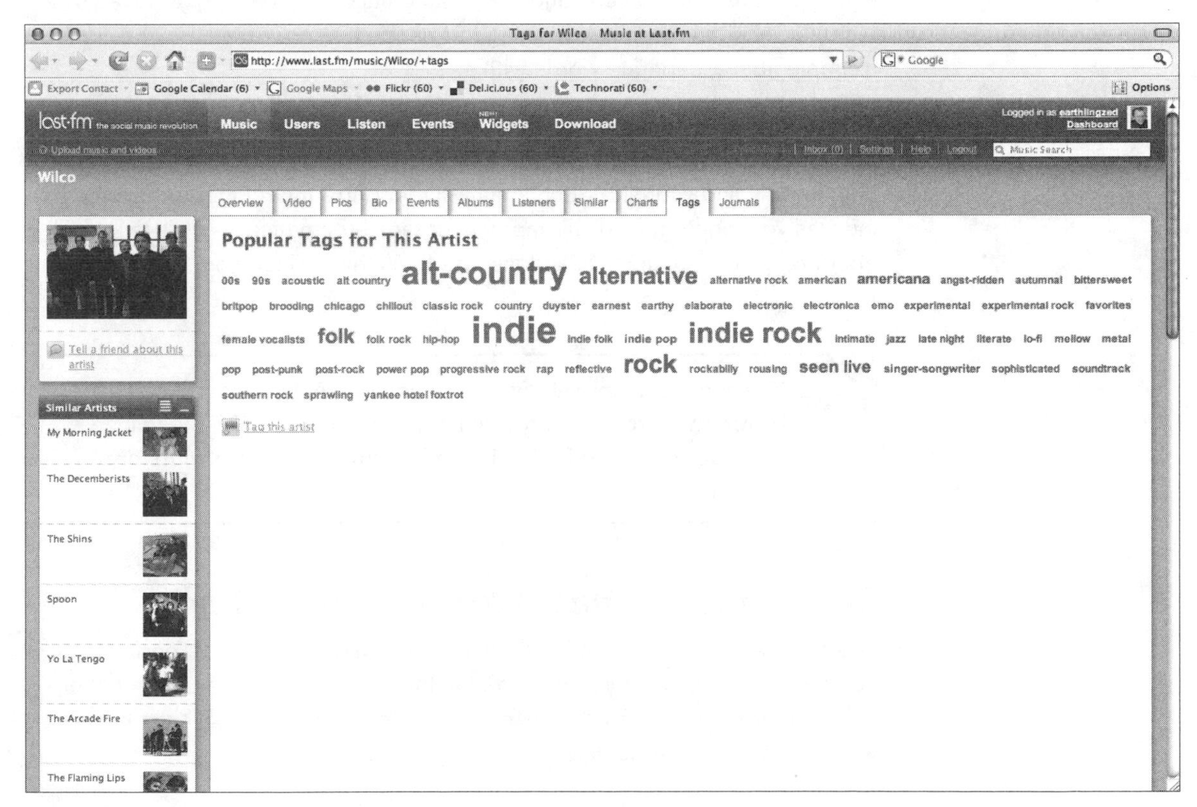

FIGURE 2.6 *Last.fm uses social tagging to help users learn about artists and find others that may be similar.*

Using rel-tag allows third-party services like Technorati to relate keywords to your content effectively labeling what it's about. These keywords help connect users searching Technorati to your content and can lead to an increase in traffic.

Tags usually link to external sources where the user can find related content with the same tag, or to a section of the same site where a server-side technology can grab all other content with the same tag.

Marking up a tag using the rel-tag microformat is quite simple.

```
<a href="http://www.last.fm/tag/indie+rock" rel="tag">
Indie Rock</a>
```

Defining this link as a tag is done by adding the `rel="tag"` attribute. The destination of your tag is required to be a page that collates or defines tags; in this case, we link to the Last.fm tag collation page. The end of the URL we are linking to is the tag content, and will be automatically gleaned by the tag system that receives the link. If your tag text needs a space, as is the case in the example above, separate words with a +.

The tags you add to describe your content like photos, or blog posts will provide more descriptive keywords that search engines can index and use to help people find your site. Technorati will recognize the rel-tag format when it indexes your content, and will import your tags automatically. We'll talk more about tagging in Chapter 5, and discuss tools that will tag your blog posts for you.

NOTE You can learn more about how to use the rel-tag microformat at **http://microformats.org/wiki/rel-tag**, and read about its close relative xFolk, used for bookmarks, at **http://microformats.org/wiki/xfolk**.

More Microformats Worth Investigating

There are a slew of useful microformats in the wild that offer the perfect solution for marking up all sorts of content in the most findable way. In fact, there are too many to be covered here, but I'd like to point out a few that you may wish to learn more about later.

All of these microformats and more are deftly explained with links to real world examples on the microformats wiki (**http://microformats.org/wiki/**).

hResume

hResume is for marking up resumes. The easiest way to get started is using the hResume builder at **http://hresume.weblogswork.com/hresumecreator/**, which includes an automatic ping to Technorati once your resume is complete.

hReview

hReview facilitates the writing of reviews of all sorts. Use the hReview creator at **http://microformats.org/code/hreview/creator** to easily convert any reviews to this findable format. hReviews are searchable using Technorati's microformat search engine (**http://kitchen.technorati.com/search/**)

VoteLinks

Search engine indexing systems view links to a site as an automatic endorsement, which can be problematic as there are times you want to link to a site with which you disagree. VoteLinks provides simple standards that indicate whether you support or disagree with the content you link to.

Using Icons To Point Out Microformat Content

Once you've so skillfully marked up your content using microformats, you'll need to tip off your users to the functionality that lies within. Using icons that are recognizable is the most efficient solution. Icon designs are still being standardized for microformats, and may not yet be recognized by many users. Bartelme Design has created a great icon development kit available for free download at **http://www.bartelme.at/journal/archive/microformats_icons/**, providing Photoshop and Illustrator source files so you can customize the color palette to fit your site. Once the Web community adopts a standard icon set, more users will start to recognize the presence of microformats on a page. See **FIGURE 2.7** and **FIGURE 2.8**.

Showing the icons next to your links—as **FIGURE 2.8** illustrates—is achieved with some basic CSS classes:

CSS

```
.hcal-icon {background:url(i/hcal.gif) no-repeat left;
padding-left:33px;}
.hcard-icon {background:url(i/hcard.gif) no-repeat left;
padding-left:33px;}
```

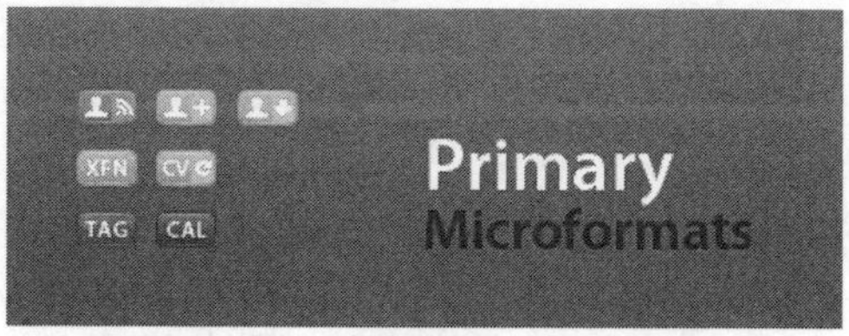

FIGURE 2.7 *Icons for hCard, hCalendar, rel-tag, and other microformats can be an effective way of informing your users about the microformats on the page.*

FIGURE 2.8 *Icons used to indicate microformat content.*

XHTML

```
<a href="http://technorati.com/contacts/http://example.com/events.
html" class=".hcal-icon">Download this event</a> |
<a href="http://technorati.com/events/http://example.com/events.
html" class=".hcard-icon">Download venue information</a>
```

Do Search Engines Recognize Microformat Content?

After gaining a great deal of support from developers, microformats are now finally being adopted by major companies on the Web who are both publishing large databases of content in hCard, hCalendar, and other microformats, and just beginning to index this content for more precise, segmented search results. Yahoo! is one of the largest publishers of microformat content, delivering hCalendar and hCard on Upcoming.org, over 15 million hCards in Yahoo! Local, and hCard, XFN (indicates friendships), and the geo (indicates location) microformats on Flickr. Google recently introduced hCard into Google Maps search results (**http://googlemapsapi.blogspot.com/2007/06/microformats-in-google-maps.html**), making the storage of addresses you've found much easier. Publication of content in microformats on a massive scale is great for findability, but more progress is needed still, especially from the major search engines.

At the time of publishing this book the major search engines were still watching with interest from the sidelines not yet implementing significant support for microformat searching. Google (**http://www.google.com/support/bin/answer.py?answer=29508**) and Yahoo! (**http://search.yahoo.com/cc**) currently do offer search services that look for content released under Creative Commons licensing using the rel-license microformat, which identifies content that can be reused under more open terms and conditions. It's still just a small step in the grand scheme of things, though. Imagine the power search engines could provide users if they indexed content with an informed algorithm that could tell the difference between an event, contact information, a recipe, a book review, and random text on a page. With microformats search has the potential to return much more precise and meaningful results to users.

Yahoo! and MSN Support Microformats–What Chance Google?
http://blogs.zdnet.com/web2explorer/?p=217

As more and more content is published using microformats, search engines will be hard pressed to pass up the opportunity to provide the unprecedented content indexing and search segmentation that microformats can facilitate. Currently, because the major search engines do not integrate microformat recognition into their algorithms, the findability boost that most microformats provide is not via SEO, but rather in the flexibility offered to users who could move your content to a location where they are sure to find and use it later. When the major search engines do start to introduce microformat searching, which will hopefully be the near future, your content will already be a step ahead of the competition.

Though the big three are currently somewhat passive on the implementation of microformat recognition algorithms into their systems, Technorati is blazing the trail, already introducing a microformat search engine (**http://kitchen.technorati.com/search/**) that allows users to find events, contact information, and reviews across the Web that are marked up with microformats. If your content is marked up correctly, you can wait for Technorati's search spiders to index your content or, better yet, be proactive and submit it yourself at **http://pingerati.net**. Pingerati.net notifies a number of microformat friendly services like Alexa, Eventful, and the rest of Technorati's services of your content, so a wider audience can index it.

Creative Commons Licensing

Creative Commons (**http://creativecommons.org**) offers a free, legal means of simultaneously protecting and sharing content of all sorts. Rather than a wholesale lockdown on usage and publication rights, a Creative Commons license outlines the ways people can share or remix your content into something new. Each license is delivered as an HTML page that can be linked to from the location of your content. By simply adding the `rel="license"` attribute to your link to the license, your content will be searchable by the Google (http://www.google.com/support/bin/answer.py?answer=29508) and Yahoo! (**http://search.yahoo.com/cc**) Creative Commons search systems.

```
<a href="http://creativecommons.
org/licenses/by/3.0/"
rel="license">Creative Commons
License</a>
```

3

Server-Side Strategies

Findability strategies extend beyond the client-side. The way you structure your files, build your URLs, design your 404 pages, and optimize your server for speed can significantly improve the findability of your site.

Oftentimes search engine optimization best practices are hyper-focused on making changes client-side. There are many simple things you can do sever-side as well that will make your site easier for search engines to index and help your audience find their way around better. You can significantly improve the findability of your site with file naming, choosing the right domain name, creating search engine friendly URLs, serving custom 404 pages, and plenty of server optimization for fast indexing.

File and Folders: The Power of a Name

What's in a name? Well, when it comes to the names of the files and folders in your site, a lot. Creating keyword density on your pages can help lift your site in search listings, but there are other places besides in your markup that can help out. Search engines index keywords in the names of files and folders in order to understand the content of your pages so choosing relevant, descriptive names for them is important. Here are a few recommendations to keep in mind when naming your files:

- Include keywords in file and folder names where natural, and certain ubiquitous files such as in the name of the logo, and default style sheet.
- Separate keywords in file and folder names with a hyphen rather than an underscore to ensure that search engines can read each word individually rather than as one large word. For example, most search engines will read a file named my-page.html as "my" "page," whereas my_page.html would be read as "my_page," which is not likely to match a search query. Google recently updated its system to recognize individual words in file names separated by an underscore. Since other search engines could be tripped up by the underscore, stick with hyphen-delimited keywords in your file names to be safe.

- Keep your keywords brief, and relevant to your audience. The more keywords you add, the more you dilute the power of each one.
- Contrary to rumors, a .html file extension will not rank higher than a .php extension, so feel free to use the one that is appropriate for your page.

Choosing and Managing Domain Names

Domain names are also a great place to include keywords that can help users find you. When choosing a domain name, it doesn't matter which extension you choose: .com, .net, .biz and all other extensions start on equal footing and will not in any way impact search engine rankings. Of course, .com domains tend to be more memorable to users because of their popularity, and therefore may be more desirable for word-of-mouth referrals.

Just as keywords in file names can help boost search listings, keywords in domain names are important as well. Keywords in a domain name separated by hyphens are individually readable, and are more desirable for search engine indexing, but can be a little trickier for users to remember. It may be a good idea to register your domain name with hyphens for search engines, and without for the memorability and easy verbal referral by users. You can park both domain names on the same server, pointing them to the same site. List the hyphen-delimited domain with search engines, and include the domain without the hyphens on print collateral and advertisements.

An added benefit of including your target keywords in your domain name is that it will help encourage all inbound links to your site to contain the same keywords, making your site more relevant to search queries.

The age of a domain name can play a significant role in the assigning of a Google PageRank (a mathematical formula that defines the reputation of a site specific to Google). Young domains are generally ranked low, since many disreputable link-farm sites created by spammers pop up temporarily to make money from link referrals then quickly disappear before search engines blacklist them. Consequently, older domains are always preferable. However, if you buy a recently expired domain name that has a high PageRank because of its age and accumulated reputation, the PageRank does not transfer to the new owner. Search engines can usually see when domain names change ownership, and will reset their rankings in such situations. You'll just have to buy a domain name that is relevant to your audience, and wait for it to age like a fine wine.

Determining Your Google PageRank

Using the free Google Toolbar (**http://toolbar.Google.com**), you can determine your site's PageRank just by viewing it in your browser. Pages are ranked on a 0–10 scale, where 10 is the highest ranking. When indexed for the first time, most sites start with a PageRank of around 2. As your domain name ages and you gain inbound links, the credibility of the site will increase along with your PageRank. PageRank is updated about four times a year, so be patient waiting for dividends from your efforts.

A high PageRank will make your site a stronger competitor for the keywords you target, thus raising your listing position on search engine return pages. See **FIGURE 3.1**.

FIGURE 3.1 *The Google toolbar is an easy way to view PageRank.*

Solving the Google Canonical Problem

When Google indexes sites, it sees URLs with and without the preceding *www* as entirely different sites. Referred to as the *Google canonical problem*, this indexing approach can negatively affect your PageRank as some inbound links to your site may include the www while others may not, which divides the number of links to your site from Google's perspective and splits your PageRank. You can tell if your site is suffering from the Google canonical problem by checking the PageRank of a page with and without the www in the URL. If you see two different PageRanks, then you'll want to fix this issue. We can solve the problem using an Apache module called `mod_rewrite`, which can automatically map all requests to a single, consistent format.

`mod_rewrite` is a handy Apache module that rewrites URLs when specified patterns are detected. It's exceptionally powerful, and can provide solutions to a number of SEO-related challenges including the Google canonical problem. We'll use it to execute a 301 redirect, sending the user's browser to a URL with the www included in the URL.

Servers provide different HTTP status codes to indicate a response to a request. You're probably familiar with a 404 status code that indicates the page requested was not found. A 301 status code is a redirect from the URL requested to another one specified by the server administrator.

To send out a 301 redirect status code, create a file called `htaccess.txt` with the following code to give Apache the message:

Force WWW

```
RewriteEngine On
RewriteCond %{HTTP_HOST} ^example.com$ [NC]
RewriteRule ^(.*)$ http://www.example.com/$1 [R=301,L]
```

This code uses regular expressions to locate specific patterns when evaluating URLs. Regular expressions are commonly used in many scripting and programming languages to identify patterns in strings—a series of text characters. They can be intimidating because of the cryptic characters they use to locate specific text, and aren't exactly an intuitive read without some prior research.

In this example we see strange characters that indicate text pattern scenarios. For example, the ^ indicates the start of the string, and the $ indicates the end of the string. Each special character has some pattern matching meaning. You can print out a quick reference to demystify regular expressions at http://www.ilovejackdaniels.com/cheat-sheets/regular-expressions-cheat-sheet/.

Now that you've got your rewrite code in place, upload the `htaccess.txt` file to the Web root of your server, then rename it to `.htaccess`. Naming the file `.htaccess` locally can cause problems, as it is a reserved name recognized by some operating systems such as Mac OS X, which would automatically hide it.

In case you are new to working with Apache, the `.htaccess` file provides on-the-fly configuration commands to the server and the various modules associated with it. Apache looks for this file whenever it needs to send out a response, and supports the use of unique `.htaccess` files in different directories for very granular control of the server's configuration. We'll be using it often to configure Apache to meet our findability goals.

301 Redirects and URL Rewriting on a Windows Server

If you are running a Windows server with IIS (Internet Information Services) you can still rewrite URLs, create 301 redirects and build search engine friendly URLs, but the method is a little different. Just like Apache uses modules to extend its feature set, IIS uses ISAPI (Internet Services Application Programming Interface) filters to provide features that are not available by default. An ISAPI filter can be used to rewrite URLs on the fly very much like `mod_rewrite` for Apache.

It's possible to create your own ISAPI rewrite filter, but it can be rather complex. Instead, you may want to use one of the many that have already been developed. There are a lot of ISAPI rewrite filters that you could track down with a quick Google search, but most of them you'd have to pay for. IIRF (Ionic's IIS Rewrite Filter) is a free rewrite filter that can do the same things as Apache's `mod_rewrite` and with a similar syntax (**http://cheeso.members.winisp.net/IIRF.aspx**).

Using the mod_rewrite Cheat Sheet

mod_rewrite can be intimidating and cryptic if you are new to it because of the many mysterious regular expression characters. You may want to refer to Dave Child's handy PDF mod_rewrite cheat sheet, which will introduce you to the basics, and even show you some common solutions for other SEO-related issues.

http://www.ilovejackdaniels.com/mod_rewrite_cheat_sheet.pdf

You can also learn more about mod_rewrite and see some good examples in the official documentation at **http://httpd.apache.org/docs/1.3/mod/mod_rewrite.html**.

The first line in the code example turns mod_rewrite on, and the next one sets a condition to be on the lookout for any page request with the domain name in the URL. Of course, example.com will need to be changed to your domain name in order for this to work. The last line creates a rewrite rule that redirects users to their intended destination with the www in the URL.

If you'd like to do the inverse and remove the www, just make sure your rewrite condition contains the www, and remove it from the rewrite rule.

Remove WWW

```
RewriteEngine On
RewriteCond %{HTTP_HOST} ^www.example.com$ [NC]
RewriteRule ^(.*)$ http://example.com/$1 [R=301,L]
```

There is one other way to ensure Google is using the desired URL structure when ranking your pages. The Google Web Master tools at **http://www.google.com/webmasters/sitemaps/**, which are discussed further in the bonus chapter entitled "Free Search Engine Tools and Services" on the companion site (**http://buildingfindablewebsites.com**), allow you to define your preference to include or exclude the www in your URLs when indexing. Taking this approach is good, but doesn't address canonical problems with other search engines, so it's still a good idea to employ the mod_rewrite solution as well.

Building Search Engine Friendly URLs

Poorly designed URLs can stop a search engine spider dead in its tracks, resulting in an incomplete indexing of your site. URLs with GET variable strings or session IDs in them are sometimes viewed incorrectly by search engines, and at other times are ignored completely. A URL like this, though very common in many ecommerce sites and Web applications, is not conducive to search engine indexing, nor is it very usable for humans:

```
http://example.com/top-sellers/products.php?color=red&prodId=12
```

Everything after the question mark, called GET variables or a query string, is often ignored by search engines, which would likely result in the display of the page without the necessary variables required to render it with content from a database. Though search engines may not care for them, dynamic pages that use GET data are still essential to many websites, so it's not an option to abandon them entirely in favor of static pages. There are a few different ways to build search engine friendly URLS, and we'll explore two popular solutions, both of which assume you are running an Apache server and have the ability use a `.htaccess` file to configure it, as is typical of most shared hosting environments. In both cases, we'll be rebuilding the above URL to something like this, which search engines and users will appreciate.

```
http://example.com/top-sellers/products/red/12
```

A Simple Solution

The simplest solution requires that your dynamic pages that use GET variables be named without their typical extension like `.php` so they can appear in the URL as if they were a directory. If you are creating a new site rather than modifying an existing one where changing file names is inconvenient, you can create extension-less file names then force Apache to recognize their file type. Again we'll use a `.htaccess` file to configure Apache.

```
<Files products>
 ForceType application/x-httpd-php
</Files>
```

The `<Files products>` tag indicates the file the server should keep an eye out for, and `ForceType application/x-httpd-php` forces the file to be recognized as PHP. If you had many dynamic pages that used GET variables, you'd need to replicate the above code in your .htaccess file to identify each page that should be forced to be PHP. Now that Apache will once again parse the PHP code, we'll need to create an easy way to grab the GET variables off the end of the URL, as PHP will no longer recognize the GET variables at the end of the URL. To do this, we'll need to split the URL into separate pieces then assign them to variables that PHP can once again use.

This function, saved in an external include file called `getParams.php`, receives a string indicating the base path from the Web root directory to the PHP page so it can locate where the parameter list starts in the URL, then returns an array for easy use. In this case, the base path will be /top-sellers/products/.

```
<?php
// Pull parameters off URL and return as an array
function getParams($baseUrl){
  if (!strstr($_SERVER['REQUEST_URI'],$baseUrl)){
      // error, base path is not in the URL
      trigger_error('$baseUrl is invalid: '.$baseUrl );
  }

  // pull paramters off of URI, replacing with an empty string
  if ($baseUrl != '/'){
      $fragment = str_replace($baseUrl,'',$_SERVER['REQUEST_
URI']);
  }else{
      $fragment = $_SERVER['REQUEST_URI'];
  }

  // convert "/" seperated params to an array
  $params = explode('/',$fragment);
  return $params;
}
?>
```

The $_SERVER['REQUEST_URI'] super global variable, which is built into the PHP language, retrieves the URL. Using PHP's strstr() function to search for a string within a string, the base path can be found so we know where to start looking for the parameters we are after. An error is thrown if the base path is not found as the parameters would be impossible to locate without it. Assuming the base path was found, it gets deleted from the URL string by replacing it with an empty string. Finally, using the explode() function, which splits strings into an array with many values, the parameters string is turned into an array by looking for the / which separates them. The resulting array is then returned to the location where the function was called. Here's what that array would look like if we used print_r() to write it to the page for a quick evaluation:

```
Array ( [0] => red [1] => 12 )
```

On the product page where the parameters need to be used, we simply include the file, call the function sending it the base path, then use the parameters as we like:

```
<?
require_once('inc/getParams.php');
$parameters = getParams('/top-sellers/products/');
$color = $parameters[0];
$prodId = $parameters[1];

// Do some database query with retrieved parameters
?>
```

Though a few extra lines of code are required in your dynamic pages to retrieve the GET data, the search engine friendly URLs are well worth the effort.

Using mod_rewrite

If you have `mod_rewrite` installed on your server, as is the case on most Unix/Linux hosting environments, then you may prefer to have it automatically rewrite your URLs for you, rather than having to name files without an extension. `mod_rewrite` maps URLs to other locations using regular expressions, which were introduced earlier in this chapter in the section entitled "Solving the Google Canonical Problem." Let's take a look at a simple rewrite rule that will remap the URL for the `products.php` script:

```
RewriteEngine On
RewriteRule ^products/([a-zA-Z0-9]+)\/([0-9]+) products.
php?color=$1&id=$2
```

The first line simply turns `mod_rewrite` on to execute the following command. The `RewriteRule` looks for the products script with a query string trailing, then converts it to `products/`first GET variable in letters or numbers/second GET variable in numbers. You could add slots for more GET variables in your URLs by modifying the rewrite rule:

```
RewriteRule ^products/([a-zA-Z0-9]+)\/([0-9]+)/([a-zA-Z0-9]+)
products.php?color=$1&id=$2&newVar=string
```

The function we used in the first example would also be used with the `mod_rewrite` approach, and could accommodate any number of GET variables you need to grab from the URL.

An important thing to note when testing this is that the above rewrite is not an auto redirection, just a remapping. If you try testing this by entering the original URL with the query string, it will not automatically redirect you to the new search engine friendly URL. It simply points the search engine friendly URL to the `products.php` page.

General Guidelines for URL Design

Before getting too far into the development of your site, you'll want to take some time to consider the structure of your URLs, and the variables that will need to be passed within them. Keep these guidelines in mind as you hatch your search engine friendly URL plans:

- Try to make your URLs predictable to users. Define a system that users will instantly understand, such as naming directories and/or files with the same names as the navigation labels, and be sure to stay consistent.
- Where possible, avoid including too many dynamic parameters that can make the URL cumbersome to reference and impossible to type. Even a search engine friendly URL can quickly become unwieldy for humans.
- Shorter, descriptive URLs are more convenient for people who wish to link to your site, thus encouraging inbound links or reference in printed materials.

If you can make good on these three simple recommendations, your site is going to be much more navigable for search engines, and your users.

Moving Pages and Domains with 301 Redirects

From time to time it's necessary to move the location of a page, change its name, or even move to a totally different domain name. In these situations you want to make sure you get your users and search engines informed about the new location. As mentioned in Chapter 2, a meta refresh, which automatically sends users to a new URL using a special meta tag, is the wrong solution for the problem, as it is used by spammers to trick search engines into incorrectly indexing pages. You can redirect requests for the old URLs directly from the server using `mod_rewrite` to do a 301 redirection. There's no negative stigma around 301 redirects in the eyes of search engines as there is with meta refresh, so there are no worries of being mistaken for a spammer. When search engines receive a 301 redirect, they automatically update their records to replace the old URL with the new one.

Imagine we've updated a contact page that was once simply HTML with the typical contact info, but now we've decided to add a PHP contact form so users can more conveniently contact the organization. To do this, the extension of the page needs to change from `.html` to `.php` so the server will run the page through the PHP engine. It's a good idea to automatically send people to the new location in case users try to access the old HTML page that no longer exists. To make this happen, add the following code to your .htaccess file on your server:

```
# Redirect to new contact page
RewriteEngine On
RewriteRule ^contact.html(.*)$ /contact.php [L,R=301]
```

If you already have another rewrite rule in your file, you won't need to turn the rewrite engine on again as is shown in the second line. Note that you can comment your .htaccess files by preceding your notes with the #. The last line simply looks for any URL that points to contact.html in the Web root directory, and sends a 301 HTTP response to redirect the request to contact.php.

This same approach is equally useful if you are moving to an entirely new domain name. Although the code is slightly more verbose, the ideas are the same:

```
RewriteEngine On
RewriteCond %{HTTP_HOST} ^(www\.)?old-site\.com$ [NC]
RewriteRule ^(.*)$ http://www.new-site.com/$1 [R=301,L]
```

After the rewrite engine is enabled, a condition is set looking for the domain name with or without the proceeding www, and regardless of capitalization. Next, requests are redirected to the new domain name with the preceding www and with the trailing path that may have been entered for the original request. Keep in mind this assumes you have the same directory and file structure with the new domain as the old one.

Using the 301 redirect will help ensure the Google PageRank of the old domain gets transferred to the new one, but be aware that redirects can slow down the user experience, and Apache as it will have additional lookup tasks on top of serving the requested file. In most situations this will not be very perceptible, but on high-traffic sites redirects can cause a noticeable slowdown in server performance. With this in mind, keep your use of 301 redirects to a minimum for simple tasks like correcting changed directory structures, file names, or domain names.

A little forward thinking can help you avoid having to do a lot of redirecting when your site changes. If a number of files in your site have to switch from HTML to PHP, rather than changing the file extensions, you could force Apache to run all HTML files through the PHP engine. By taking this approach all of your existing file extensions can stay the same. You can change Apache's configuration in your .htaccess file as follows:

```
AddType application/x-httpd-php .php .html
```

This simple line of code tells the server that all files with a .php or .html extension need to be run through the PHP parsing engine.

Alternatively you could just not include an extension on your files so you have the flexibility in the future to have the server deliver them as plain HTML or run them through the PHP parsing engine. This can be a little more tedious to manage, as you'd need to tell Apache what file type is to be used on your anonymous files. You can do this using ForceType in your .htaccess file as illustrated earlier in this chapter in the section about creating search engine friendly URLs, entitled "A Simple Solution." Extension-less files can be troublesome when you are building them in your development application because they will probably not show color-coding, code hints, and other features the software offers that are dependant upon knowing the file type.

Getting Users Back on Track with Custom 404 Pages

The default 404 error pages displayed by servers are cryptic to novice Web users, provide no explanation of why the error occured, and offer no means of getting back on track. They are a dead end that can frustrate users, and cause them to leave your site. The solution to the problem is to create a custom error page that can provide a clearer description of the problem, and offer solutions that could get your visitors back on track. Triggering the display of custom error pages is as simple as modifying your .htaccess file to tell the Apache server what to do when a URL can't be resolved:

```
ErrorDocument 404 http://www.example.com/404.php
```

Hunting Down Broken Links

Serving up helpful 404 pages is great, but it's even better to locate and fix broken links so your users don't have to deal with 404 errors at all. The W3C has a handy link validation tool (**http://validator.w3.org/checklink**) that will do your dirty work for you as you sip coffee and watch the magic happen. You give it a URL, and it will dig through your site, providing a detailed report of the problems and how to fix them.

This single line of code is all it takes to trigger the display of 404.php in the Web root directory when a requested file is not found. Many shared hosting environments actually have 404 page handling options in their control panels, and may even have a template to get you started. Should your server not support the method shown above, you could instead use `mod_rewrite` to determine when a request is neither a file nor a directory, then trigger the display of the custom 404 page. This is a little less desirable because it is slightly more complex, but is still a great solution if your options are limited:

```
# Request is not a file
RewriteCond %{REQUEST_FILENAME} !-f
# Request is not a directory
RewriteCond %{REQUEST_FILENAME} !-d
RewriteRule .? /404.php [L]
```

Windows users can download and install Xenu (**http://home.snafu.de/tilman/xenulink.html**), which also helps you identify broken links but from your local machine. If you're running a Windows IIS server you can set custom 404 error pages just by changing a few properties for your site. 404 error handling is built right into IIS. Microsoft offers a helpful tutorial on the subject at **http://www.microsoft.com/technet/prodtechnol/windows2000serv/technologies/iis/tips/custerr.mspx**.

The Elements of a Successful 404 Page

Beyond knowing how to trigger a custom 404 page, it's even more important know how to design one. A well-designed 404 page should help users recover from wrong turns or broken links without technical jargon or finger-pointing messages admonishing your users for their ignorant navigation choices. It's a great opportunity to turn an otherwise frustrating user experience into a positive one, and keep users on the site longer. To get the best results, keep these simple guidelines in mind:

- The design should be consistent with the rest of the site.
- Include a clear message acknowledging the problem, indicating the possible cause (don't admonish your users), and offering solutions.
- Avoid technical jargon as many users may not know what a 404 error means.
- Include the search box so users can find what they are looking for.
- Include a link to the home page.

- Include a link to the site map that provides links to all of the main sections of the site.
- Include an option to report a broken link (contact form link).
- Optionally, suggest popular destinations on the site.
- Never auto-redirect users to another page, such as the home page, as users will have no idea that an error occurred and will be confused about what happened.

Don't be afraid to inject some humor into your copy for your 404 pages. No one likes getting lost on a site, but finding something funny on the page makes the experience like finding an Easter egg. **FIGURES 3.2–3.5** show a variety of examples of successful 404 error pages.

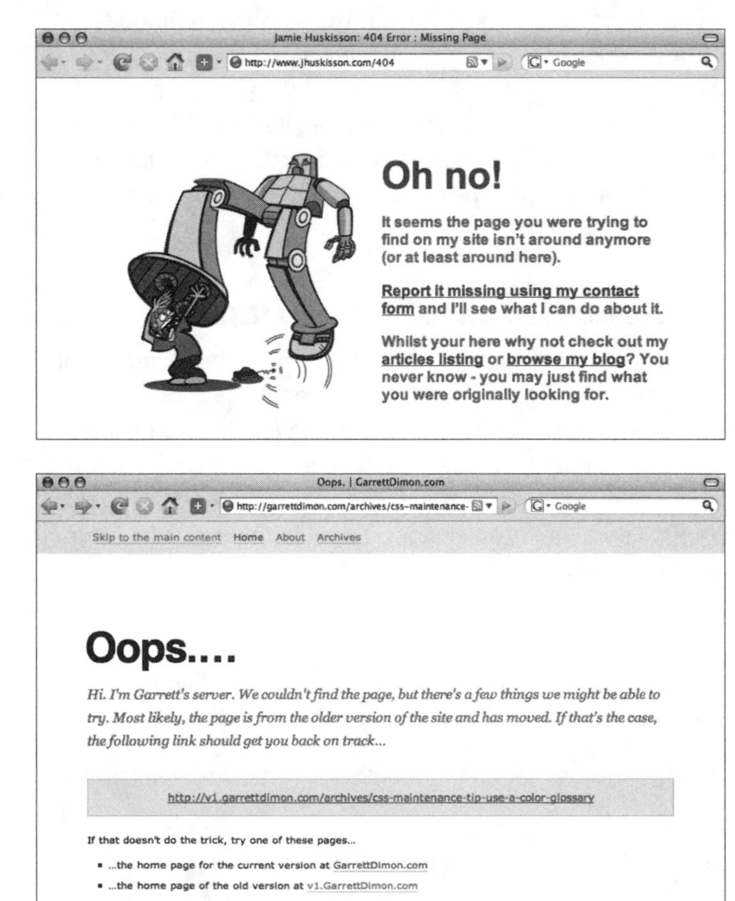

FIGURE 3.2 *Jamie Huskisson (**http://www.jhuskisson.com**) uses humor to make the experience of getting lost on his site a little more like finding an Easter egg.*

FIGURE 3.3 *Garrett Dimon's (**http://garrettdimon.com**) 404 page points lost users to areas in the previous version of his site which may contain the content they seek.*

SimpleBits ~ Oops!

http://www.simplebits.com/404

SimpleBits

HOME NOTEBOOK WORK PUBLICATIONS T-SHIRTS ABOUT CONTACT

Oops!

File Not Found

404 Error: The page you are looking for can't be found. Sorry!

There could be a few different reasons for this:

- The page was moved.
- The page no longer exists.
- The URL is slightly incorrect.

To get you back on track, I'd suggest one of the following:

- Notebook archives
- About SimpleBits
- Report a broken link

FROM THE NOTEBOOK

Search the Notebook SEARCH

- After Media
- Gone Fishing
- Cork'd Finds a New Home
- Compatriots

BOOKS *by* DAN CEDERHOLM

Bulletproof Web Design
Improving flexibility and protecting against worst-case scenarios, Second Edition

Web Standards Solutions
The Markup and Style Handbook

SNAPSHOTS

FIGURE 3.4 *Dan Cederholm's site* ***http://simplebits.com*** *provides a number of options to get the user back on track.*

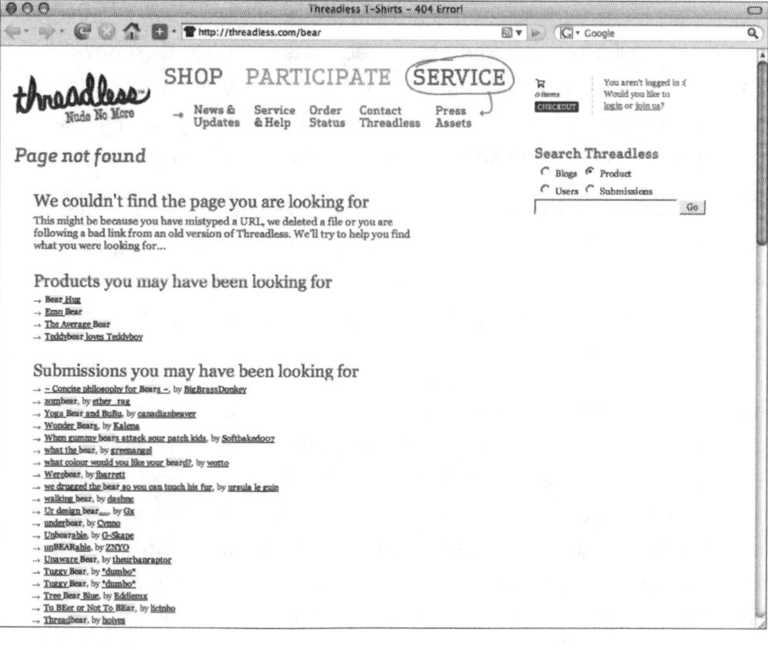

FIGURE 3.5 *The popular designer T-shirt site Threadless* ***(http://threadless.com)*** *uses server-side scripting to look at the keywords in the URL so it can suggest links to the pages the user may have been searching for.*

Optimizing Performance for Efficient Indexing

The loading speed of pages is a significant issue for search engine spiders, which have the mandate to crawl and index the Web as fast as possible. Optimizing content delivery can help ensure that spiders can crawl pages quickly, efficiently, and create more complete listings. As an added bonus, your users will appreciate the performance boost too, as they'll spend less time waiting for content, and more time enjoying your site!

The speed at which your content is served can be affected primarily by the way the server is set up to send responses and by the files that are being served. Achieving optimal performance is a bit like alchemy, requiring a number of smaller tasks that can add up to a big increase in response and rendering speeds. Let's start our performance optimization with some simple server configuration that will make a significant difference in indexing speed.

Cache and Dash: Getting Clients To Cache Files

The temporary memory of a client, known as the *cache*, can significantly speed up the browsing of a site. By the way, the term *client* refers to any browser, search engine spider, or other entity making a request of the server. As a client views a site, it stores common files in the cache so it doesn't have to continually make redundant trips to the server for the files it's already requested. Clients will often skip redundant requests if the file they have stored in memory is still current. Usually servers are not by default set up to define the expiration date of files, which prevents clients from taking full advantage of caching and thus significantly slows the crawling/viewing of a site.

In order to really wrap our heads around the idea of caching files, and understand how to configure Apache to give us the speed boost we want, we'll need a working knowledge of HTTP, the protocol used when servers and clients communicate on the Web. Here's a quick primer to set the stage for our server-side optimizations.

The back-and-forth dialog between a client and a server is delivered via HTTP or Hypertext Transfer Protocol, a standardized communication protocol that is split into requests and responses. All HTTP communication includes some simple bits of text at the top of the message, called headers, that provide lots of information about the communiqué including date and time information, which are central to our optimization goals. The HTTP headers in a request from a client are different from those in a response from a server.

HTTP headers are normally invisible to the average Web user, but you can take a peek behind the scenes using a shareware HTTP monitoring program called Charles (**http://www.xk72.com/charles/**). Charles acts as a proxy through which all HTTP request and response headers pass as you navigate sites in a browser. It can be used on Mac OS X, Windows, and Linux and will work with any browser. If you're using Firefox you'll need to download the free add-on from the Charles site to route all request and response traffic through Charles. **FIGURE 3.6** shows Charles revealing some typical HTTP request headers sent by the client to the server, the last of which is centrally important for search engines.

TIP If you're doing any work with Ajax, Charles can be an exceptionally useful tool, as it will show your XMLHttpRequests (XHR) as each call to the server is made.

The very last request header shown in **FIGURE 3.6** is `If-Last-Modified`, one that search engine spiders often use to determine if they have to re-index a file or if they can instead rely on their cached content. As its name suggests, `If-Last-Modified` compares the modification/expiration date of a file to the date of the cached file. If the file has changed then the spider will re-index it, but

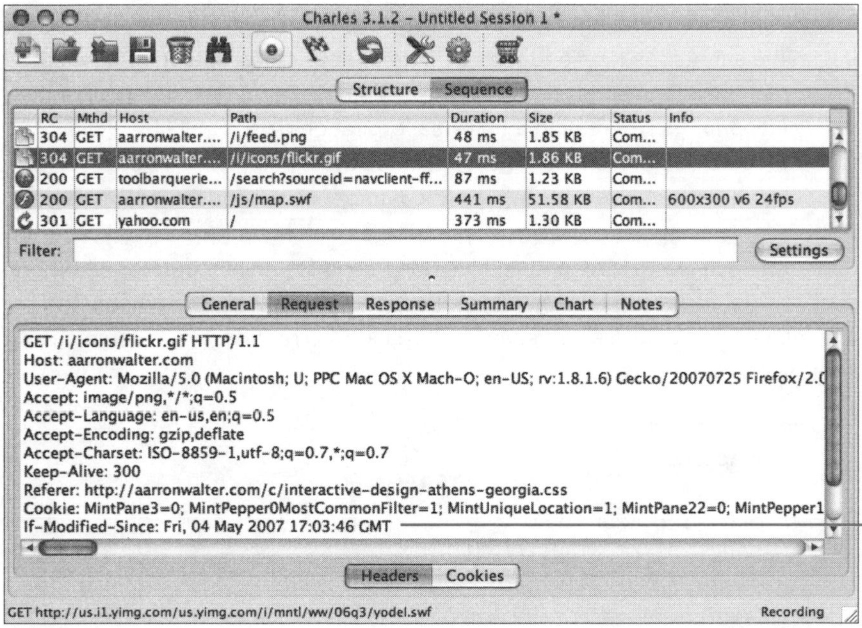

FIGURE 3.6 *Using Charles, a shareware HTTP monitor/proxy, you can observe HTTP requests and responses for any website in your browser. The* `If-Last-Modified` *request header shown here sent by the client to determine if the file requested has changed since it was last downloaded.*

Date file was last modified

if it hasn't the server sends out a 304 response, meaning there is no need to request this file.

It may, at first, sound like a negative thing to encourage spiders to skip the indexing of certain content, but it's actually a huge benefit. If spiders are able to rely more on their cached files from a previous crawl of your site then they will be able to cruise through at a much faster speed, grabbing only the new stuff. Files like your logo, master style sheet, or common JavaScript libraries can take a long time to download, but do not get updated regularly. The files you want search engines to re-index regularly are likely to be your HTML or PHP files where you've added new content or made changes. Using an `.htaccess` file, you can configure your server to tell clients to regularly index the important file types, and only periodically download others that rarely change.

Our `.htaccess` file will configure the Apache module called `mod_expires`, which is typically installed with most Apache servers, to set the expiration headers in HTTP responses. Here's a simplified example of how it works:

```
<IfModule mod_expires.c>
  ExpiresActive On
  # All Files: 1 month from access date
  ExpiresDefault A2592000
</IfModule>
```

To be cautious we first check to see if `mod_expires` is available on the server; if it is, the script fires it up and then defines the expiration date to one month from when the client accessed the file. The `ExpiresDefault` is doing all of the heavy lifting for us by creating a universal expiration date for all files downloaded regardless of file type. The `A` indicates the time the client accessed the file, and the number following it is the number of seconds in one month. Although handy, this is not quite as practical as setting unique expiration dates for each file type as certain files don't need frequent indexing but others certainly do. Following the same idea, here's an example that segments the expiration dates of all files so some can be indexed regularly and others can be passed over:

```
<IfModule mod_expires.c>
  ExpiresActive On

   # 1 Year: Ico, PDF, FLV
  <FilesMatch "\.(ico|pdf|flv)$">
    ExpiresDefault A2419200
  </FilesMatch>
```

```
  # 1 Month: Jpg, PNG, GIF, SWF
  <FilesMatch "\.(jpg|jpeg|png|gif|swf)$">
    ExpiresDefault A2419200
  </FilesMatch>

  # 1 Month: XML, TXT, CSS, JS
  <FilesMatch "\.(xml|txt|css|js)$">
    ExpiresDefault A2419200
  </FilesMatch>

  # 2 Days: HTML, PHP
  <FilesMatch "\.(html|htm|php)$">
    ExpiresDefault A172800
  </FilesMatch>
</IfModule>
```

The `FilesMatch` condition can be used to group certain file types to share a common expiration date. Files such as PDF and FLV, which are less likely to change and can significantly slow down the indexing of your site, will be cached for an entire year. HTML and PHP, on the other hand, are cached for just two days to maintain freshness. With the expiration dates logically assigned, you remove a significant burden from search engines, which will have to download fewer files when indexing your site. Some added benefits of this optimization are that you will conserve server bandwidth, thus saving on the costs associated with it, and your human users will also see much faster load times when their cache is primed with your site files.

Another way to set the expiration date of files is by using the Apache module called `mod_headers` to define the `cache-control`. The ideas are very similar, as is the code, and both do essentially the same thing. The difference between using `mod_headers` and `mod_expires` is that `mod_headers` will actually override all other cache settings, but will not work with the older HTTP 1.0 specification. Since most browsers from the late 1990s and on have supported HTTP 1.1 or better, this caveat seems less compelling. Let's take a look at the `mod_headers` approach, which would also make use of an `.htaccess` file to modify Apache's configuration:

```
<IfModule mod_headers.c>
  # Default: 1 Week
  Header set Cache-Control "max-age=2592000, public"

  # 1 Year: Ico, PDF, FLV
  <FilesMatch "\.(ico|pdf|flv)$">
    Header set Cache-Control "max-age=29030400, public"
```

```
  </FilesMatch>

  # 1 Month: Jpg, PNG, GIF, SWF
  <FilesMatch "\.(jpg|jpeg|png|gif|swf)$">
    Header set Cache-Control "max-age=2592000, public"
  </FilesMatch>

  # 1 Month: XML, TXT, CSS, JS
  <FilesMatch "\.(xml|txt|css|js)$">
    Header set Cache-Control "max-age=2592000, public"
  </FilesMatch>

  # 2 Days: HTML, PHP
  <FilesMatch "\.(html|htm|php)$">
    Header set Cache-Control "max-age=172800, public"
  </FilesMatch>
</IfModule>
```

Again, we start by determining if the module is installed, and if it is we execute the header modifications. The first `cache-control` sets a default expiration of one month for all files unless specified otherwise. Again, the times are set in seconds, so you'll need to break out your calculator to modify the expiration times to fit your needs.

With the `cache-control` or `ExpiresDefault` set, clients like search spiders can take advantage of caching, relying more on their archives and spending less time making redundant requests to the server. If you have content that changes regularly you can certainly adjust the expiration and caching threshold to ensure your audience is finding your latest content.

Setting Expiration Date Headers for Dynamic Content

If your content is coming from a database it's likely to have a different modification date than the file itself. The expiration date you'll want to deliver will need to be calculated from the date the content in the database was modified, rather than by the file modification date. To do this you'll need to have some sort of date/time stamp associated with each record entered when it is created or updated. When you pull the content from the database, you can manually set the expiration headers using the built in PHP function `header()`. Be sure to set these headers before outputting any content to the page, as the HTTP headers get sent to the client immediately when anything is written to the page. Once the HTTP headers ship has sailed, you can't make changes as needed.

The W3C provides further explanation of this issue along with a couple of simple PHP examples at **http://www.w3.org/QA/2007/07/the_way_of_web_standards.html**.

Managing File Size

Obviously, the size of the files the server is sending to the client can really slow down the download speed of a page. There are many techniques to keep the size of your files down, all of which can and should work in concert to shave off download time wherever possible.

A very general rule of thumb to keep in mind is that the collective weight of a page including HTML, images, CSS, JavaScript, and other accoutrements should stay below 100k if possible to facilitate speedy downloads. Of course, life isn't always so utopian, and there are situations where larger file sizes can't be avoided.

Inside of your HTML files you can trim file size by simply avoiding excessive white space, and overly verbose commenting. Compact your code and trim comments as much as possible without compromising legibility for you and your teammates who have to manage the files.

Naming utility folders such as your images, JavaScript, and CSS folders with shorter names like i, js, and c eliminates text in your files where frequent links are made to content in these directories. Since this type of content is not what we want search engines to index, short, keyword-poor names like this will have no bearing on the keyword density that we desire.

Externalizing all CSS and JavaScript and avoiding inline or local style sheets and obtrusive in-page embedding of JavaScript allows clients to cache this content, which is often shared between pages on a site. Internalizing this type of code defeats the server-side caching efforts discussed above. Although we'll be discussing some JavaScript best practices in Chapter 7, consult Jeremy Keith's book *DOM Scripting* (**http://domscripting.com/**), published by Friends of Ed, for further explanation of the concepts and benefits of unobtrusive JavaScript.

JavaScript files, such as the popular frameworks and libraries used in many Web applications today, are notoriously bloated with white space, comments, and functionality that may not even be desired. Purist JavaScript developers like Peter Paul Koch (aka PPK, **http://quirksmode.com**) argue that the best solution to this bloat is to build your own JavaScript libraries to include just the essential functionality that you need. Other developers argue that this is unnecessarily reinventing the wheel, and is not always the most practical solution. Whichever side of the argument you come down on, there are some useful methods for keeping your JavaScript files smaller.

Minifying is the process of removing white space (such as tabs, new lines, and spaces), and comments, leaving a lean file that is not very practical while you're making updates, but it's great when development and testing are complete. Amazingly, minifying your JavaScript can reduce file size significantly, sometimes by 50 percent or more. It would be painfully tedious to do this by hand, but there are a number of great, free tools on the Web that will do it for you. Some minification tools go even further to shrink your files by renaming variables and all references to them with shorter names, shaving even more off the file size.

Dean Edwards has created an exceptionally useful JavaScript minifier called Packer (**http://dean.edwards.name/packer/**). Packer (see **FIGURE 3.7**) is a simple little Web app in which you paste your code, click "pack," and out comes a minified version of the script without comments or white space. It provides the option of renaming variables in the packing process to further decrease the files size of your JavaScript. Packer is also available in .Net, PHP, and Perl scripts that could be integrated into your Web applications to automate file compression.

In order for Packer to produce a working, compressed version of your JavaScript you'll need to make sure your code is well formed with proper syntax.

FIGURE 3.7 *Dean Edwards' JavaScript minification tool Packer can significantly decrease the file size of your external JavaScript. The file size of this script has been decreased 44 percent.*

44% decrease in file size

All of your semicolons and curly braces need to be in order for it to work properly. Be sure to test your JavaScript files in your browser after minification, as the process can sometimes introduce errors.

TIP The popular JavaScript framework Prototype (**http://www.prototypejs.org**) doesn't take well to minification because it uses a slightly less formal coding approach. Running Prototype through Dean Edwards' Packer will produce an unusable file. Instead of minifying Prototype yourself, use one of Steve Kallestad's working compressed versions (**http://www.stevekallestad.com/blog/prototype_and_scriptaculous_compressed.html**) or run Prototype through jscompact (**http://jscompact.sourceforge.net/**) before running it through Packer.

Some JavaScript libraries like MooTools (**http://mootools.net/**) offer the option of building a custom version *a la carte*, selecting just the functionality you need. Once you've selected the features you want, MooTools also offers compression options, including running the code through Dean Edwards' Packer automatically. Choose compression when you are ready to deploy your site, but avoid it while you are still in development so you can explore or change the file if needed.

CSS files can also be minified in much the same way as JavaScript, removing comments and white space. CSS files written with each declaration on its own line can increase file size exponentially because of the huge amount of added white space. CSS Drive (see **FIGURE 3.8**) has a useful CSS minification tool that can crunch your files down to their most efficient sizes (**http://www.cssdrive.com/index.php/main/csscompressor/**).

Compressing Files with Gzip

Yet another way to save file size and download time is by using a standard HTTP compression called Gzip. Gzip can compress common text files such as CSS, JavaScript, and XML, making significant file size reductions. Most modern browsers now support HTTP 1.1 or greater, which is required to decompress Gzip files once they've been downloaded, making Gzip compression a safe option for most any project. Manually Gzipping your files before posting them would get old quickly; an automated approach would be much more convenient.

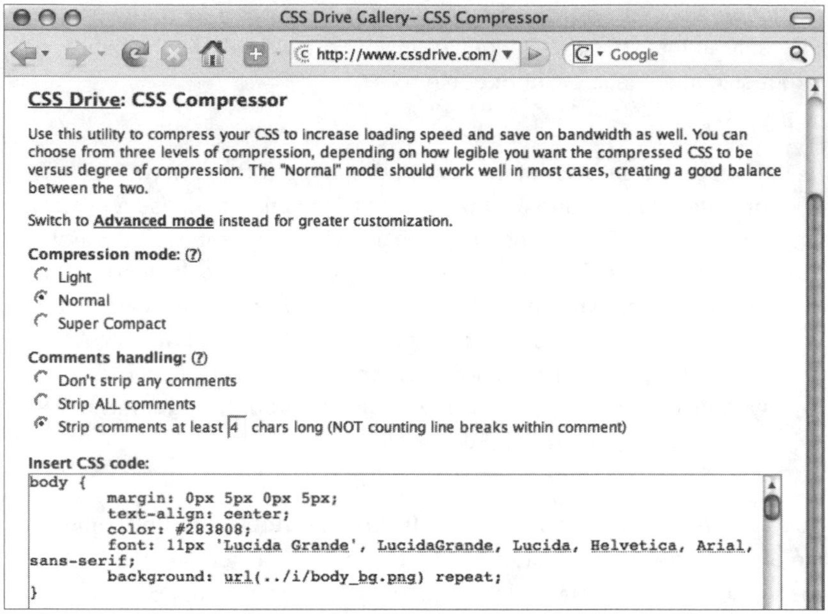

FIGURE 3.8 *The CSS compression tool from CSS Drive can create further file size savings to help your site load efficiently for search engines and users.*

Niels Leenheer of **http://rakaz.nl/** has developed a brilliant yet simple solution[1] that fits the bill, compressing each file on the fly when requested from the server. Anytime a client requests a CSS or JavaScript file, the Leenheer technique routes them through a PHP script that works its compression magic. Leenheer's script does more than simple Gzip compression, though; it actually combines multiple JavaScript and CSS files into one larger Gzip file so only one HTTP request is necessary from the server, improving download times even further. Each HTTP request to a server slows down the load time of a page, so combining many requests into one can be a huge time saver.

It actually ends up saving HTML code too. Rather than listing multiple script tags in your HTML to connect to JavaScript files, you instead make just a single call, separating the file names with commas:

```
<script type="text/javascript" src="http://example.com/js/prototype.
js,builder.js,effects.js,dragdrop.js,slider.js"></script>
```

One drawback of Leenheer's approach is that the time required to compress many files on the fly can be rather long, negatively offsetting a good portion of the speed increase. Leenheer solves this problem by creating a writable

1. http://rakaz.nl/item/make_your_pages_load_faster_by_combining_and_compressing_javascript_and_css_files

Using Apache's mod_deflate and mod_gzip

There are other options for on-the-fly compression of your files. Apache 2.0 supports a module called `mod_deflate` that can be configured to automatically compress your files for you. If your server is running Apache 1.3 you'll need to use `mod_gzip` for your compression. Stephen Pierzchala's articles on SitePoint.com do a good job of walking you through the configuration of each module.

http://www.sitepoint.com/article/web-output-mod_gzip-apache

http://www.sitepoint.com/article/mod_deflate-apache-2-0-x

cache folder on the server where the combined and compressed file can be stored for immediate access, circumventing the need to continually perform processor intensive compression.

According to Leenheer, with his combine and compress approach eight external JavaScript files collectively weighing in at around 168kb and taking 1905ms to download can be compressed down to 37kb, downloading in just 400ms. That's an 88 percent decrease in file size and an 80 percent decrease in load time!

Leenheer's solution uses `mod_rewrite` to run all CSS and JavaScript through the PHP script automatically, making setup and maintenance a snap. Place the following code in your `.htaccess` file to set up the automatic routing through the PHP script:

```
RewriteRule ^css/(.*\.css) /combine.php?type=css&files=$1
RewriteRule ^js/(.*\.js) /combine.php?type=javascript&files=$1
```

Assuming you have folders called "js" and "css" in the root directory of your server, Apache will send any request for files within them through `combine.php` appending two GET variables indicating the file type and file name so the script can correctly fetch, combine, compress, and serve the files. You can download the `combine.php` file at **http://rakaz.nl/projects/combine/combine.phps**. You'll need to make a few simple configuration changes at the top of the script to fit the directory structure of your server, upload it to the root directory on your server along with your newly modified `.htaccess` file, and you're site is ready for super speedy deliveries.

Reducing HTTP Requests

As mentioned above, the number of HTTP requests a page has to make to the server can really slow down the load and render time of your pages. Only two or four HTTP requests can be processed from a single domain at a time by browsers, depending on the version of HTTP being used and the browser itself. This means that regardless of file size, when the browser encounters multiple JavaScript file requests in the head of an HTML page, it has to wait for two to load before loading two more, or continuing to the images, CSS, and other elements on the page. It's like a planned traffic jam! Each HTTP request requires some set up and tear down to execute, and can be taxing on the server especially on high-traffic sites. Reducing the number of trips to the server is one of the most effective ways to speed up the delivery of your content to clients.

Already we've seen some solutions to the problem. By setting the HTTP expires headers to future dates we avoid unnecessary requests to the server, as clients will not request files that are still fresh in their cache. Leenheer's combine script cuts out a number of requests to the server by concatenating multiple files into one compressed file.

Some Web designers and developers opt to split their style sheets into logically organized, separate files creating one document for fonts, one for colors, one for layout, one to reset the browser to default values, etc. This practice unnecessarily increases the number of server requests required for a page to render. It's a better idea to keep your core style rules in one document, only adding additional documents when absolutely necessary such as when working with browser specific or print style sheets.

Keeping images in one larger file rather than in many separate files can save many server requests. Dave Shea's CSS sprites technique described in issue 173 of A List Apart (**http://alistapart.com/articles/sprites**) is a great way to conserve HTTP requests. The basic idea is to combine the main images in your design into one file, then with a little CSS kung fu you can position this image in the background of elements, revealing just the subsection of the larger image you want. Although originally intended for rollover and image map effects, CSS sprites could be used as a simple HTTP request elimination technique.

Be a miser with your HTTP requests wherever possible, and you will notice significant speed increases that users and search spiders will appreciate.

Diagnosing Performance Problems with YSlow

As you complete the various optimization recommendations outlined so far, it's a good idea to check your work with YSlow (see **FIGURE 3.9**) to see how much you've decreased the load time of your pages. Developed by Yahoo!, YSlow is a handy Firefox add-on that extends Firebug (**http://getfirebug.com**)—another Firefox add-on with a number of Web developer tools—to provide a 13-point checklist and scoring system for evaluating the various factors that can negatively impact the load speed of your site. To use YSlow, you'll need to first install Firebug, restart Firefox, and then install YSlow. YSlow evaluates your page as it loads, checking it against the Yahoo! page performance rules (**http://developer.yahoo.com/performance/rules.html**).

When you score poorly on a performance rule, YSlow provides a more detailed explanation of what specifically is affecting the rating (see **FIGURE 3.10**). In addition to performance testing, it also provides stats about your page and information about each component associated such as images, CSS, and JavaScript.

FIGURE 3.9 *YSlow grades you on each of Yahoo!'s page performance rules, then assigns an overall performance grade.*

```
F   1. Make fewer HTTP requests
      This page has 7 external JavaScript files.
      This page has 16 CSS background images.
```

FIGURE 3.10 *YSlow lets you know why your page scores poorly, so you can fix it.*

If you've followed the performance optimization tips we've covered so far, chances are your page performance score will be reasonably good. Whether you are optimizing an existing site or developing a new one, YSlow is a great way to pinpoint problem areas that will slow down search engine indexing.

Controlling Search Engine Indexing with Robots.txt

There are situations when you don't want search engines digging through some files and directories that need to remain private. By creating a file called `robots.txt` in your Web root directory, you can prevent spiders from indexing certain content on your site such as dynamic search results pages that may display improperly without user input, 404 pages, image directories, login pages, or general content to which you don't want to direct search traffic. All search spiders automatically look for this file in your root directory, so all you need to do is create it, upload it, and wait for the spiders to read it. The `robots.txt` file does not secure your content in any way; it simply prevents search engine indexing. In fact, anyone can read your `robots.txt` file by simply going to the domain name `/robots.txt`. For an entertaining example, try out this much-viewed `robots.txt` file:

```
http://whitehouse.gov/robots.txt
```

Writing the file is a piece of cake. Here's a short example of the important elements:

```
User-agent: *
# My private folder
Disallow: /private-folder/
Disallow: /404.php
```

Start your `robots.txt` file by defining the search spider user-agent you want to receive the message. The asterisk indicates that you are universally communi-

Validate Your robots.txt Files

Before publishing your robots.txt file, it's a good idea to validate your code to ensure you have no errors that could make it unreadable by search engines. A convenient validator is available at **http://tool.motoricerca.info/robots-checker.phtml**.

cating to all spiders. Preventing spiders from indexing content is done with the keyword `Disallow:` followed by the path to the private content. This example hides both the 404 error page, and a private directory. The # is used to create comments in your file so you can keep track of what you've done.

Each user-agent has a unique name you'll need to know if you wish to segment your commands. Here's a quick reference of the popular user-agents you can target with your `robots.txt` file:

- Google: "googlebot"
- Google's Image Search: "Googlebot-Image"
- MSN Live Search: "msnbot"
- Inktomi: "Slurp"
- AllTheWeb: "fast"
- AskJeeves: "teomaagent1" or "directhit"
- Lycos: "lycos"

Let's take a look at another example, this time preventing the Google Image Search spider from indexing a folder with photos in it:

```
User-agent: Googlebot-Image
Disallow: /photos/
```

You can find the `robots.txt` mother ship at **http://www.robotstxt.org/** along with plenty of explanation and more examples.

4

Creating Content that Drives Traffic

A site that is brilliantly optimized for search engines is folly if it's shy on quality content that's relevant to the target audience. As it turns out, your content is the best tool to generate traffic.

Although your audience may discover you via one of your many findability strategies, they stay on your site and return often only if your content is engaging. Findability and content have a very symbiotic relationship that is degraded if either is not pulling its weight.

Great content presented without consideration for findability is destined to remain on its undiscovered island in a sea of millions of websites. Conversely, poor content that is perfectly optimized to be findable may draw traffic but users are likely to leave immediately, never to return again, if they find nothing of use to them.

Content that Sucks (Users In)

Well-produced, valuable content on a website has a gravity that can suck users in with great force. When people find something on the Web that's exciting, they love to be the first to introduce others to it. Perhaps it's ego or maybe it's altruism. Combine this fact of human nature with the inherent connectivity of the Web and you have a recipe to unite a large number of people around your website.

Let's examine a scenario of an e-commerce site that provides a user with content that is exceptionally valuable.

The Story of Tom

A user named Tom wants to buy a home theater system but he's unsure what equipment he'll need and how to set it up properly. Naturally, he turns to the Web to find answers to his questions. Using one of the major search engines he types in the key phrase "home theater system advice" and runs across a site that matches his search criteria. The site is for a small retail chain that sells high quality home theater paraphernalia. Beyond the typical online store this website has expert- and user-authored reviews about equipment, and articles discussing the requirements and setup of a top-notch system. The site also provides links to other useful sites that cover home theater culture. The welcoming voice of the content makes Tom feel like this otherwise very complex task is achievable even for a novice. Links within the articles and reviews make it easy for Tom to connect his new knowledge to the various products the site sells.

Because Tom is able to learn all he needs to know from a site that also sells the products he needs, he makes all of his purchases for his home theater on this site. Once his order arrives at his home Tom returns to the website so he can get guidance on the setup process.

Because Tom's experience was so positive, he recommends the site to his friends and family. He returns to the website again to write his own reviews of the products he's purchased. Finally, Tom posts on his personal blog about the new home theater he's so excited about and mentions the wonderful information he found on the site, providing a link.

All three of the goals of findability–help people find your site, help people find what they're looking for within your site, encourage repeat traffic–were realized in this scenario because of the presence of quality content on the site.

Let's examine more closely how the content served the goals of findability.

1. Keywords and phrases in the articles and reviews created a search engine referral.
2. The user was able to find the products he needed for his home theater through the links in the articles and reviews.
3. The user returned to the site multiple times to reread useful content and created more valuable content for the site in the form of user-generated product reviews.
4. The user was so satisfied he helped others find the site and created a link on his blog.

Not only was findability improved for Tom's experience by including relevant, well-produced content on the site, it actually caused Tom to improve the findability of the site for future users. The great content turned Tom into an evangelist for the site. He told his friends and family, and created a link to the site from his blog. Tom actually generated more traffic himself! His inbound link to the site will also help boost search engine rankings because inbound links are an indicator of the trustworthiness of a site.

The product reviews that Tom wrote also increased the amount of useful content on the site that could turn other visitors into customers. Keywords within his reviews could help foster more search traffic referrals.

The moral of Tom's story is that when you create quality content that serves the needs of your audience you will be rewarded. Your reward might be increased sales, better brand awareness, more user involvement, or simply more traffic on your site that could make any business or communication goal a reality. This story speaks to the beauty of the Web. If you solve a problem for people, provide something that's useful, create something entertaining, or produce something unique, your good deeds come back to you.

Content Karma

As illustrated in the story of Tom, when you solve a problem or provide something useful for your users you improve the findability of your site. Users want to tell others about the great things they find on the Web.

Karma, an ancient Hindu concept of cause and effect, could be applied to the practice of content development. A very simplified explanation of karma is that our deeds create reciprocal returns.

When you create content that altruistically serves the needs of your audience you are likely to receive positive benefits in the form of inbound links to your site, more online sales, flattering blog posts about your site, improved brand awareness/perception, and more traffic. A site without quality content will have a hard time achieving these goals. To further illustrate the power of content karma let's take a look at a real-world example of content good deeds that have generated huge findability returns.

Blueprint CSS Framework

Norwegian tech student Olav Frihagen Bjorkoy created an exceptionally useful CSS framework called Blueprint (**http://code.google.com/p/blueprintcss/**) that quickly became a huge sensation in the Web design world.

The secret to the success of Blueprint is that it adroitly addresses a pain point that many Web designers experience: The process of setting up page layouts and the extensive cross-browser testing that ensues can be tedious. Although many helpful articles and tools already exist to assist Web designers with their work, nothing actually unites theory and practice in a practical fashion. Olav's Blueprint was the solution that many designers had been searching for, and word of it spread like wildfire.

When Blueprint was released many well-known Web designers like Khoi Vinh (**http://subtraction.com**), Jeff Croft (**http://jeffcroft.com**), and Mark Boulton (**http://markboulton.co.uk**) wrote posts on their blogs that broadcast word of Olav's project to thousands of Web designers. Hundreds of blog posts from

Web designers all over the world followed, singing Blueprint's praises and providing inbound links to Olav's site.

Within the first week of the release of his project Olav saw a giant traffic spike and a number of new subscriptions to his blog's RSS feed.

> *"My blog went from about 300 visitors a day to just over 20,000 each day during the following week. The number of people subscribing to my feed went up from about 200 to 3000"*

In about three weeks Blueprint had been downloaded more than 25,000 times. By watching the number of bookmarks stored at **http://del.icio.us**–a popular social bookmarking site–Olav was able to further gauge the success of the project.

> *"I also like to count how many people bookmark my articles at* ***http://del.icio.us****, as I think that gives a good clue of how many people actually plan on using this in the future. [The current number of individual bookmarks is] closing in on 6000 ..."*

Blueprint was not a marketing initiative. As Olav describes it himself in his 2007 interview with Khoi Vinh (**http://www.subtraction.com/archives/2007/0807_the_framewor.php**)

> *"Blueprint is an unknown, untested and unused framework from an unknown guy launched from a highly irregular blog. This should make it quite clear that the craving for a proper designer's framework almost couldn't be greater."*

Although part of the success of Blueprint can be attributed to the timing of its release, ultimately it was Olav's desire to share with his community that made it the phenomenon that it is. By publishing a useful solution to a common problem Olav generated throngs of visits to his site. According to Google his site now has 22,500 inbound links.

Blueprint is an amazing example of a good deed returning huge findability benefits.

Open Content Generates Attribution

Often when people develop great content their first impulse is to prevent others from using or modifying it by creating copyright restrictions. There are certainly times when you need to employ a restrictive license on your work.

"Open Content, Remix Culture, and the Sharing Economy: Rights, Ownership, and Getting Paid"

http://audio.sxsw.com/podcast/interactive/panel/2007/SXSW07.INT.20070312.OpenContentRemixCulture.mp3

Google, for example, would not want to open up its search algorithm to the public, as it would be the downfall of its business. However, there are plenty of situations where large and small organizations alike can reap significant findability benefits by adopting a more open license that allows others to use and modify their content.

As mentioned at the end of Chapter 2 in the sidebar "Creative Commons Licensing," Creative Commons (**http://creativecommons.org**) offers a free, legal means of simultaneously protecting and sharing content of all sorts. Rather than completely blocking usage and publication rights, a Creative Commons license outlines the ways people can share or remix your content into something new.

One popular Creative Commons license prevents commercial gain from your content while allowing users to remix it as long as they provide attribution to you and allows others to make further modifications under the same stipulations. When users create derivations of your works under this license they'll be required to identify you and your site as the source of the original version. Their attribution is likely to create new inbound links to your site and generate more traffic for you.

Improvements that your users make on your content can also allow your ideas to become bigger than you might have been able to make them. Your good karma of sharing the original idea and letting it grow in a community will not go unnoticed. Open licensing can bolster your site's reputation in ways that would have been impossible if you had opted for a closed approach.

Olav Frihagen Bjorkoy's CSS framework is distributed under an open source MIT license (**http://www.opensource.org/licenses/mit-license.php**) that allows others to improve upon what he's created. The openness of the project actually helped contribute to the excitement around it and the quality of the initial release, which incorporates other designers' ideas as well.

The good karma of sharing your ideas and keeping them open can bolster the findability of your site. Good ideas tend to generate buzz and support, both of which lead to an increase in traffic on your site.

The Mark of Quality Content

Creating content can be a daunting task. Sometimes it's hard to know where to begin. The secret to success is to simply know the traits of quality content.

Quality content...

- is on topic
- fills a niche
- is authoritative and passionate
- is trustworthy
- is actionable, entertaining, or otherwise appeals to audience interests
- is original
- uses an appropriate voice for the audience

Each of these traits of quality in some way relates back to the relevance of your content to your audience. Beneath all of the technical complexities of the medium the Web is fundamentally about communication. Sending the wrong message, an irrelevant message, an untrustworthy message, or delivering the message in the wrong package can be the downfall of a website. Let's examine each mark of quality in further detail to ensure your content serves your audience well.

Stay on Topic

When building your content identify a topic or small series of topics and stick to them religiously. We've probably all run across blogs that were at one point interesting, but then took a turn towards the irrelevant when the author began posting about his honeymoon. If your blog is the personal account of your life, then this content is entirely on target. If your readers are lured to your site by your brilliant posts about the history of design, then a post about off-topic personal matters may cost you a few readers. Staying on topic helps ensure your message is relevant to your audience.

Fill a Niche

A generalized topic like architecture is very difficult to do justice even with a whole team of content creators. Instead of targeting nebulous topics that could have many different meanings to many different people, find the niche that is not being addressed well or at all by other websites. Attempts at addressing very broad topics often result in content that is generic and meaningless to everyone. Broad topics also put you in the company of stiffer competition who may already have captured your audience's loyalties.

A brilliant teacher of mine once told me, "Never say candy bar when you can say Snickers." His advice speaks to the point that specificity makes your message more powerful and relevant to your audience than if you are generalizing.

A site about rural, vernacular architecture in 20th century Alabama will be exceptionally relevant to a very specific audience who is likely to be engaged because the topic focuses precisely on something that interests them but may not be addressed elsewhere.

Regardless of how obscure a niche you may be filling, there's someone on the Web who will be interested. A niche audience is much more likely to be instantly loyal, visit regularly, create links to your site, and tell others about it as well. This is exactly the type of audience you want to build!

Be Passionate and Authoritative

Nothing inspires passion in an audience more than the passion of the speaker. Whatever your subject matter is, make sure it's one that you believe in with gusto and let that shine through in the content of your site. Part of being passionate is wanting to know as much about a subject as possible. When you target a niche subject and address it in a very comprehensive way you become an authority that your audience will start to trust.

Sometimes being authoritative doesn't require that you actually author all of the content yourself. Assembling a link library that outlines where all worthwhile knowledge on a subject can be located is exceptionally useful and relevant to your audience, making you an authority on the subject just by association. Such a resource would also generate repeat traffic, as many people would use it as a frequent reference. Taking the time to carefully compile a refined link library illustrates the passion you have for your subject, which your audience will appreciate.

We'll be tackling this problem later in this chapter by building a link library of our own.

Be Trustworthy

In order to be seen as an authority on a subject, your audience must trust you. Once you've established trust you don't want to do anything to jeopardize it as it doesn't come easy, and is even more difficult to restore. Trust is perhaps the most crucial and complex mark of quality to understand, as it can be quickly undermined and the etiquette of preserving it can get fuzzy at times.

One thing that is not fuzzy about maintaining trust is that your audience will be more apt to trust your content if it is factually sound. Be sure to research where necessary to confirm that you are presenting content that is based on fact, not conjecture.

When you make a number of typos and spelling or grammar errors you erode audience trust in your authority. Be sure to proofread, and spell-check before presenting your copy. Production values of your content are just as important as the ideas within. It's better to delay publication of your content than to post it with typos or spelling errors that will make you look like a knucklehead.

One thing you can count on is that you will make mistakes in your content at some point. Hey, to err is human! One of the great things about the Web is that you can quickly correct small errors and redistribute your content immediately.

If you make factual mistakes, though, be sure to transparently present your corrections indicating when and why you made the changes. Doing so indicates to your audience that you are not hiding your mistakes and you are genuinely concerned about the credibility of your content. HTML conveniently supports this practice with the `<del>` tag—indicating a deletion—and the `<ins>` tag—indicating an insertion. Here's a simple example of how to correctly indicate a factual change in your content:

```
The second US president was <del cite="http://www.whitehouse.gov/
history/presidents/" datetime="20070818">Thomas Jefferson</del>
<ins>John Adams</ins>.
```

As shown in **FIGURE 4.1**, browsers will by default display the deleted text with a strikethrough, and the correct inserted text will be displayed with an underline. Using the `datetime` and `cite` attributes you can provide further information in either `<del>` or `<ins>` to indicate when the correction was made, and provide a link to a document that indicates why the information was changed.

You may want to use a little CSS to change the default underline style of the `<ins>` to ensure that your users don't mistake it for a text link. In this simple example I replace the underline with a bold font weight for emphasis

```
ins {text-decoration:none; font-weight:bold;}
```

The second US president was ~~Thomas Jefferson~~ John Adams.

FIGURE 4.1 *Using the <del> and <ins> tags you can correct your mistakes transparently.*

You can learn more about <del> and <ins> at **http://www.w3schools.com/tags/tag_del.asp**

Audience trust in your content can also be degraded if you are not honest about affiliations that may impact your perspective on a subject. For example, if you write a glowing review on your personal blog of a product that is built by a company you work for, it's probably a good idea to disclose this fact. As someone who may have a personal stake in the success of the product the perspective you are offering your audience on this product could be skewed, and therefore be perceived as a bit subversive. Disclosure to your readers of your affiliation with the company shows them that the information you are presenting is not trying to dupe them into buying it. They can either accept or reject your subjective recommendation. Either way, you are much better off letting your audience decide than run the risk of being perceived as having sneaky, ulterior motives.

Appeal to Your Audience's Interests

People usually visit websites for very specific reasons. They want to solve a specific problem, learn about a subject, or be entertained. There are, of course, other reasons one might visit a site, but a user's goals can often be placed in one of these categories. Knowing what your audience's goals and interests are can help you identify what type of content you need to include on your site to encourage them to return.

If you are working in a team environment chances are an information architect has already researched your audience and outlined the type of content that will best serve their needs. If you are flying solo you'll need to do a little research of your own. Although a complete discussion of user research is beyond the scope of this book, here are a few simple things you can do to help ensure your content is on target:

- List the target audience groups identifying primary, secondary, and tertiary users.
- List the goals and motivations of these users to identify what they would want from the site.
- Thinking from your audience's perspective, create a list of the types of content that you think would be desirable for your users.
- If at all possible, speak to people in your target audience. Ask them if the type of content you plan on including in your site would be interesting.

- After launching the site, solicit user feedback about the value of the content on your site.
- Watch your traffic stats when the site is live to see what sections are the most popular and where users are browsing the longest.

When your content successfully addresses your users' needs you increase the likelihood that they'll come back again. Initial user research before planning and building your site is worth its weight in gold, as it will reveal the type of content you should include on your site.

Norm Carr and Tim Meehan do a nice job of introducing the user research process in their article "What's the Problem?" on A List Apart http://www.alistapart.com/articles/whatstheproblem.

You'll find a number of consistently brilliant articles on information architecture at http://informationarchitects.jp/.

Be Original

The Web is by nature a very competitive place. If your site offers similar things with the same approach as your competitors, then what motivation will users have to come to your site? Your content needs to be original in order to draw traffic and compel users to return. Originality is what will distinguish you among the crowds.

Ironically, originality doesn't necessarily mean that your content or ideas are new to the world. You can present existing content in new ways to create an original perspective that people will enjoy.

Smashing Magazine (**http://smashingmagazine.com**) is a brilliant example of creating valuable, original content out of preexisting stuff–see **FIGURE 4.2**. As a Web design blog, Smashing Magazine often creates comprehensive lists of

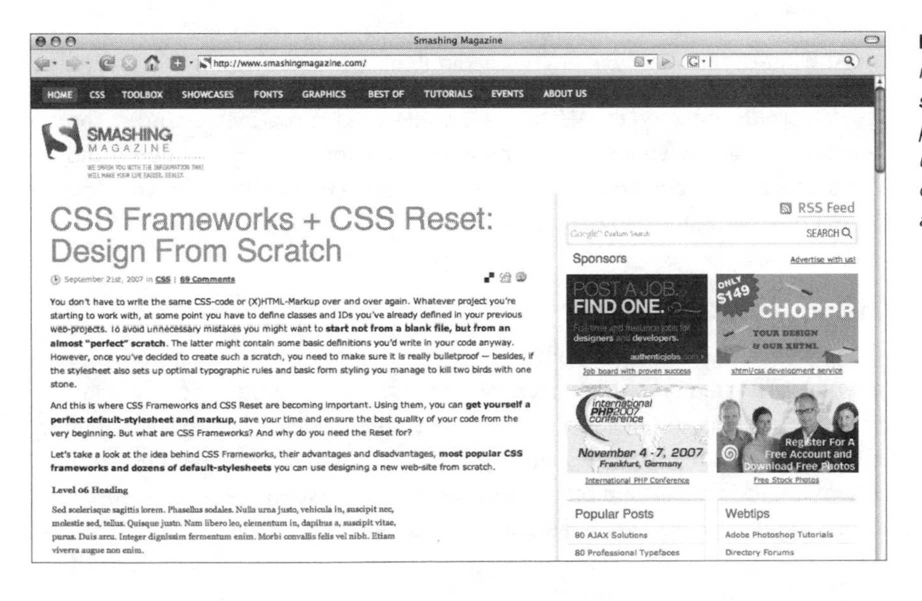

FIGURE 4.2 *Smashing Magazine (**http://smashingmagazine.com**) provides its readers with unique content by creating comprehensive lists of valuable resources.*

valuable resources that address a particular pain point in Web design. As the title suggests, the popular post "70 Expert Ideas for Better CSS Coding" provides a supremely comprehensive listing of CSS best coding practices culled from other sources. So what's so original about that, if many of the ideas are from other places? No one else has assembled a solution so comprehensively and as well. Their originality is in how they identify a problem and then edit down a complete answer that only contains the best stuff. Sometimes that's all it takes.

Use an Appropriate Voice

The way you say something is often as important and what you are saying. Let's revisit the earlier example of Tom shopping online for a home theater system. If the website that sold Tom his home theater equipment had provided its articles in a condescending tone, or had used too many technical terms that a novice wouldn't understand, they would have probably lost his business.

"Writing Better" http://odeo.com/audio/11797773/play

You can find the appropriate voice for your content by considering the profile and needs of your target audience. Ask yourself these questions before writing your content:

- What sort of reading level does my audience have?
- Are they experts or novices on this subject?
- Do users expect this site to be authoritative, or entertaining? Is it familiar or formal?
- At what speed will my users be reading?

As is often the case on the Web where users tend to read faster and in shorter bursts, the voice of your message may need to avoid flowery discourse and get to the point. Sometimes photos or illustrations can be the right voice rather than a paragraph that may not be read.

Keep It Coming

Once you've found your content niche be sure to publish often and on regular intervals. The frequency of publication depends on the type of content that you are providing. Articles about CSS techniques would need to be refreshed more often than a one page summary of a CSS property. Frequent updates where applicable will help bring users back to your website and build loyalty. Defining the update interval fosters planned visits to your site.

The hugely popular, homegrown cartoon site **http://homestarrunner.com** updates its content every Monday. Because its users know when to expect the next cartoon, each Monday 250,000 people return for some regularly scheduled entertainment. The underlying reason it draws so much traffic, though, is that its content is great!

A common myth in SEO is that search engines reward higher page ranking to sites that update their content often. This is untrue. A site that has not been updated since its original publication can rank equally as well as a site that is updated daily. Many factors can affect your search engine ranking but update frequency is not one of them.

All Roads Lead to Content

Once you've created great content you'll want to make sure your users are finding it. Especially on large sites that have many subsections it's important to create avenues into the areas where you want to funnel your traffic. The home page is a great place to create call outs that help users find the content you want to direct them towards.

FIGURE 4.3 shows a home page for photographer Stephen Grote (**http://stephengrote.com**) that draws the users' attention to recently added photos

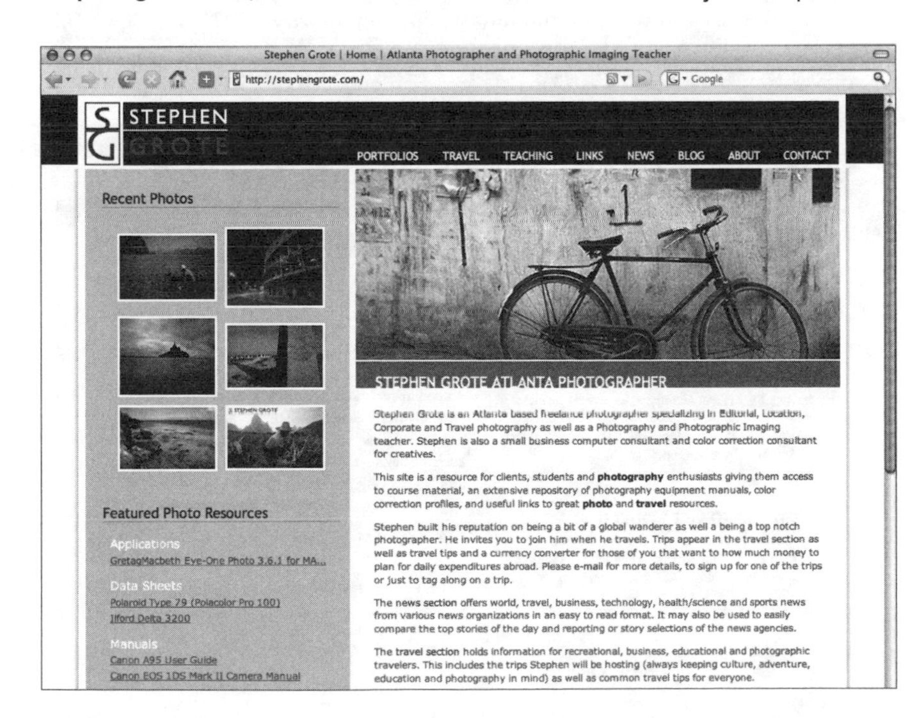

FIGURE 4.3 *On the left side of the home page of **http://stephengrote.com** recently added content is showcased to funnel traffic into various portions of the site that users may have otherwise missed.*

and featured photography resources. Highlighting content updates makes the home page seem continually fresh while catering to repeat visitors who often search for what's new on the site. The featured content directs users to various areas of the site that may otherwise have been overlooked.

Happy Cog (**http://happycog.com**) also does a great job of directing traffic to all of the important places (see **FIGURE 4.4**). To educate new visitors about the company the home page provides a quick synopsis of who they are and what they do.

A site that doesn't make the proper introductions to new visitors runs the risk of an increased bounce rate—the number of immediate exits from a site. The brief introduction acts like a "You Are Here" label on a map, providing users some orientation so they can confirm they're in a place that may have what they're looking for. When users stay on your site longer you increase the odds that they'll do or learn something that achieves the goals of the site.

FIGURE 4.4 *The Happy Cog website provides a number of quickly recognizable avenues into the content. The quick synopsis of the company at the top cleverly links to key sections where a user can learn more. Images in the center of the page capture attention and further funnel traffic to target areas.*

A solid home page design is a very powerful tool for pulling people into your content and making them stick around longer. Spend some time thinking about the hierarchy of the business and communication objectives for your website, and make sure your home page design reflects them.

NOTE Derek Powazek provides further advice for your home page in his article entitled "Home Page Goals" on A List Apart **http://www.alistapart.com/articles/homepagegoals**.

Content of Many Flavors

The types of content you choose to add to your site all depend on the goals of your organization and the amount of time you'll be able to dedicate to content production. Plans to add content can start with the best of intentions and end with a reality check when time and resources make content production difficult. Knowing a little about popular content types and the amount of production time required can help you define a content strategy that attracts your target audience without monopolizing your time.

Blogs

Blogs can be exceptionally effective content delivery platforms. They're easy to set up, posts are often rich in keywords that attract search traffic, and they can be managed by a single person or an entire team of writers. Blog content is usually syndicated to other websites and platforms using a standardized form of XML called RSS or Really Simple Syndication. Users can subscribe to RSS feeds in aggregators such as Bloglines (**http://bloglines.com**), Netvibes (**http://netvibes.com**), or Google Reader (**http://google.com/reader**). These tools pull headlines from many sources and display them in a concise format so users can stay up to date with many sites without having to visit each one.

When content from your site is syndicated to other locations it increases readership and tends to improve repeat traffic. When users stay up to date on a site's content changes they are more likely return.

If you're new to the concept of RSS you may want to watch the brilliantly simple video explanation of it provided by Common Craft http://www.commoncraft.com/rss_plain_english.

Most blog platforms automatically publish RSS feeds, allowing you to focus on your content rather than the technical aspects of publishing. We'll explore blogs and their findability benefits in further detail in the following chapter.

Blogging should be avoided if your time and interest in creating new content is low. When blogs stagnate, users often stop returning to a site and will discontinue their subscription to the RSS feed. This creates a negative perception of your site that will deter traffic.

Team blogging makes keeping your content fresh much easier. Rather than resting all content production obligations on the shoulders of one person you can distribute them among many people. If you know you are going to be busy in the near future you can pre-author blog posts when your schedule is free and release them incrementally when your writing time is limited.

It's a good idea to write about and link to other blog posts when possible. This will automatically publish an excerpt of your post as a comment on the other person's blog. In addition to the excerpt a link to your site will be created from the site you are writing about. Inbound links to your site increase traffic and your page rank with search engines. This automatic publication between blogs is called a trackback and is a standard feature with most blogging platforms.

Although blogs are one of the most powerful content publication tools for generating traffic to your site they are also the most time-consuming. They require constant maintenance and a passion for your subject, but can provide huge traffic increases.

Articles, Case Studies, and White Papers

You may already have articles you've written, case studies on client projects, or white papers that provide a comprehensive explanation of a subject relevant to your audience. These are all valuable assets that can be published on your site with little or no modification. Assets like these are often already produced for clients and could potentially be shared with your audience who may be seeking advice on the same issues.

If possible, keep these assets in HTML format so search engines can easily index them. Search engines do index PDF files but HTML delivery offers better SEO opportunities.

Articles, case studies, and white papers tend to have a lot of keywords that can attract search engine traffic. Although they may take a long time to author if you are starting from scratch, they don't require the maintenance that a blog does making them a practical solution if you are too busy to make regular content updates.

Writing articles for popular online publications is a great way to create exposure for your site while doing something positive for your online community.

Taking the time to write an article that shares a solution others may find useful not only builds your reputation among your audience but it also creates a very powerful inbound link to your site.

Online publications tend to have very high page rankings with search engines. A link from a site with a high page rank can exponentially build your page rank too. After the traffic spike that follows publication of an article your site will receive a lasting increase in search engine traffic.

Andy Rutledge, designer and principle of UNIT Interactive, regularly writes intelligent articles extolling the principles of design on his website (**http://andyrutledge.com**)—see **FIGURE 4.5**. His articles are read by about 3300 people daily, and have made a huge impact on his reputation in the industry.

> *"... publishing articles on my site ... is almost wholly responsible for my entire site traffic and is greatly responsible for my reputation in the industry. I find that the value of articles as demonstrations of my thinking, reasoning, insights, and approach to design-related issues is appreciated by both my peers and potential clients. I'd say that likely 70 percent of potential clients that contact me say that they decided to do so based on some article that I had published. This is not why I write or publish articles, but it is certainly a nice benefit."*

Andy's also written for popular online publications like A List Apart, which has expanded awareness of his work in the industry. His 2007 article "Contrast and Meaning" (**http://www.alistapart.com/articles/contrastandmeaning/**) directed 1333 new visitors to his site in the first week of publication. By regularly sharing his ideas Andy Rutledge has not only built a loyal audience for his website, he's also built a successful business.

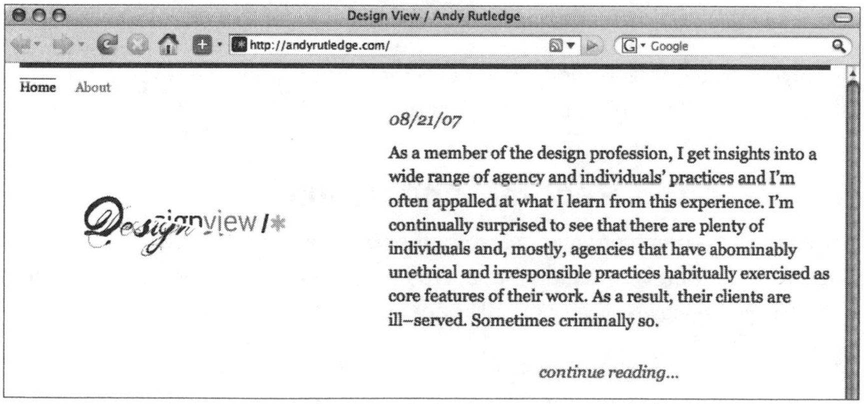

FIGURE 4.5 *Andy Rutledge's site (**http://andyrutledge.com**) receives on average 3300 visitors a day because of his brilliant design articles.*

Link Libraries

A link library is a collection of useful links to resources that your audience would find valuable. Rather than including every bookmark in your browser, a good link library should include only the most useful links that relate to a single theme or topic.

Link libraries require less maintenance and writing than many other content options. For someone with an exceptionally busy schedule a link library can be a practical content option that is feasible to maintain and is of great value to users. Good link libraries that contain a concise listing of resources tend to generate inbound links and blog posts that point new users to your site.

Later in this chapter we'll see some practical code examples of how to build a link library using the popular bookmark management services Delicious (**http://del.icio.us**) and Magnolia (**http://ma.gnolia.com**).

Document Templates, Code Examples, and Other Tools

Publishing useful templates, code examples, and tools not only generate traffic to your site and buzz in the blogoshphere but also builds respect and a positive perception of your brand. These are assets that you may already have created for your personal use that could be shared with your audience.

Jonathan Snook's color contrast checker (**http://snook.ca/technical/colour_contrast/colour.html**) is a handy little tool that compares the color of type to its background color in order to determine if it has enough contrast to be legible and accessible to users with color perception deficits (see **FIGURE 4.6**). Snook's simple tool was created to serve his purposes and published to benefit his audience of Web designers.

According to Google, Snook's color contrast checker has garnered around 300 inbound links to his site, which is a great reward for his efforts.

Reviews and Recommendations

Reviews and recommendations are another great way to provide your audience with relevant information that serves their needs and interests. The type of things you review will vary greatly depending on the goals of your site.

As we saw earlier in the story of Tom, e-commerce sites can improve sales and draw in more search traffic by providing expert reviews of products that help customers make informed purchases.

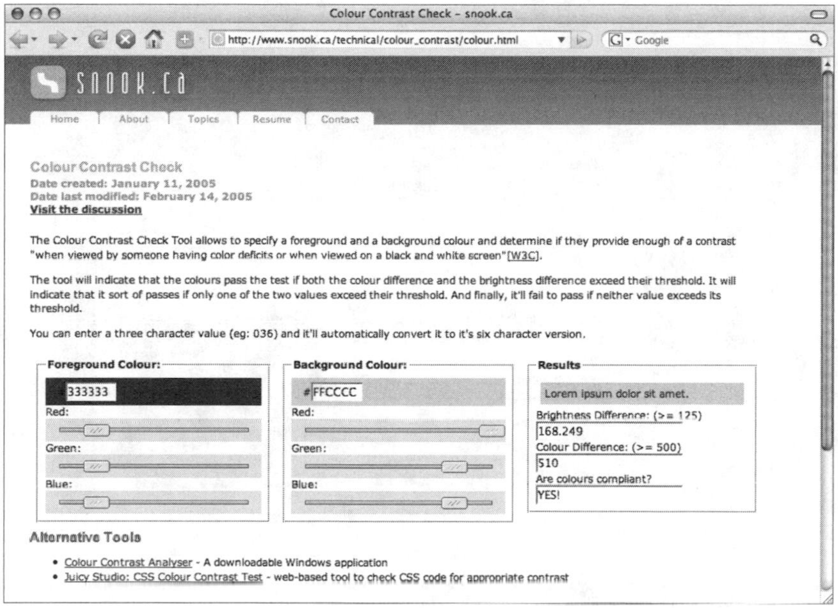

FIGURE 4.6 *Jonathan Snook's color contrast checker is a useful tool that has generated a great deal of traffic for his site.*

Sites that are focused on educating their audience might benefit by adding a book review section. Book reviews can supplement articles by providing further reading on a subject being discussed. They can also simply act as intriguing branches of secondary content that your audience can explore.

Terra Incognita (**http://terraincognita.com**)—an award-winning interactive narrative design firm in Austin, TX—provides book recommendations on their company website that relate to the various projects they've worked on and the principles that guide their work (see **FIGURE 4.7**). Their recommendations provide engaging secondary content that their audience enjoys browsing. They also embody the value system of the company, which produces educational content for clients such as National Geographic and the Smithsonian Museum.

When you write reviews of anything on your site it's a good idea to mark them up using the hReview microformat. As Chapter 2 pointed out in the section "More Microformats Worth Investigating," reviews that employ hReview can be located using Technorati's microformat search engine (**http://kitchen.technorati.com/search/**). The microformats site has a brilliant hReview creator (**http://microformats.org/code/hreview/creator**) that will build the markup for you as you type your content into a simple form. When you've posted your reviews to your server you can let Technorati know the location of your hReviews so users can easily find them. Just submit your URL to Pingerati (**http://pingerati.net/**) and you're all set.

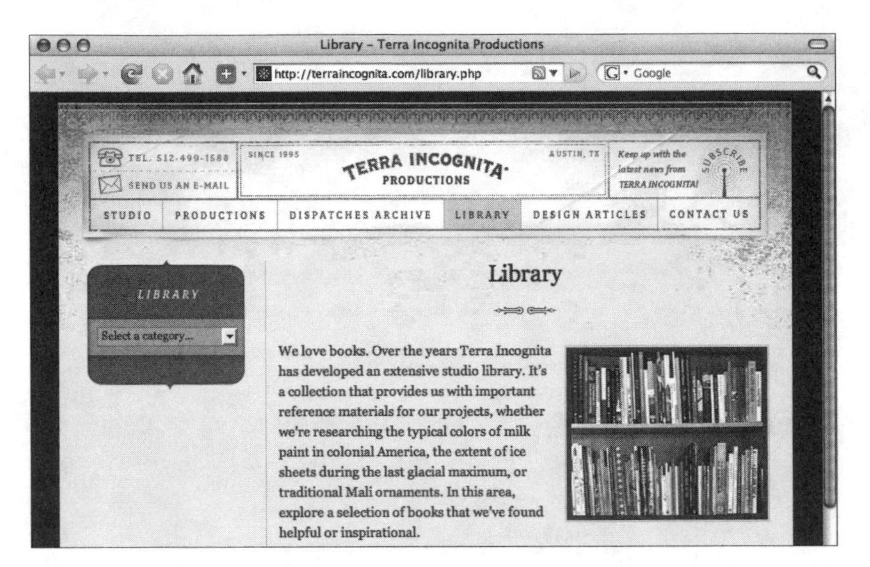

FIGURE 4.7 *Terra Incognita has included categorized book recommendations on their company website. The book recommendations serve their audience's interests and embody the educational values of the firm.*

Syndicated Content (RSS)

RSS syndication of your content provides your users with a convenient way to stay up to date with your site. Any sort of content can be syndicated with RSS 2.0, including text, images, files, and audio.

Most blogs and content management systems publish RSS feeds automatically and even notify blog tracking services like Technorati when you publish. Blog tracking services then notify all subscribers to your RSS feed that new information is available for download. It's a great way to keep users aware of your site and encourages repeat visits.

RSS also helps you to more widely distribute your content. RSS content can be displayed on many platforms and on many websites, all with links back to your site.

User-Generated Content (UGC)

User-generated content (UGC) is a powerful tool in the right situations. Most sites require some time to build an audience before UGC is a viable option. For UGC to work you'll not only need a decent-sized audience, but you'll also need a certain level of interest and loyalty that will change lurking users into content contributors.

In the best situations UGC is free content that generates search traffic and a great deal of buzz. At its worst UGC can be critical of the host site or organization or could absolutely fail by not generating any user contributions.

UGC comes in many shapes and sizes. Reviews, forums, media, and comments are just a few of the many options that can get your users involved on your site.

User-authored reviews of your products and services can help provide other users with some third-party validation of things you're selling. Amazon does a brilliant job of letting users leave product feedback that may influence sales. Regardless of the positive or negative spin on a review, users reading it will greatly appreciate the added information that can help them make an informed purchase. As we saw in the previous story of Tom, providing users with useful information can promote sales and encourage repeat visits.

Forums are another popular platform for UGC. If your site is focused on providing users with information and solutions to common problems then a forum may be a good way to let users solve problems for one another. By watching hot topics on the forums you can decide the topic of your next article or blog post. Because posts tend to be keyword-rich, a thriving forum can be a huge attractor of search traffic.

Forums can be problematic, though. Spam is inevitably the bane of every forum moderator. You'll need to make sure you use a forum platform that has sophisticated spam prevention if you want it to survive.

Forum moderation is important too and can be time-consuming. Every forum has some knucklehead who will say inappropriate or hurtful things. Although moderation can be time-consuming it is essential to making sure your users are comfortable enough to stick around.

Forums can also be an absolute flop if no one participates. Sometimes it just takes a few people asking some interesting questions to get the conversation started. If after a little prodding your forum doesn't take off, then pull the plug, as a dormant forum speaks poorly of a site.

Look at your site traffic stats and blog comments before deciding to set up a forum. If your blog is getting only a few comments you can infer that a forum will probably not get the participation it needs.

TIP If you are considering adding a forum to your site you may want to research some of the popular systems that are on the market. PHPBB (**http://www.phpbb.com/**) and vBulletin (**http://www.vbulletin.com**) are popular, feature-rich forums worth considering.

With the rise in popularity of UGC many organizations have jumped on the bandwagon before considering how appropriate it may be for their site. Lack of participation is not nearly as bad as what Chevy experienced in its contest to create the 2007 Tahoe video ad. Users submitted more than 30,000 videos, most of which actually promoted the Tahoe. But some of the ads subverted Chevy's marketing goals by pointing out the poor fuel economy and impact the SUV has on the environment.

Although UGC can reduce the authoring time required to deliver good content, it's not a cakewalk. Closely consider the ramifications and worst-case scenarios before jumping into something that could have a negative impact on your site and business.

NOTE To learn more about the 2007 Chevy Tahoe user-generated ad campaign that went awry and view some of the controversial videos visit **http://www.wired.com/wired/archive/14.12/tahoe.html**.

Targeting Keywords in Your Content

In Chapter 2 we learned about the many places within your HTML documents where you can place keywords and phrases to generate more search referrals. Knowing where to place keywords is only half the battle. You'll also need to know with which keywords you can be most successful.

Researching and Selecting Keywords

Blog posts, articles, reviews, and all of the other types of content previously mentioned would naturally be filled with keywords that will attract your target audience. But there are places on your site where it's beneficial to include very targeted keywords in order to improve your placement on search results pages. These places include the title tag, meta description, headings, and copy for the home page. Targeted keywords in strategic areas of your HTML in conjunction with keyword-rich content can generate a lot of search traffic.

You may have a general idea of search terms to target, but sometimes our assumptions about keyword popularity don't match reality. Rather than trying to guess which keywords will best match users' search habits, you can get definitive answers through research.

One place to start your keyword research is on search engines themselves. Searching for the terms you think may be valuable will show you your competitors and potentially reveal additional terms that you may not have considered.

If you have an existing site you can learn a lot about the keywords your audience uses to locate it by searching social bookmarking sites like Delicious (**http://del.icio.us**) and Magnolia (**http://ma.gnolia.com**) for your URL (see **FIGURE 4.8**). The tags that people use on these sites to describe your content can reveal user search behaviors. If you see reoccurring tags then you may want to add those keywords to your list.

FIGURE 4.8 *By searching for your URL on a social bookmarking site like Magnolia (**http://ma.gnolia.com**) you can identify what tags people are using to describe your content.*

Even if you don't have an existing site or it's not yet bookmarked in Magnolia or Delicious, you can still search social bookmarking systems for your initial keyword ideas to see what other keywords are related. With thousands of people bookmarking and tagging content daily Delicious and Magnolia can offer a wealth of knowledge about user search habits.

Wordtracker

To gain even more detailed keyword data you'll need to consult tools built specifically for the task. Wordtracker (**http://wordtracker.com**) is a powerful tool used to identify which keywords have the most competition and how often users are searching for them. Wordtracker searches other websites that score well with search engines and shows you the keywords they use. It also gathers query statistics from the major search engines to help you determine what terms were recently popular, and which are likely to be popular in the future.

Wordtracker (see **FIGURE 4.9**) is a paid service, but it does have a free trial that allows you limited capabilities to see if the tool fits your needs. The costs are generally pretty reasonable and vary according to the duration of access to their tools.

Wordtracker's lateral and thesaurus keyword search features can help you find terms that are similar to the one you're searching for. Figure 4.9 illustrates a search for the keyword "espresso," which produces synonyms like "coffee" and "latte" as well as lateral terms such as "coffee beans" and "barista." Using Wordtracker you can discover many terms you've overlooked.

Once you find terms you can do a little further research to see how many users search for them and how many sites already target them. Broad terms that are searched for often such as "espresso" are much harder to successfully target because so many sites already compete for them. You'll want to identify more niche terms that have fewer competitors but are still being searched for often.

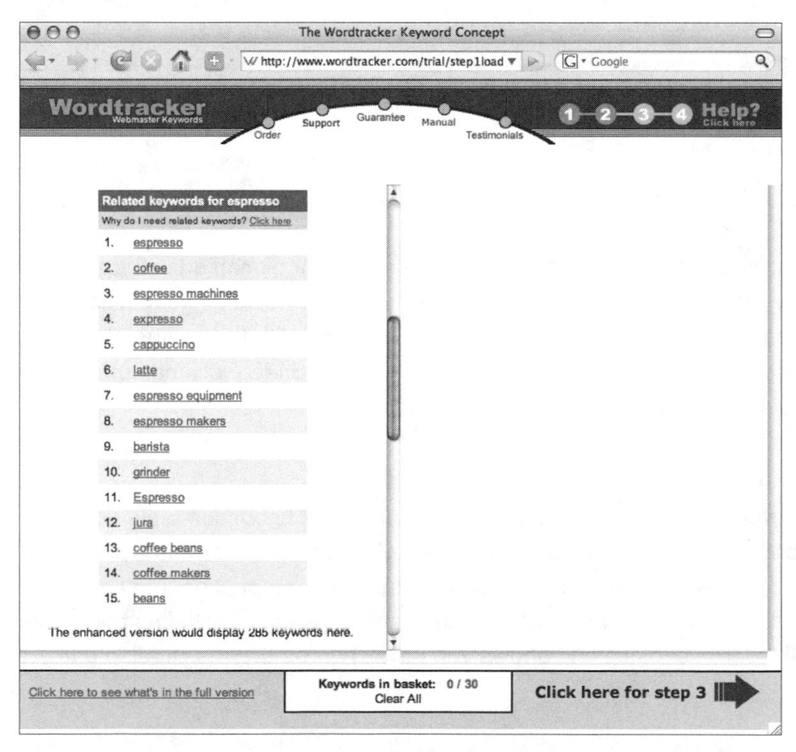

FIGURE 4.9 *Wordtracker is a handy tool to research the best keywords to target.*

When users search they tend to start with general terms and refine their search once they know more about the subject. It's when users search for niche terms that they are most likely to make a purchase or take some other action on a website.

Wordtracker looks at the popularity of keywords and compares it to the amount of competition it has using a mathematical formula. The result of the formula is called a KEI or Keyword Effectiveness Index. Here's how Wordtracker calculates the KEI of keywords.

KEI = (P2/C)

KEI: Keyword Effectiveness Index

P2: Popularity of Keyword Squared

C: Competitiveness (number of other sites optimized for that keyword)

A KEI between 10 and 100 is a good niche keyword or phrase to use as the balance between search frequency and competition for the term is good. Anything above 100 is even better but is very hard to find. See **FIGURE 4.10**.

No.	Keyword Why quotes?	KEI Analysis (?)	Count (?)	24Hrs (?)	Competing (?)
1	"imported espresso"	1.191	47	7	1854
2	"espresso supplies"	0.398	38	6	3627
3	"espresso coffee beans"	0.176	42	7	10002
4	"italian espresso machine"	0.167	40	6	9580
5	"espresso machines"	0.088	182	29	376972
6	"espresso beans"	0.081	75	12	69717
7	"espresso machine"	0.074	149	24	301594
8	"espresso cups"	0.058	60	10	61985
9	"espresso coffee machines"	0.051	38	6	28426
10	"espresso coffee"	0.021	80	13	309002
11	"espresso"	0.012	260	41	5539898

FIGURE 4.10 *Wordtracker's data can help you determine which keywords will prove most successful.*

As you discover valuable keywords and phrases you can either perform further searches on them to identify more niche terms or you can add them to a keyword basket. The keyword basket is the final outcome of your research. It serves as the master list you'll reference when building your site to target the search terms that will attract your target audience.

Other Keyword Research Services

If you're not keen on forking out a few bucks to research your keywords with Wordtracker there are some free alternatives. Both Google and Yahoo! provide keyword research tools for current or prospective users of their text ad services. Both are absolutely free to use and do a nice job of providing lateral search terms and data on keyword popularity.

Google's AdWords keyword tool (**https://adwords.google.com/select/KeywordToolExternal**) allows you to gather keyword data in two ways. If you are working on a new site you can enter a list of keywords to find related and synonymous terms. If you have an existing site you can enter the URL and the system will recommend keywords based on those it finds on your site.

In both situations the Google keyword research tool displays side-by-side bar charts that visually present the number of competitors and the number of searches for the term in the past month. Comparing the two charts makes it easy to identify the terms that will give you your best results.

It should be noted that the data Google displays is based on paid search competition for Google AdWords, not on the number of sites across the Web that prominently display the keywords. Because Google AdWords is a hugely popular advertising platform their data tends to closely parallel the competition for organic search terms, making the data still very relevant to your research. See **FIGURE 4.11**.

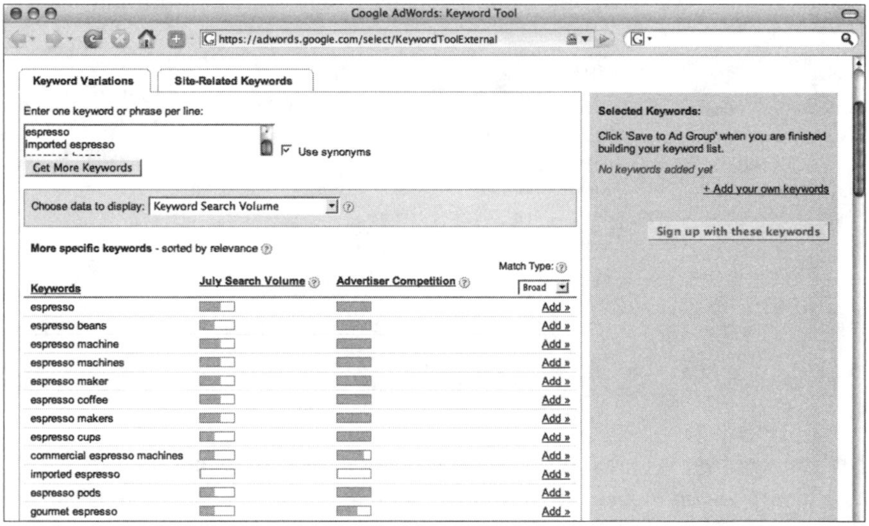

FIGURE 4.11 *Google's AdWords keyword research tool provides data about the frequency of searches for keywords and indicates how heavy the competition is for them. Their keyword research tool will even examine an existing site to identify recommended terms.*

NOTE Organic search terms are those that sites feature in key areas of their markup to achieve prominent search engine rankings. Paid search terms are those that people bid on with search engines so their text ad will be featured above competitors.

Yahoo!'s keyword research tool provides similar data, but with less detail and fewer features than Google's AdWords keyword tool. Enter a keyword into Yahoo!'s system and out pops a list of lateral and synonymous terms along with the number of times it was searched for in previous months.

The data tends to be a little older than Google's and no information is provided about the competition for each keyword. Yahoo!'s keyword research tool is good but is perhaps best used as a supplement to confirm data from other sources. See **FIGURE 4.12**.

Searches done in January 2007	
Count	Search Term
6440	coffee espresso
3491	cappuccino coffee espresso maker salton three
3406	coffee espresso maker
3071	coffee espresso machine
524	coffee espresso pod
433	coffee espresso krups maker
293	bean coffee espresso
281	cappuccino coffee espresso maker
253	business coffee espresso own running specialty starting
242	coffee espresso maker mr
240	coffee dual espresso maker

FIGURE 4.12 *Yahoo!'s keyword research tool provides good lateral and synonymous keywords.*

TIP You can find a few other interesting and useful keyword research tools as well as articles about keyword research at **http://searchenginewatch.com/facts/article.php/2156041**.

Placing Keywords in Your Content

Once you've identified the keywords that are most relevant to user search behaviors you'll need to insert your keywords into your content and HTML. Chapter 2 identified a number of important areas in your documents to feature your keywords. Some of the most important areas include

- `<title>`
- heading tags, especially `<h1>`, `<h2>`, and `<h3>`
- `<strong>` and `<em>`
- link labels
- file names (logo image file name, external CSS file name)
- `alt` attributes
- `title` attributes
- table elements such as `<th>`, `<caption>`, and the `summary` attribute
- `<acronym>` and `<abbr>`
- first line of first paragraph of a page
- meta description
- within the URL

In addition to placing keywords in your HTML document be sure to add them to your content as well. It's pretty easy to get caught up in a frenzy of keyword optimization and before you know it your content starts to read strangely.

Although keyword optimization can improve your search referral traffic, don't sacrifice the quality of your content in the process. Your content should always be written for humans first, and search engines second!

When keywords appear in a page too often it will be conspicuous to search engines that you are trying to dishonestly stuff your pages in order to generate traffic. Search engines use a simple mathematical formula and some basic logic about language to determine if a page unnaturally features a word. This formula helps determine the density of a keyword in a page.

Keyword frequency / Total number of words in a page = Keyword density

Following this formula, if there were 50 instances of a keyword in a page that had a total of 500 words the keyword density would be 10 percent. By studying written language researchers have discovered that keyword density is typically not higher than 7 percent. A page that has a keyword density of 10 percent would look suspicious and could possibly receive a penalty in search engine rankings.

Search engines also look for the presence of other words around prominent keywords to see if they are naturally included in the content or are part of a list of terms aimed at dishonestly stuffing the page.

In order to do a good job of optimizing your pages for keywords without crossing the natural 7 percent keyword density threshold you'll need a utility that can help you evaluate your work.

Evaluating Keyword Density

Evaluating your keyword density by counting words in your page would get old pretty quickly. Luckily there are some good, free utilities that will do the dirty work for you.

You'll find one of the most full featured keyword density analyzers at **http://www.ranks.nl/cgi-bin/ranksnl/spider/spider.cgi**. In addition to analyzing keyword density this tool will also provide information about the prominence of keywords (see **FIGURE 4.13**). Keywords placed in `<title>` and heading tags receive higher prominence ratings than those featured in a paragraph. By evaluating both density and prominence simultaneously you can get a good idea of what keywords search engines will rank highest in your page.

You'll get loads of other information when you run your URLs through the Ranks.nl keyword analyzer. It indicates the Google PageRank for the page, shows the HTTP headers, provides links to discover what sites are linking to

Total 2 word phrases : 57 - Total Repeats : 167			
phrase	repeats	density	Prominence
user insight	10 T,D,H	4.81 %	52.40
user experience	8 T,K,H,B,I	3.85 %	48.89
the user	7 T,H,L	3.37 %	53.64
user research	7 L,B,I	3.37 %	42.27
about the	5 L	2.40 %	43.32
accessibility testing	5 T,L,I,A	2.40 %	65.62

Total 3 word phrases : 49 - Total Repeats : 109			
phrase	repeats	density	Prominence
read about the	5 L	3.61 %	43.56
section 508 accessibility	4 D,L,B,I	2.88 %	50.66
usability and accessibility	4 T,H,A	2.88 %	83.71
and accessibility testing	3 T,A	2.16 %	85.34
insight usability and	3 T,H	2.16 %	87.42
the user experience	3 T,H	2.16 %	85.02

FIGURE 4.13 *The Ranks.nl keyword density and prominence evaluation tool provides information about single and multi-word phrases in your page so you can quickly identify how search engines will perceive your content.*

yours, and a host of other useful things. Adjacent to the keywords and phrases detected you'll see a series of capital letters that indicate the places within your HTML that the term is featured. In Figure 4.13 the key phrase "user experience" appears eight times and is included in the `<title>`, the keywords meta tag, headings, bold and italic text.

If you find that any of your terms have a low density or prominence you can simply add instances of them in the page, targeting more of the strategic locations mentioned earlier in this chapter.

Content Development Strategies

You don't always have to author every word on your site. With some fancy Web development techniques you can actually pull content into your site from other locations dynamically.

Earlier in this chapter in the section entitled "Syndicated Content (RSS)" you learned that RSS—Really Simple Syndication—is a standard XML format that many blogs and content management systems use to syndicate their content to other platforms and websites. There are thousands of websites that publish RSS feeds in order to reach more people in their audience. Just as TV stations air syndicated content from other channels to supplement their original programming, a website can display syndicated content from other sites.

Let's take a look at some practical examples of how RSS can make your site more findable.

Displaying RSS Content on Your Site

Headlines and excerpts from blogs or other sites that provide content relating to yours can be displayed in the sidebar of a home page, or in a page of their own where your users can see the top news from many sites in a single

All of the source code for the following examples can be downloaded from this book's companion website at http://buildingfindablewebsites.com.

location. All of the headlines can link back to the host site so users can read more of the syndicated story. The result is a symbiotic relationship that gives RSS content providers more traffic from your inbound links to their site and gives your site content relevant to your audience that can also draw traffic. Everybody wins!

Transforming RSS content into a usable HTML display is not very difficult. In the example that follows we'll use a popular set of open source PHP classes called Magpie (**http://magpierss.sourceforge.net/**) to extract the content we want from the RSS files.

Before attempting to parse RSS it may help to see what a typical feed file looks like:

```
<?xml version="1.0" encoding="UTF-8"?>
<rss version="2.0" xmlns:dc="http://purl.org/dc/elements/1.1/">
  <channel>
    <title>Crazy Monkey News</title>
    <link>http://www.crazymonkeynews.com/</link>
    <language>en-us</language>
    <description>The craziest news about monkeys</description>
    <item>
      <title>Rare Species of Blue Monkeys Discovered!</title>
      <description>A rare breed of blue monkeys was recently
discovered living in an ink pen factory. Scientists are still
baffled about what causes the azure skin color of the little
devils.</description>
      <pubDate>Fri, 10 Aug 2007 05:19:47 GMT</pubDate>
      <author>nospam@example.com (Simean Mandrake)</author>
      <guid isPermaLink="true">http://www.crazymonkeynews.com/
bluemonkeys</guid>
      <link>http://www.crazymonkeynews.com/bluemonkeys</link>
      <category>Monkey News</category>
    </item>
  </channel>
</rss>
```

RSS looks a bit like HTML and even shares some of the same tags. The tags that contain the information we'll display include `<channel>`, which provides information about the site publishing the feed, and `<item>`, which contains information about a single blog post or other bit of content. There are usually many item tags—one for each blog post.

Let's get an overview of how we'll go about parsing and displaying RSS feeds. We're going to have three main components in our system:

- The Magpie RSS class that can be downloaded at **http://magpierss.sourceforge.net/**
- A PHP script that uses Magpie to transform RSS into HTML
- A page where the headlines will be displayed

We'll be following these basic steps:

1. We'll create a PHP file called `parseRSS.php` that connects to the Magpie RSS parsing engine. This file will contain a function we build to handle the conversion of RSS content into HTML by using the member functions of the Magpie class. The function will be aptly named `parseRSS()`.
2. We'll create a page called `index.php` that connects to the file containing the `parseRSS()` function. It will then call the function, defining which feeds to display and how many headlines to show.

An Object-Oriented Programming Primer

Using Magpie requires a very basic understanding of Object-Oriented Programming, or OOP. In OOP a series of functions—called member functions—and variables—called member variables—are encapsulated in a class and work together to perform a series of related tasks. The contents of all member variables can be accessed and manipulated by all member functions. With all of the pieces of a class working together it's like a little factory built of code to simplify and expedite otherwise very complicated tasks.

If you've ever used Flash you're probably familiar with the idea of movie clips. A movie clip stored in the library can be dragged onto the stage to create a new instance of it. Although each instance comes from the same movie clip they are all autonomous and can be individually manipulated.

OOP follows a similar paradigm. You make a new instance of a class—called an object—to use its functionality. Each new object instance has a set of capabilities that is defined by the member functions and properties defined by the member variables. As we're about to see, one of the wonderful benefits of OOP is that it makes using other programmers' code solutions very convenient. Once you understand the principles of OOP you can use any of the thousands of PHP classes that are freely available on the Web to solve most any programming challenge you can imagine.

If you're brand new to OOP you're probably not going to master its fundamental principles from this very brief explanation. You can find good examples and some useful explanations to get you up to speed in these articles:

http://www.sitepoint.com/article/object-oriented-php

http://devzone.zend.com/node/view/id/638

http://www.php.net/oop

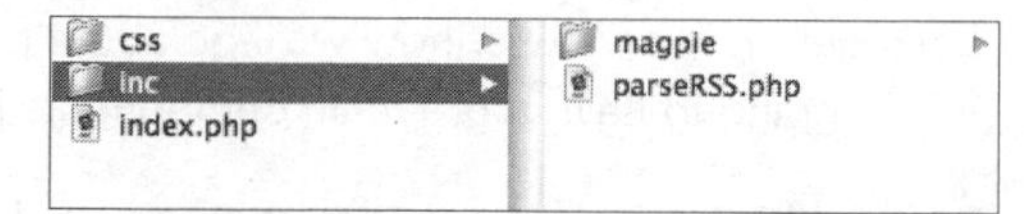

FIGURE 4.14 *To complete the RSS parsing example you'll need to set up a directory structure as illustrated.*

We'll get lots of mileage out of the parseRSS() function, as it will be used in later examples as well. Before getting started, see **FIGURE 4.14** for the directory structure you'll need to create.

Once you've downloaded Magpie and have set up a directory structure as shown in Figure 4.14, you're ready to start.

1. Create a new file called parseRSS.php and save it in your "inc" (includes) folder.

2. Start the file by including Magpie's RSS fetch class and defining the parseRSS() function.

```
// Include Magpie to do the RSS parsing
require_once('magpie/rss_fetch.inc');

function parseRSS($url,$numHeadlines){

}
```

Notice that the parseRSS() function accepts two variables—called parameters when passed to a function. The first parameter defines the URL of the feed to be parsed and the second defines the number of headlines to be displayed.

The first task the parseRSS() function executes is a call to Magpie's fetch_rss() function. We'll store the parsed RSS that Magpie returns in a variable called $rss for easy use throughout the script.

```
function parseRSS($url,$numHeadlines){

    // Call Magpie's fetch_rss function to grab feed items
    $rss = @fetch_rss($url);

}
```

When the fetch_rss() function is called it returns the feed in the form of an object with a series of properties—also known as member variables. Each property represents a tag from the RSS feed and will contain the same text as the original tag.

Notice that the call to the fetch_rss() function is preceded with an @. This will suppress the display of error messages that might be returned. We'll do a little error checking of our own to let users know when the process failed without the cryptic techno-babble that would otherwise be displayed.

Following the fetch_rss() function call, a simple conditional can be used to stop the process if there was some problem grabbing the feed. If it was fetched and parsed successfully we'll remove any unwanted headlines, leaving just the number requested when the parseRSS() function is called.

```
// Does the $rss varaible have anything in it?
if($rss){
    // Get number of headlines defined by $numHeadlines
    $items = array_slice($rss->items, 0, $numHeadlines);
}else{
    return '<div class="error">
    Sorry! Couldn\'t retrieve RSS feed</div>';
    exit;
}
```

If the $rss variable does have something stored in it a new variable called $items is created to store just the number of headlines defined by the $numHeadlines parameter. We gain access to the parsed <items> content with $rss->items. There are often many <items> in an RSS feed so Magpie returns them as an array—a variable with many values. Using the PHP function array_slice() we can cut off all extra <items> in the array beyond the number of headlines that we want to display.

If something went awry in the fetching of the RSS feed we'll send out an error inside a <div> that lets the user know the content couldn't be retrieved. The class="error" in the <div> makes styling error messages using CSS easier.

With all of the basic preparation out of the way we're now ready to convert the parsed RSS content into HTML. All of the HTML transformations we make will be collected in a variable called $feed. The HTML that the script builds will have a heading displaying the source of the headlines and link back to the original source followed by an unordered list of headlines. Let's take a look at the retrieval of the channel information first.

```
    // Feed heading
    $feed .= '<h4><a href="' . $rss->channel['link'] . '"
target="_blank">' . $rss->channel['title'] . '</a></h4>'; // Link
to channel source
```

The <channel> tag has tags within it including <link> and <title>. The object that Magpie's fetch_rss() function returned has placed these inside the channel property as an array so they can be easily accessed like this: $rss->channel['title'].

Building the unordered list of headlines requires a foreach loop because, like the channel property, the item property also has its nested tags stored in an array.

```
// Build feed list
$feed .= '<ul class="feed">';

foreach ($items as $item) {
    $href = strip_tags($item['link']);
    $title = strip_tags($item['title']);

    // truncate headlines if needed, comment out if not
    if(strlen($title) > 50){ $title = substr_replace($title,"...",
50); }

    $feed .= '
    <li><a href="'.$href.'" target="_blank" title="Read full post
in new window">'.$title.'</a></li>';

} // End loop

// Close feed list
$feed .= "</ul>";
```

The <ul> and </ul> are added to the $feed variable outside of the loop so we don't end up with a bunch of lists with just one headline. Inside the loop the strip_tags() function built into PHP removes any rogue HTML tags added by the feed's author to prevent accidental display explosions. When you're pulling content from other sources it's prudent to take such precautions as a random </div> in an RSS feed could make your page break into an unintended mess.

Like the <channel> tag, each <item> tag has tags nested within it that are also returned by the fetch_rss() function in an array. Each nested tag in <item> is accessed using $item['tagname'] where 'tagname' is the name of the tag.

Although this example doesn't display the <description> text, it could be easily added using $item['description']. We'll add it into the script in the link library example we'll see shortly.

RSS content is often displayed in small spaces such as the sidebar of a home page. Long headlines could compromise the display by awkwardly occupying multiple lines. You can limit the number of characters to be included in the headlines–called truncation–with a simple condition and the `strlen()` function built into PHP.

This example limits headlines to 50 characters. Those that exceed this number will have an ellipsis (...) added to the end where excess characters have been trimmed.

With the feed successfully transformed into HTML all that's left to do is return the HTML to the location where the function is called and close the function:

```
    return $feed;
}
?>
```

When we bring it all together, here's what it looks like:

```
<?
// Include Magpie to do the RSS parsing
require_once('magpie/rss_fetch.inc');

function parseRSS($url,$numHeadlines){

    // Call Magpie's fetch_rss function to grab feed items
    $rss = @fetch_rss($url);

    // Does the $rss varaible have anything in it?
    if($rss){
        // Get number of headlines defined by $numHeadlines
        $items = array_slice($rss->items, 0, $numHeadlines);
    }else{
        return '<div class="error">
        Sorry! Couldn\'t retrieve RSS feed</div>';
        exit;
    }

       // Feed heading
       $feed .= '<h4><a href="' . $rss->channel['link'] . '"
target="_blank">' . $rss->channel['title'] . '</a></h4>'; // Link
to channel source

   // Build feed list
   $feed .= '<ul class="feed">';
```

```
    foreach ($items as $item) {
        $href = strip_tags($item['link']);
        $title = strip_tags($item['title']);

        // truncate headlines if needed, comment out if not
        if(strlen($title) > 50){ $title = substr_replace($title,".
..",50); }

        $feed .= '
        <li><a href="'.$href.'" target="_blank" title="Read full
post in new   window">'.$title.'</a></li>';

     } // End loop

    // Close feed list
    $feed .= "</ul>";

    return $feed;
}
?>
```

Once you have the parseRSS.php file built you're ready to begin showing feed content anywhere on your site. There are two simple steps to displaying RSS content using parseRSS.php:

1. Include the parseRSS.php file into the page where you'll be displaying feed content.
2. Call the parseRSS() function defining the feed URL and the number of headlines to be displayed.

See a variation on this RSS parsing example that uses Ajax to load feeds at DMXZone http://www.dmxzone.com/ShowDetail.asp?NewsId=12757.

With the tricky part out of the way, adding syndicated content to your site is a piece of cake. Here's a simple example that demonstrates a feed display column being added to a page:

```
<div id="feed-col">
    <? require_once('inc/parseRSS.php'); ?>
    <div class="feedbox">
        <?=parseRSS('http://feeds.feedburner.com/AarronWalter',5)?>
    </div>

    <div class="feedbox">
        <?=parseRSS('http://snook.ca/jonathan/index.rdf',5)?>
    </div>
</div>
```

Once you include the parseRSS.php file you can call the parseRSS() function wherever you want to show RSS content. It's that simple. I've added a few <div> tags with classes and ids that will make layout and styling with CSS more convenient. **FIGURE 4.15** illustrates what the feed output might look like in a styled page.

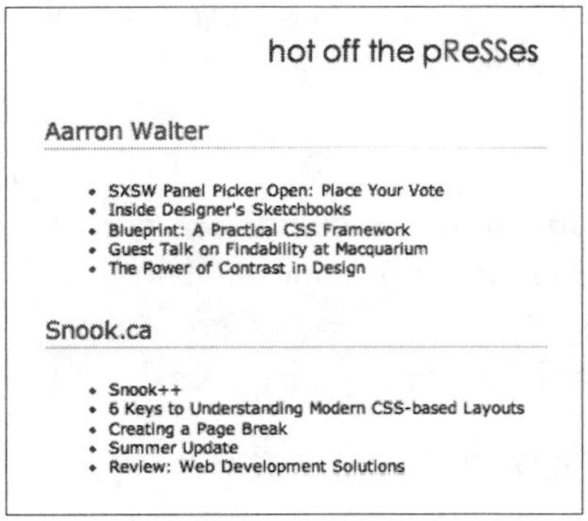

hot off the pReSSes

Aarron Walter

- SXSW Panel Picker Open: Place Your Vote
- Inside Designer's Sketchbooks
- Blueprint: A Practical CSS Framework
- Guest Talk on Findability at Macquarium
- The Power of Contrast in Design

Snook.ca

- Snook++
- 6 Keys to Understanding Modern CSS-based Layouts
- Creating a Page Break
- Summer Update
- Review: Web Development Solutions

FIGURE 4.15 *The latest headlines from sites that produce content related to yours can be displayed anywhere on your site with RSS and PHP.*

More RSS Parsing Opportunities

Headlines from blogs are just the beginning of the syndicated content opportunities your site could take advantage of. RSS is a low-hanging fruit that can provide relevant content your audience will enjoy and can attract more search traffic. Anytime new content is published the associated RSS feed is redistributed, automatically updating any site that displays it. Using RSS is a great way to keep your site's content fresh without investing a lot of time.

Now that you know how to parse RSS you could display information from any of the following sites with ease.

Music: Last.fm

Last.fm (**http://last.fm**) is a social music site that provides you with tools to upload information about the music you've been listening to. It provides suggestions of music you may like based on your listening habits, and connects you with users who have similar tastes.

Last.fm publishes a wealth of interesting RSS feeds that you could tap into including a list of your recent tracks, your most-listened-to artists, and much more. Each track listing links back to the Last.fm site where more information is available about the artist and the album. Last.fm offers both paid and free services.

Photos: Flickr

Flickr (**http://flickr.com**) is a popular photo-sharing Web application. When users post photos they tag them with descriptive keywords so they can be easily located in broad searches. Flickr published RSS feeds–called photo streams–for each individual account, and all tags.

You could use Flickr's RSS feeds to display photos you've recently taken, or photos anyone has tagged with a particular term.

Jobs: Authenticjobs.com

Cameron Moll's job listing site Authentic Jobs (**http://authenticjobs.com/**) publishes information about design and development positions in the Web industry. All of the job listings are available via RSS in a single feed or separately by full-time, part-time, design, and development positions.

Many Web designers display these job listings on their site because it's content that is relevant to their audience.

Events: Upcoming.org

Upcoming (**http://upcoming.org**), a Yahoo! property, publishes listings for events of all kinds around the world. Besides publishing generalized RSS feeds of different event categories, it also offers feeds for events taking place in a specific location.

Upcoming offers RSS feeds that could be used to display all events that pertain to a certain topic, events at a single venue, tour dates for a band, or just events happening in a local area.

Bookmarks: Del.icio.us and Ma.gnolia.com

The popular social bookmarking sites Delicious (**http://del.icio.us**) and Magnolia (**http://ma.gnolia.com**) both offer a similar feature set. Each allows users to store their bookmarks, tag them, work in teams to create larger bookmark groups, and share them with others. Both Delicious and Magnolia offer great RSS features that allow you to subscribe to anyone's bookmarks or grab all bookmarks that have a shared tag.

As we'll see shortly, using Delicious and Magnolia you can create a very useful link library that can generate traffic on your site.

Movies: Netflix.com

Netflix (**http://netflix.com**)–the online movie rental service–provides RSS feeds of new DVD releases, movie reviews, and most popular rentals. If you have an account with them you could use the RSS feeds of your recently viewed movies and your rental queue to publish your film interests.

Files: Box.net

Box.net (**http://box.net**) is an online file storage application that offers file sharing and collaboration services. Users with an account can grab their RSS feed to display links to files stored on the Box.net system.

Using the RSS Parsing System To Create a Link Library

Because Magnolia and Delicious both publish all bookmarks in their system via RSS it's easy to use the `parseRSS.php` file we've already built to create a link library on your site. As we saw earlier in this chapter in the section entitled "Content of Many Flavors," a well-constructed link library is a valuable resource that users are likely to return to often, and can increase search traffic.

The goal of a link library is to provide a series of top-notch resources that address a single topic. A good link library is not flooded with irrelevant links. Identify an important topic for your audience and create an authoritative library of all resources on the Web that can help your users solve a problem.

Using a bookmark management system like Magnolia or Delicious to build your link library will make keeping it updated very convenient. Both services offer bookmarklets you can use while browsing the Web to quickly save a link to your account. A bookmarklet is a little JavaScript link that you can drag into your browser's bookmark toolbar. When clicked a bookmarklet performs a task like connecting to a site to record information.

Each time you save a bookmark to Delicious or Magnolia your link library page will automatically update because it pulls its information from your bookmark management system's RSS feed. When you build a link library to be this easy to update it's sure to stay fresh with relevant content for your users.

You can find bookmarklets and handy browser extensions for Delicious at http://del.icio.us/help/.

If you're not already using Delicious (**http://del.icio.us**) or Magnolia (**http://ma.gnolia.com**) you may want to visit both sites to try out their features and interface. Both are free to use so there's really no risk in using both or changing your mind later on.

Magnolia also has a number of good bookmarklets that you can grab at http://ma.gnolia.com/support/bookmarklets.

Delicious and Magnolia offer a JavaScript-based method for syndicating your bookmarks onto your site called a linkroll. Because linkrolls are dependent on

JavaScript, search engines won't see the links, which undermines the reason for including them. A server-side approach using PHP is preferable to make sure your link library is visible to all search engine spiders.

In order to use the parseRSS.php file to build our link library, we'll make a couple simple modifications to the foreach loop to show the description information as well. I've highlighted the areas that have changed from the previous example.

```
foreach ($items as $item) {
    $href = strip_tags($item['link']);
    $title = strip_tags($item['title']);
    $desc = $item['description'];

    // truncate headlines if needed, comment out if not
    if(strlen($title) > 50){ $title = substr_replace($title,"...",
50); }
    if(strlen($desc) > 200){ $desc = substr_replace($desc,"...",20
0); }

    $feed .= '
    <li>
        <h4><a href="'.$href.'" target="_blank" title="Read full
post in new window">'.$title.'</a></h4>
        '.$desc.'
    </li>
    ';

} // End loop
```

The script will now include the <description> information in the HTML output and can be optionally truncated to any number of characters if you like. Adding description text will be especially important when using Magnolia as it provides some unique features in its <description> tags. Notice that the description does not have tags stripped from its contents. This is because Magnolia includes some HTML in their <description> that is worth preserving.

Now that we have the necessary changes to parseRSS.php in place all we really need to know is how Delicious and Magnolia build their RSS URLs. Each provides very specific control to access a user's entire library, a user's bookmarks with a specific tag, or everyone's bookmarks with a specific tag. Here's how they work.

Delicious

Delicious has a rather simple approach to their RSS URL structure. Here are some basic examples of feed URLs you might use to display bookmarks from Delicious:

- Grabbing all of a user's bookmarks:
  http://del.icio.us/rss/username
- Grabbing a user's bookmarks with a specific tag:
  http://del.icio.us/rss/username/tagname
- Grabbing every user's bookmarks with a specific tag:
  http://del.icio.us/rss/tag/tagname

Choosing any of the above types of RSS information, simply include `parseRSS.php` into a page and call the `parseRSS()` function to see your link library come to life. In this example the 20 most recent bookmarks tagged with the term "seo" will be displayed. See **FIGURE 4.16**.

```
<? require_once('inc/parseRSS.php'); ?>
<div id="library">
    <?=parseRSS('http://del.icio.us/rss/tag/seo,20)?>
</div>
```

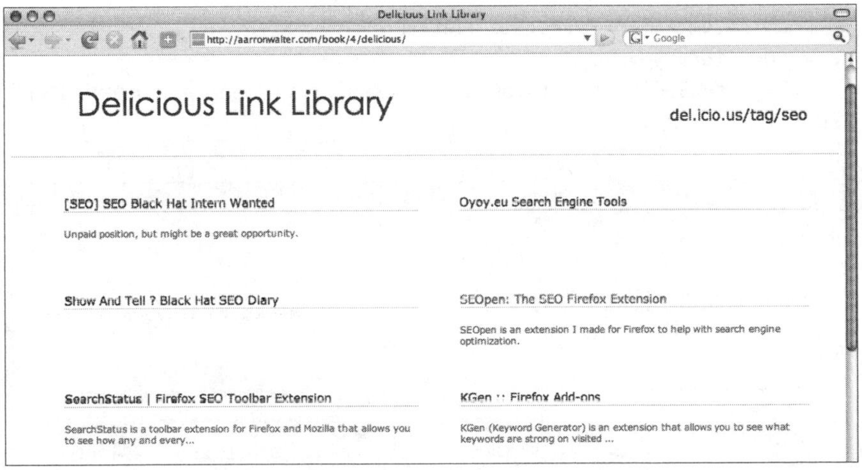

FIGURE 4.16 *Twenty links from Delicious with the tag "seo" are displayed in this link library. Because this example draws from everyone's bookmarks, anytime someone tags a new link with the term "seo" it will automatically show up on the page.*

Magnolia

Magnolia provides full and lite feed options to give you more control over what information is included in your RSS feeds. Full feeds include a text description of the link, tags, and thumbnail images for each bookmark. Lite feeds only include the title, description, and link for each bookmark. If you're displaying your bookmarks in a sidebar of a blog or home page then the lite option is the best bet. For a full-page link library, use the full feed.

Here's how Magnolia structures its feed URLs:

- Grabbing all of a user's bookmarks with all possible content:
  http://ma.gnolia.com/rss/full/people/aarron/
- Grabbing a user's bookmarks with a specific tag with all possible content:
  http://ma.gnolia.com/rss/full/people/aarron/tags/findability
- Grabbing every user's bookmarks with a specific tag with all possible content:
  http://ma.gnolia.com/rss/full/tags/findability

To grab the lite version, just replace the word "full" in the URL with "lite" and you're all set.

The Magnolia link library works exactly the same as the Delicious example we just saw. This example (see **FIGURE 4.17**) uses the full feed in order to display thumbnails, tag links, and a link for users to say thanks for the information, which creates a much more compelling display than the one created by the plain text in a Delicious feed.

```
<? require_once('inc/parseRSS.php'); ?>
<div id="library">
    <?=parseRSS('http://ma.gnolia.com/rss/full/people/aarron',20)?>
</div>
```

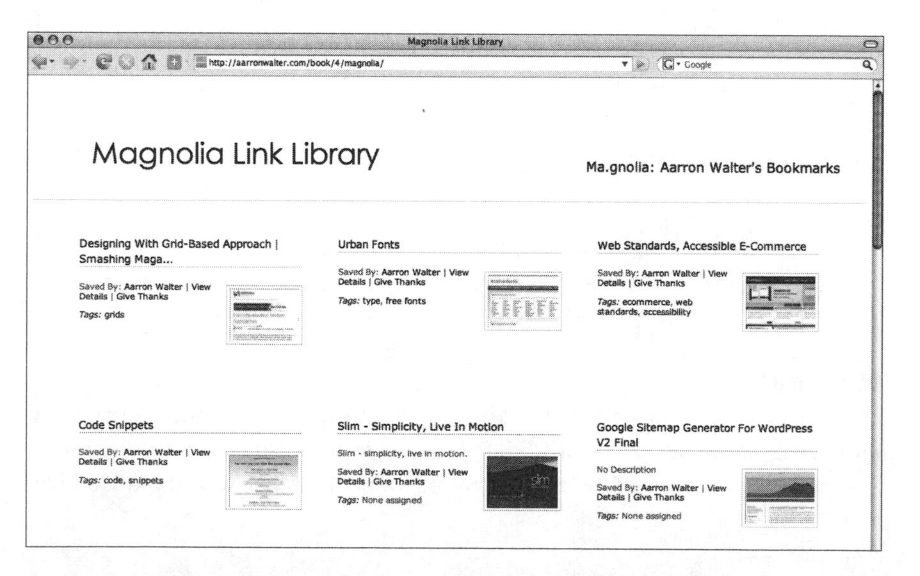

FIGURE 4.17 *Using Magnolia's full RSS feed option you can display thumbnails of the sites bookmarked. It also includes links to view other bookmarks on Magnolia with the same tag and a link for grateful users to say "thanks" for sharing the link.*

Tapping into More Social Bookmarking Features

Delicious and Magnolia both provide APIs that allow developers to create new applications that make use of their features. An API–or Application Programming Interface–opens up the feature set of an application to other applications so developers can create new and interesting mashups. Just as RSS syndicates content, an API syndicates functionality.

If you are interested in exploring the Delicious and Magnolia APIs to create more advanced bookmarking features on your site, take a look at these resources:

PHPDelicious: a class for accessing the Delicious API **http://www.ejeliot.com/pages/5**

Magnolia API Wiki **http://wiki.ma.gnolia.com/Ma.gnolia_API**

Although link libraries from any of these feeds will add a lot of great content to your site, grabbing links with a single tag will keep your resource listing focused on one topic. You could always create a series of pages each displaying links with a different tag to provide some variety.

Users won't like digging through a mountain of links to find the ones that are relevant to them, so narrowing it down using tags is preferable.

Good link libraries get referenced often and draw inbound links. If you keep your link library on topic and only include the best stuff you'll certainly increase traffic on your site.

5

Building a Findable Blog

By following some simple best practices and using intelligent configuration techniques your blog is sure to be a pillar of findability that helps your site communicate with a broader audience and inspires repeat traffic.

As we saw in the previous chapter, blogs are a powerful content-delivery platform that can generate interest in your site, increase your inbound links, and create more search referrals. A blog can either function autonomously with few or no additional pages in your site, or it can be used as supporting content for a larger site funneling traffic into other areas of importance.

In this chapter we'll explore some practical solutions that will help you configure your blog to promote search engine traffic, RSS readership, and see how social bookmarking and news sites can springboard your blog's visibility on the Web. Before getting into the nuts and bolts of configuring your blog to be more findable, let's take a look at some blogging best practices that can generate traffic and keep users on your site longer.

Blogging Best Practices To Improve Findability

The content and structure of your blog play a big role in generating search traffic and helping users find points of interest on your site. After blogging for a while you'll start to discover what types of content your users are most interested in. Using some traffic analysis tools, you can see which posts are read the most and which keywords in your posts are generating the most traffic. This information can help you define the topics of future posts so you can continue to provide content relevant to your audience. You'll find this information in the bonus chapter entitled "Analyzing Your Traffic" on the companion website **http://buildingfindablewebsites.com**.

Blogs are an amazing tool for discovering niche issues that attract a surprising amount of interest because they cover a lot of sub-topics within a primary subject. When you discover that one of your posts has generated a lot of interest, follow it up with a related post. Look for posts that have received the most comments. If you're getting mostly positive comments or you've discovered a hot-button issue that people want to debate, keep the momentum with more posts.

There are a lot of simple but critical ways to make your blog successful. Following these best practices will help you bring in new readers and keep them on your site longer. We'll explore the technical solutions for many of these recommendations later in this chapter.

Matt Cutts (http://www.mattcutts.com/blog/), head of Google's Webspam team, spoke at WordCamp in 2007 and offered some insight into SEO for blogging.

Part 1 is at http://one.revver.com/watch/352281.

Part 2 is at http://one.revver.com/watch/352486.

Write Regularly on a Focused Topic

Although it was already mentioned in Chapter 4 in the section entitled "Content of Many Flavors," it's worth repeating that in order for any blog to be successful you need to stay on topic. Define your primary subject for your blog and stick to it. It's OK for your topic to have many sub-topics, but try not to veer too far off course or you may begin to lose readers.

People will visit your blog because they find it entertaining, inspiring, or educational. If your blog stops delivering the content that brought them in initially, they'll stop coming back.

Link Often, and Link to Other Blog Posts To Generate Trackbacks

Make sure your blog posts include plenty of links to other sites to provide value for your readers. Rather than just writing about interesting things, show your readers where to find more. Although links in your post may draw users away temporarily to explore another site, they'll return for more of your link recommendations.

Linking to blog posts on other websites can help build the number of inbound links to your site. Blogs that are the recipients of links in your posts will automatically be notified when you publish. An excerpt of your post and a link to your site will be displayed in the comments section of the recipient blog. This is called a trackback. It should be noted that the recipient blog's author could choose to approve or reject your trackback. If they do approve it, though, you'll have created a new inbound link to your site, which can help you build your Google PageRank.

Trackbacks often get abused by spam bloggers who write nonsense and include links to other blog posts so they can dishonestly build their inbound links. When used as intended, trackbacks are a great way to build a discussion within a community, and share traffic among peer sites.

Create Your Own Blog Template

If you want your audience to take your blog seriously you'll need to ditch the default templates the application often comes with and create your own. By creating your own template design you can establish your blog's identity or tie it into the look of the rest of your site. It also affords you the opportunity to build your HTML to be more search engine friendly as outlined in Chapter 2.

Because life's not always so utopian, you may find that you don't have either the time or knowledge to build your own blog template. For small, personal blogs a pre-built template might be an option worth considering. Templates for different blogging platforms are readily available from many sites on the Web that you can track down with a quick Google search. Also, check the official site of the blogging platform you're using, as it may provide links to recommended template sources. Since third party template designs aren't built into the blogging platform they're less likely to be used by quite as many other bloggers, and they can still seem unique to your audience. Once you've settled on a template you like, make some quick modifications to the HTML to improve SEO.

Put Keywords in Your Post Titles

As we discovered in Chapter 2, heading tags are an important place to position your keywords to help encourage search referrals. When you build your custom template for your blog, use a prominent heading tag such as <h2> to assign greater prominence to the keywords within your post titles. If you recall from the section in Chapter 2 entitled "How to Use Heading Tags, it's a good idea to reserve the <h1> tag for the name of your site or organization as it is top in any site's information hierarchy.

As you write your posts you can use headings of other levels to delineate subsections. This will make your content easier for your readers to quickly scan and provides even more opportunity to make your keywords more prominent from the perspective of search engines.

A good post title will sum up the post using some of its important keywords and phrases. The text in headings often gets automatically repeated in the `<title>` tag by the blogging application, and sometimes in the meta description tag, depending on how your blog is configured. Choosing your post titles wisely can create a good keyword density and prominence that can generate search referrals.

Consider these two headings for the same blog post:

"One More Thing"

"Steve Jobs Unveils New iPods at Press Conference in Cupertino"

When presented in context with a few descriptive paragraphs, the first headline might make sense to people who know this is Steve Jobs' catch phrase when revealing new Apple products. But because it contains no descriptive keywords it's not likely to generate the volume of search referrals that the second headline will. A concise but descriptive headline that includes relevant keywords will communicate more clearly to search engines and users alike.

Remember that your blog headlines will often be read in news aggregators like Bloglines (**http://bloglines.com**) or Google Reader (**http://google.com/reader**). In this context your headline might be shown without the accompanying text. The quality of the headline will determine whether your users will read further and potentially visit your site for more detailed information.

Don't overengineer your post titles. Although it's important that they contain keywords, make sure they still communicate to your users first and search engines second.

Archive by Topics

Blogs have automatic archiving systems that organize old posts so users can easily browse through them. Blogging systems often offer a number of options for generating your archiving system, including archive by date and archive by topic or category.

Archiving by date is usually a bad idea for two reasons:

1. Users don't care when a post was made. They just want to find the content they're looking for. An archive by topic makes it a lot easier for users to explore posts that are most relevant to them.

2. Archiving by topic places important keywords in your page that can help optimize your site for search engines. Topic titles tend to closely parallel the keywords you might be targeting already, thus helping improve your keyword density.

As shown in **FIGURE 5.1**, Internet marketing consultant Ed Shull's site Net Results (**http://netresults.com**) displays its categories prominently at the top right of the layout to promote browsing by topic. Net Results also offers RSS feeds for each category so users can stay abreast of the stories in categories they find most interesting.

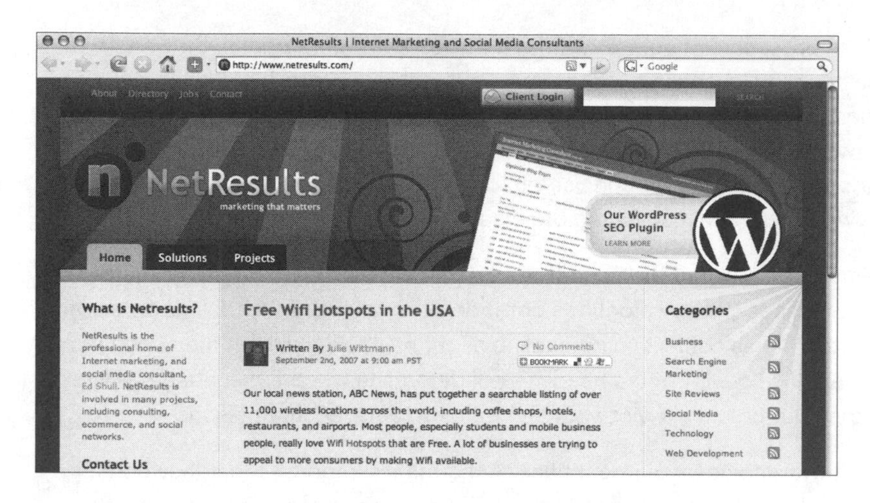

FIGURE 5.1 *Net Results (**http://netresults.com**) displays category links at the top of the page to promote browsing by topic. The site's topics also mirror target keywords featured in the* `<title>` *tag and elsewhere in the page.*

Summarize Posts To Direct Traffic Better

The home page of your blog can direct your traffic best if it displays short summaries of posts rather than the full text. A prominent headline followed by a short summary gives users enough information to know whether they want to read further. More headlines on a page means your users can get a bird's eye view of content options, and will be able to explore your site more thoroughly. Full post displays bury older posts way at the bottom of the page where users are likely to miss them.

Shaun Inman's blog (**http://shauninman.com**), as shown in **FIGURE 5.2**, displays just headlines and the date of each post. With this approach he's able to present a lot of posts to his users in a limited space.

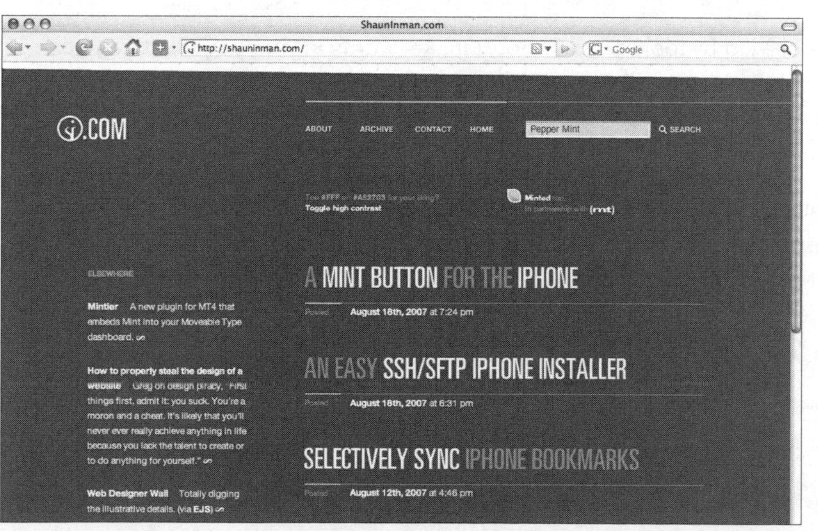

FIGURE 5.2 *Shaun Inman's blog (**http://shauninman.com**) displays headlines on the home page, which gives users a good overview of the most recent posts and encourages broader exploration of the site.*

Add a Popular Posts Section

Your best posts that have attracted the most traffic can get lost in your archives if you don't help users find them. Including a popular posts section on your blog can help users find the content that many other users have found useful.

Though a post might be old it can still be very relevant to your audience's needs. As shown in **FIGURE 5.3**, Problogger (**http://problogger.net**) provides its users with a really great tabbed browsing system to quickly view the most popular posts of all time, popular posts of the past month, recommended posts for beginners, and the author's favorites. This simple system brings 35 posts to the user's attention that would have otherwise been buried.

Add a Recent Posts Section

Repeat visitors to your site will look for your latest blog posts. You can make it easy for them to see what's new by adding a recent posts section to your blog. Display your recent posts in a prominent location on the page so users don't miss them.

As shown in **FIGURE 5.4**, Dave Shea's site Mezzoblue (**http://mezzoblue.com**) features a concise listing of his recent posts at the top of the page, making it easy for users to dig into his content.

Best of Problogger

All Time | This Month | For Beginners | Darren's Favs

How to Draw StumbleUpon Users Into Your Blog
by Darren Rowse / 90 comments

Why StumbleUpon Sends More Traffic Than Digg
by Darren Rowse / 74 comments

How Bloggers Make Money from Blogs
by Darren Rowse / 326 comments

FIGURE 5.3 *Problogger (**http://problogger.net**) provides a brilliant popular posts menu.*

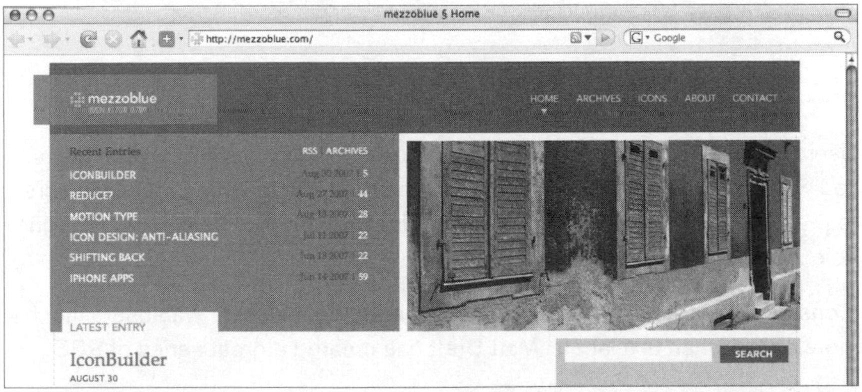

mezzoblue § Home

http://mezzoblue.com/

mezzoblue

HOME ARCHIVES ICONS ABOUT CONTACT

Recent Entries RSS ARCHIVES

ICONBUILDER

REDUCE?

MOTION TYPE

ICON DESIGN: ANTI-ALIASING

SHIFTING BACK

IPHONE APPS

LATEST ENTRY

IconBuilder

AUGUST 30

SEARCH

FIGURE 5.4 *Dave Shea's site Mezzoblue (**http://mezzoblue.com**) lets users know what's new on his blog by prominently displaying a concise list at the top of the page.*

Tell People Who You Are and What Your Blog Is About

When new users arrive at your site they usually have no idea who you are, and what your site's about. Adding a short introduction answering these questions can help users figure out if your site might have the type of information they are looking for.

Lifting the curtain to reveal the author behind the blog also helps create a sense of trust and connection with users. Adding a photo can literally put a human face on your blog that can strengthen your audience's trust in the content. Adding links to a profile and contact page within your introduction lets people learn more about you if they're interested or get in touch with you.

As shown in **FIGURE 5.5**, Jesse Bennett-Chamberlain does a nice job of introducing himself to his audience on his blog 31Three (**http://31three.com/Weblog**). A photo and a friendly paragraph let users know where he's from, what he does, and how to get in touch with him. At the top of the page a tagline gives users an idea of what this site is about.

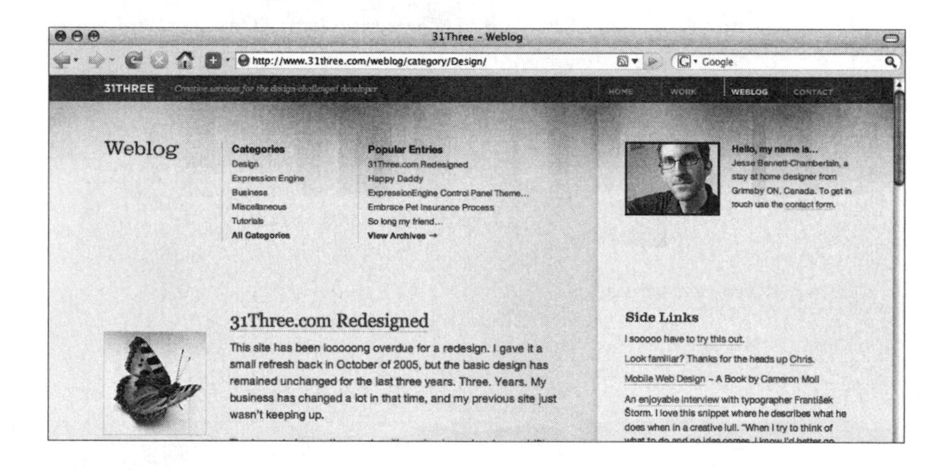

FIGURE 5.5 *Jesse Bennett-Chamberlain's blog 31Three (**http://31three.com/Weblog**) provides visitors with a friendly introduction that can instill trust in his content.*

Promote Your RSS Feed

Users who subscribe to your RSS feed are very likely to return to your site, so you want to convert as many new visitors as possible to subscribers. Be sure to promote your RSS feed in a prominent location on your blog using recognizable icons.

Icons work as a visual landmark in design and communicate with users much more quickly than text labels. Matt Brett has created a great series of RSS icons and Illustrator source files you can use to customize your feed icons to match your site's design (**http://feedicons.com/**).

As shown in **FIGURE 5.6**, Bartelme Design (**http://bartelme.at**) displays a slightly modified version of the typical RSS icon prominently at the top of the layout to encourage subscriptions. Users can subscribe to the blog feed or a feed of recent bookmarks.

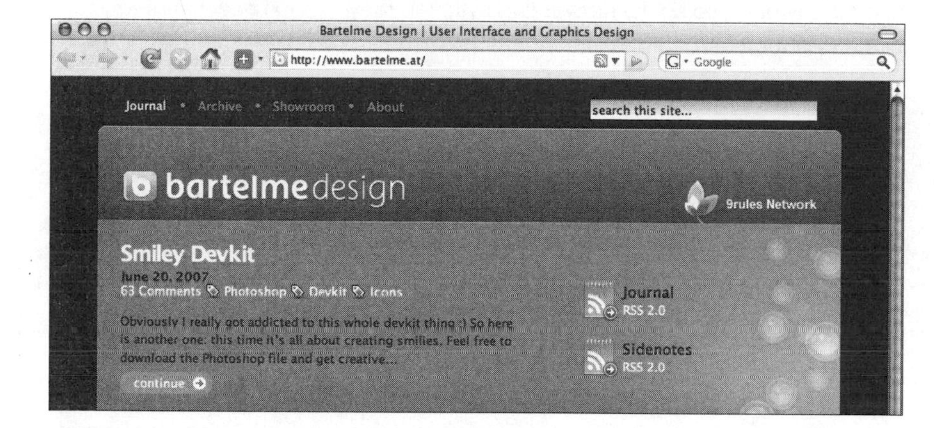

FIGURE 5.6 *Users who subscribe to your RSS feed are much more likely to return to your site.*

Cross Link To Circulate Traffic

When you write blog posts, reference and link to previous posts or other content areas on your site. Linking back to old posts can resurrect them from the archives and create greater depth to your post by providing further reading on the topic.

Remember that your blog can be a powerful tool to funnel people into other parts of your site, such as your portfolio, a products section, or any number of important areas where your business and communication objectives for your site can be accomplished. If your goal is to get more clients then write a case study blog post that links to your portfolio where users can see other projects you've worked on.

Encourage Users To Share Your Content With Others

If you read blogs yourself you've probably seen many sites that offer links at the end of their posts to share the URL in a social networking sites like Delicious (**http://del.icio.us**), Magnolia, or Digg (**http://digg.com**). As shown in **FIGURE 5.7**, some blog platforms like WordPress offer extensions to their

FIGURE 5.7 *A typical series of links at the end of a blog post that help encourage users to share a link to your site on Digg, Magnolia, Delicious, and other social networking sites.*

Share and Enjoy

system that will automatically add social networking links to the end of your blog posts to encourage users to share your URL. When users bookmark your site on any of these social networking systems they expose new users to your site and offer their personal endorsement.

Digg is a very popular social news site that lets users vote on what news should be prominently featured. Each vote for a news post is called a "digg." There are countless stories on the Web of blogs getting enough diggs to be featured on the home page of the site and then being flooded with traffic. It's a little like winning the findability lottery. It might not happen often, if at all, but if it does it will probably pay off big!

Direct Users to Related Posts

When users are done reading a post you can keep them on your site longer by suggesting related posts to read. Problogger (**http://problogger.net**) uses an automated system that identifies the same keywords in other posts as the current one and generates a list of links to connect users to other content that may be of interest. See **FIGURE 5.8**.

When users stay longer on your site they are likely to find content they value, and will come back again for further exploration.

FIGURE 5.8 *Problogger (**http://problogger.net**) includes a series of links at the end of each blog post suggesting other posts that readers may find interesting.*

Related Posts

- Website Tips from Blogging Pro
- More Google Adsense Tips
- Simple Adsense Tips

About Duplicate Content Indexing

It's a common misconception that search engines will penalize the page ranking of sites that publish duplicate content. If this were true a large part of the Web would incur significant ranking penalties.

Blogs inherently generate duplicate versions of their content. Your archives, categories, home page, and RSS feed can all feature the same content under a different URL.

There are black hat search engine optimizers on the Web that duplicate content intentionally in an effort to manipulate their page rankings and dishonestly generate more traffic to their site. When multiple pages are published with the same content a search engine could potentially return multiple link recommendations to the exact same content, which would degrade the relevance of their service. Search engines do a good job of identifying duplicate content, and can identify when it's being served with dishonest intentions.

It's very unlikely that your blog is going to incur any page ranking penalties because the archives, categories, and RSS feed present duplicate content. If you want to cover your bases anyway, eliminating redundancy can be easily done with a `robots.txt` file in the root directory of your server (discussed in Chapter 3 in the section "Controlling Search Engine Indexing with Robots.txt").

Because the URL structure and feature set of every blogging platform is different there's no-one-size-fits-all code solution. What you'd need to do is look at your blog and identify where you have duplicate listings, then use `disallow` in your `robots.txt` file to block indexing of those areas. Here's a simple example that could be used to eliminate indexing of redundant content in feed and trackback URLs:

```
User-agent: *
Disallow: /*/feed/
Disallow: /*/feed/rss/
Disallow: /*/trackback/
```

The first line of the `robots.txt` code applies the following `Disallow` rules to all search engine user agents. The next three lines use * as a wildcard indicating anything can appear at the front of the URL. Search engine spiders would ignore any of the following URLs:

```
http://example.com/feed/
http://example.com/feed/rss/
http://example.com/2007/08/31/my-post/trackback/
```

The last URL is an example of a trackback that would be used by other bloggers to link to a blog post.

Search engines do a good job of identifying the best URL to refer users to when they encounter duplicate content. It's very easy to modify your `robots.txt` file to try to cut down on some of the duplication, but so long as it's not being done as a black hat SEO trick you don't need to worry about receiving a page rank penalty.

Google on duplicate content

http://www.google.com/support/webmasters/bin/answer.py?answer=66359

http://googlewebmastercentral.blogspot.com/2007/06/duplicate-content-summit-at-smx.html.

Working with WordPress

There are a lot of really great blogging platforms on the market, so many that it would take an entire book to compare them in detail, and even more books to talk about each individually.

WordPress (**http://wordpress.org**) is one of the most widely used blogging platforms. Its popularity stems from its great features, quick setup, ease of use, and massive community support.

From a findability perspective, WordPress is pretty alluring. Its simple theme system makes building your own templates with a semantic, standards-compliant structure easy. It has an open architecture for which anyone can develop plugins to add features that were not originally included. Thousands of plugins are freely available to extend and customize your WordPress blog to do all sorts of things that can improve the findability of your blog.

Nearly all of the blogging best practices discussed earlier in this chapter can be addressed with a free, easy-to-install WordPress plugin. Generating traffic to your blog, helping users find the information they're interested in, keeping users on your site longer, and bringing them back again are all made much simpler with WordPress and the right selection of plugins.

The default WordPress installation has many features that improve findability including the following:

- Search
- Search engine friendly URLs
- Custom 404 error pages
- RSS publication of blog posts, comments, and categories

If you're interested in learning more about WordPress, take a look at Maria Langer and Miraz Jordan's book *WordPress 2 (Visual QuickStart Guide)*, published by Peachpit Press.

Setup of WordPress is famously fast, taking just 5 minutes. You can either host your blog from **http://wordpress.com** or download the PHP/MySQL application (**http://wordpress.org/download/**) and install (**http://codex.wordpress.org/Installing_WordPress**) it on your own server. The download and install approach is preferable as you have much more control over customization of the templates.

The extensive WordPress documentation (**http://codex.wordpress.org/**) and helpful forums (**http://wordpress.org/support/**) can set you straight if you run into troubles with installation or configuration.

Once you've got WordPress up and running, you're ready to configure it for findability.

Other Blogging Platforms

Although this chapter explores findability solutions for WordPress, that doesn't mean other platforms can't produce an equally findable blog. Movable Type (**http://movabletype.org**), Expression Engine (**http://expressionengine.com**), Textpattern (**http://textpattern.com**), and Type Pad (**http://typepad.com**) are just a few of the many great blogging platforms you might want to consider as you build your blog.

Installing WordPress Plugins

Most WordPress plugins can be installed following a standard, simple series of steps:

1. Download and unzip the desired plugin.
2. Upload the plugin to the plugins directory located in the wp-content directory (/wp-content/plugins/).
3. In the WordPress admin control panel navigate to the section called "plugins"
4. Click the activate link next to the name of the plugin you want to install.

Most plugins are distributed with a read-me file that provides specific instructions on the installation process. Be sure to read the plugin's instructions to ensure it follows these same steps before installing it. Once a plugin is installed it usually creates a preferences panel where you can configure its functionality in the admin control panel under the Options tab.

We'll be using this installation process for each of the plugins discussed in this chapter.

Creating Your Own Themes

WordPress can be skinned using themes, which consist of a series of PHP files that logically divide the blog into modular sections including a header, footer, sidebar, etc. Descriptive functions–called template tags–are used in themes to display dynamic content like post information or archives.

It's a good idea to create your own theme for your WordPress blog rather than using one of the preinstalled themes. Creating your own theme gives you the opportunity to optimize your code for search engines, and will let you create

To learn how to convert your XHTML/CSS blog template into a WordPress theme take a look at this article on The Undersigned entitled "From XHTML/CSS to WordPress" http://theundersigned.net/2006/05/from-xhtmlcss-to-wordpress/.

a design that is unlike thousands of other WordPress blogs. If you're creating your own theme for the first time you might want to read the WordPress documentation about the structure of themes and how to develop them (**http://codex.wordpress.org/Theme_Development**). Once you take a look at an existing theme and check out the helpful documentation it's pretty easy to whip together your own design. You may find it easiest to create a copy of the default theme and modify it to fit your needs.

Some of the blog optimization techniques we'll be talking about in this chapter require a little knowledge of WordPress's theme system, but if you're not yet comfortable with it you can still use any of the easy-to-install plugins discussed to improve your blog's findability.

Making Your WordPress Blog More Findable

WordPress can be made more findable by modifying some of its configuration options and by extending its feature set with third-party plugins. To get started, log in to your WordPress admin control panel.

Defining Update Services

Our first modification to WordPress will be to extend the number of update services that are pinged when you publish new content. Services like Technorati (**http://technorati.com**) and Google Blog Search (**http://blogsearch.google.com/**) keep tabs on all content published by blogs throughout the Web. WordPress sends a brief message—called a ping—to these services so they can update their indices with your latest content. When your blog pings the major update services, users will immediately be able to search aggregators, search engines, and directories to find your site.

To set up a comprehensive list of update services on your WordPress blog

1. In your admin control panel, go to Options and choose Writing. At the bottom of the page, you'll see a large text box labeled "Update Services" (see **FIGURE 5.9**). The WordPress site provides a great list of update services within its documentation including Technorati, FeedBurner, Google, and Yahoo!, which you can find at **http://codex.wordpress.org/Update_Services**.
2. Copy the entire list of URLs and add them to your update services to widely broadcast to the Web that you've posted new content on your blog.

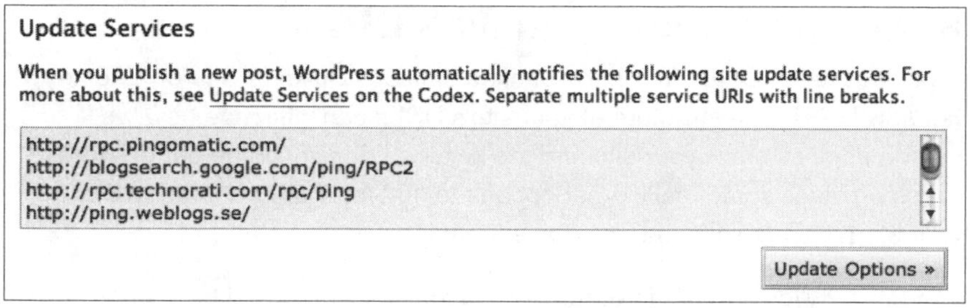

Update Services

When you publish a new post, WordPress automatically notifies the following site update services. For more about this, see Update Services on the Codex. Separate multiple service URIs with line breaks.

```
http://rpc.pingomatic.com/
http://blogsearch.google.com/ping/RPC2
http://rpc.technorati.com/rpc/ping
http://ping.weblogs.se/
```

Update Options »

FIGURE 5.9 *WordPress lets you add a number of services to automatically notify each time you publish new content on your blog.*

Keeping all of these sites updated on your blog posts can really help increase traffic to your site.

Using FeedBurner as an Update Service

Another update service option is to use FeedBurner to publish your RSS feeds. FeedBurner (**http://feedburner.com**) is a service that transforms RSS feeds into new content formats and provides enhancements like quick subscribe buttons, podcast support, and advertising that can generate revenue for your site.

You can create an account with FeedBurner, provide them with the URL for your WordPress RSS feed, and they'll give you a URL for the same RSS content that is optimized for delivery in a number of formats that will work in any reader on the desktop, Web, or on mobile devices. All subscriptions to your RSS feed through FeedBurner are tracked so you can determine how many people are subscribing and how many times they click a headline to visit your site. We'll talk more about this feature in detail in the bonus chapter entitled "Analyzing Your Traffic" on the companion website **http://buildingfindablewebsites.com**.

FeedBurner helps you publicize your new content with PingShot (**http://www.feedburner.com/fb/a/publishers/pingshot**). PingShot does the same sort of thing as WordPress' Update Services but they manage the comprehensive list of services to update. There's some overlap between the services that PingShot notifies and the list we've added to WordPress already. If your blog publishes podcasts–MP3 files linked in blog posts that get distributed by your RSS 2.0 feed–PingShot may be useful as it notifies many podcast directory sites.

Because FeedBurner's services are free including PingShot, which offers the convenience of handling the ping notifications for you, it's a really great complement to the WordPress update services. We'll see how to modify your WordPress blog to use FeedBurner for RSS distribution later in this chapter.

Remapping Your Permalink URLs

As discussed in Chapter 3 in the section entitled "Building Search Engine Friendly URLs," the structure of your site's URLs can influence how well search engines crawl your site and the keyword density of the page. WordPress provides some really great options to automatically generate URLs in your blog that are very search engine friendly.

In order for WordPress's URL remapping to work you'll need to have `mod_rewrite` installed on your Apache server and you'll need to change the permissions of your `.htaccess` file to 666 (allows read and write access) so WordPress can write the necessary code to the file. If you're not clear on how to set file permissions with an FTP client like WSFTP Pro or Fetch, you can check out the helpful tutorial on the WordPress site (**http://codex.wordpress.org/Changing_File_Permissions**).

If you're running a Windows server with IIS you'll want to take a look at these resources to help you set up WordPress's URL remapping as the process is a little bit different: **http://www.binaryfortress.com/wordpress-url-rewrite/**, **http://www.deanlee.cn/wordpress/url-rewriting-for-wordpress-under-iis/**.

To configure your URL structure in the WordPress admin control panel, go to Options and choose Permalinks.

A permalink is the permanent URL for a blog post. Because blog content can be displayed in various locations—such as in categories, on the blog home page, or in an archive—a permalink is important to create one uniform location for each post.

The default URL structure for WordPress permalinks looks something like this and is not very search engine friendly:

```
http://example.com/?p=23
```

The query string on the end of the URL (?p=23) contains no keywords, will not be very usable for your audience, and can cause indexing problems for search engines. There are a few options to change this. The simplest approach is to select the "Date and name based" URL structure (see **FIGURE 5.10**). This will change your URLs to look something like this:

```
http://example.com/2007/09/03/post-title/
```

The domain name in the URL is now followed by the date the post was published and a hyphen-delimited display of the post title text, which is much more search engine friendly.

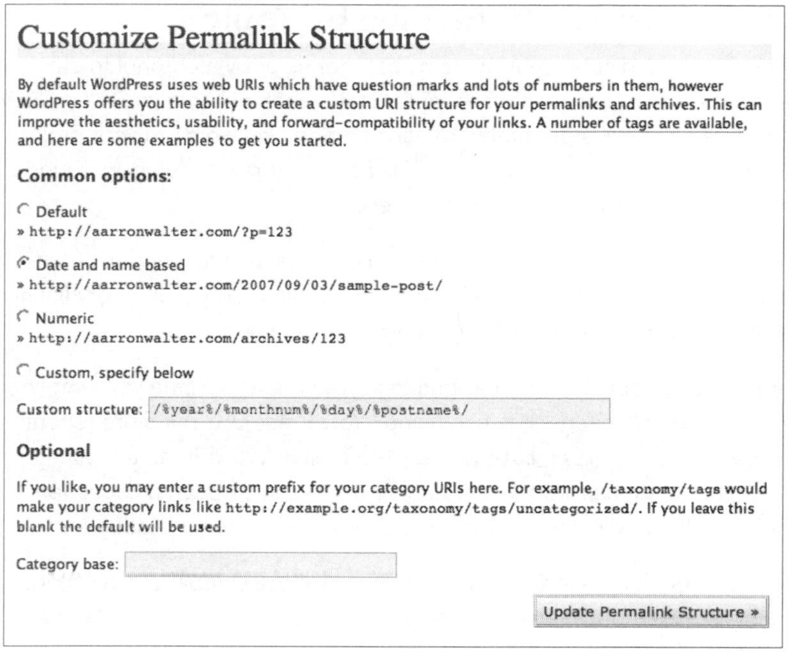

Customize Permalink Structure

By default WordPress uses web URIs which have question marks and lots of numbers in them, however WordPress offers you the ability to create a custom URI structure for your permalinks and archives. This can improve the aesthetics, usability, and forward-compatibility of your links. A number of tags are available, and here are some examples to get you started.

Common options:

Default
» http://aarronwalter.com/?p=123

Date and name based
» http://aarronwalter.com/2007/09/03/sample-post/

Numeric
» http://aarronwalter.com/archives/123

Custom, specify below

Custom structure: /%year%/%monthnum%/%day%/%postname%/

Optional

If you like, you may enter a custom prefix for your category URIs here. For example, /taxonomy/tags would make your category links like http://example.org/taxonomy/tags/uncategorized/. If you leave this blank the default will be used.

Category base:

Update Permalink Structure »

FIGURE 5.10 *You can change the structure of your URLs to include the text from your blog titles to be more search engine friendly.*

You could also create a custom URL structure by selecting the last option, labeled "Custom, specify below" (as shown in Figure 5.10). Using WordPress's predefined references to various post data you can construct your own URLs any way you'd like. For our custom URL we'll change the structure to include the category name followed by the post title text. Here's what the live URLs will look like:

```
http://example.com/findability/how-to-make-wordpress-more-
findable/
```

This URL structure includes many descriptive and relevant keywords that could help improve search engine listings of the post. To change your permalink structure, add the following code to the "Custom structure" field:

```
/%category%/%postname%/
```

That's all it takes. When you're happy with the structure you've chosen, click the "Update Permalink Structure" button and WordPress will remap all of your post permalinks accordingly. You'll find all of the post data reference codes you'll need to build your own variations and much more detail on the subject at **http://codex.wordpress.org/Using_Permalinks**.

Using Categories To Archive by Topic

WordPress lets you display your posts by categories or by a chronological archive. As discussed earlier in this chapter in the section "Archive By Topics," a topic-ordered archive is preferable because it adds keywords to your page and better suits users' search behaviors. Using WordPress's category listing will create the findable navigation system described.

Each time you write a post in WordPress you can assign it to a series of categories that you define. Most WordPress themes will display a category listing by default that will be automatically updated when you post.

In order to display your category navigation in your custom theme you simply use one of the template tags. If you're using WordPress 2.1 or a more recent version you can use `wp_list_categories()`—a built-in WordPress template tag—to display categories with a number of customizable options. Older versions of WordPress will use `wp_list_cats()` to grab a category listing.

Typically, category navigation would be displayed in the sidebar of your blog. Here's a simple example of how it might be used in the `sidebar.php` file of a custom theme:

```
<ul>
   <?php wp_list_categories('orderby=name&feed_image=/images/rss.
gif'); ?>
</ul>
```

This example would display all categories sorted alphabetically with an RSS feed icon trailing so users can easily subscribe to each category feed. Net Results—a site shown in Figure 5.1—uses this same technique to display its categories. If you don't want to display RSS feed links after each category, simply remove `&feed_image=/images/rss.gif` from the template tag.

You can learn about all of the possible category display options in the official WordPress documentation at **http://codex.wordpress.org/Template_Tags/wp_list_categories**.

Summarizing Posts To Direct Traffic Better

Creating a summary of each post on your home page can help users see more content in one place, and funnel traffic throughout your blog. Use the built-in `the_excerpt()` template tag to create home page summaries with WordPress.

This example would go on the `index.php` page of a custom theme where you want to display posts. This code runs a loop through the posts to display them if there are any. An `if else` conditional—highlighted in the following example—shows the summary of the post on the home page with a link to read more, and the full text of the post on any interior page.

```
<?php if (have_posts()) : ?>
<?php while (have_posts()) : the_post(); ?>

<div class="post" id="post-<?php the_ID(); ?>">
    <h2><a href="<?php the_permalink(); ?>"><?php the_title(); ?>
</a></h2>

    <div class="date">Posted <?php the_time('M d, Y'); ?></div>

    <div class="entry">
    <?php
        if(is_home()) {
            the_excerpt();
            ?>
            <div class="readmore">
                <a href="<?php the_permalink(); ?>">read more</a>
            </div>
                                <?
        } else {
            the_content();
        } ?>
    </div>
</div>
<?php endwhile; ?>
```

You can write your own excerpt text when you create new posts. In your admin control panel in the "Write" section where you write posts, you'll find a field labeled "Optional Excerpt" under the main post field. You can summarize your post in your own words here and it will be displayed on your home page. When users view the permalink for the post they'll see the full text.

If you choose not to write a separate excerpt, WordPress will automatically create an excerpt by truncating the first part of your post to 55 words.

Displaying Your Most Popular Posts

Alex King's Popularity Contest plugin (**http://alexking.org/projects/wordpress/readme?project=popularity-contest**) keeps track of your post, archive, and category views as well as the number of trackbacks and comments on posts so you can determine which posts are most popular. Seeing which posts your users are reading the most can help you determine what you should write about in the future. Follow up popular posts with more detail on the topic.

Once you've downloaded and installed the plugin following the same steps mentioned earlier in the chapter, you'll find its preferences panel when you go to Options and choose Popularity in your admin control panel. From the preferences panel you can reset popularity counts and learn a little about the math that makes it tick.

To display a list of your most popular posts, King has created some template tag functions you could add to your `sidebar.php` file. The plugin is actually distributed with an example file. This first example shows the all-time most popular posts when on the home page:

```
<?php if (is_home()) { ?>
<ul>
    <?php akpc_most_popular(); ?>
</ul>
<?php } ?>
```

You can also show the most popular posts for the category the user is browsing:

```
<?php if (is_category()) { ?>
<ul>
    <?php akpc_most_popular_in_cat(); ?>
</ul>
<?php } ?>
```

Or you can show the most popular posts for the past month when users are browsing your blog by the date archive:

```
<?php if (is_day()) { ?>
<ul>
    <?php akpc_most_popular_in_month(); ?>
</ul>
<?php } ?>
```

WordPress's caching features, which we'll discuss later in this chapter, will cause conflicts with Popularity Contest. Because cached WordPress pages won't trigger the plugin's tracking system, the two cannot be used together.

Displaying Your Most Recent Posts

Displaying your recent posts concisely in an area separate from your most recent post can help repeat visitors to your site easily locate what's new since their last visit. In Figure 5.4, we saw how the home page of Dave Shea's blog (**http://mezzoblue.com**) displays his six most recent posts at the top of the page and an excerpt from the most recent in the middle.

To create a similar home page structure, we can simply modify `index.php` in your custom theme just like the earlier example from the section "Summarizing Posts To Direct Traffic Better." Adding the `query_posts()` function before running the post display loop allows you to grab just one post, which is by default the latest one. The highlighted code illustrates the simple modification:

```
<?php query_posts('posts_per_page=1'); if (have_posts()) : ?>
<?php while (have_posts()) : the_post(); ?>

<div class="post" id="post-<?php the_ID(); ?>">
    <h2><a href="<?php the_permalink() ?>"><?php the_title(); ?>
</a></h2>

    <div class="date">Posted <?php the_time('M d, Y'); ?></div>

    <div class="entry">
    <?php
        if(is_home()) {
            the_excerpt();
            ?>
            <div class="readmore">
                <a href="<?php the_permalink(); ?>">read more</a>
            </div>
        <?
        } else {
            the_content();
        } ?>
    </div>
</div>
<?php endwhile; ?>
```

After the loop you can grab five recent posts, excluding the newest one, using the `get_posts()` function and display the titles in an unordered list with an id so it can be easily styled with CSS:

```
<ul id="recent-posts">
<?php $posts = get_posts('numberposts=5&offset=1');
```

```
foreach ($posts as $post) : ?>
  <li><a href="<?php the_permalink(); ?>"><?php the_title(); ?>
</a></li>
<?php endforeach; ?>
</ul>
```

Notice that the get_posts() function defines the number of posts to grab, and offsets the list by one to exclude the most recent one.

This concise home page structure will help your visitors get an overview of your content so they can quickly explore the topics most relevant to them. You could also use the same code to pull recent posts and display them at the bottom of your search results pages or on your custom 404 pages to help people find what they're looking for, or at least something else of interest.

Promoting and Tracking RSS Subscriptions with FeedBurner

WordPress publishes RSS feeds by default, but as mentioned earlier in this chapter in the section "Defining Update Services," letting FeedBurner distribute your feeds provides a number of great features beyond those WordPress offers. Subscription tracking, automatic update service notification, and advertising revenue streams are just a few of the valuable features FeedBurner offers.

Using the FeedSmith Plugin

FeedSmith (**http://www.feedburner.com/fb/a/help/wordpress_quickstart**), a popular plugin created by Steve Smith (**http://orderedlist.com**) and recently taken over by the FeedBurner folks, routes all WordPress RSS requests to your FeedBurner account so you can get detailed information about how many people are subscribing and how often they are clicking on headlines to visit your site.

After you install the plugin, go to your admin control panel, navigate to Options, and choose FeedBurner FeedSmith. Follow the directions to create your FeedBurner feeds. FeedSmith can handle both your main RSS feed with all of your posts and your comments feed.

Encouraging Social Exchanges of Your Content

Earlier in this chapter, in the section "Encourage Users To Share Your Content with Others," you learned that social bookmarking and news systems like Delicious, Magnolia, and Digg can really help you build traffic to your site by letting your users tell others about it. You can encourage your users to bookmark your site or digg it using a WordPress plugin created by Peter Harkins called Sociable (**http://push.cx/sociable**).

Sociable will automatically add a series of links under each post to some of the most popular social networking sites on the Web. Figure 5.7 illustrates what Sociable's output looks like under a blog post.

When you've installed Sociable, navigate to its preferences panel located in Options > Sociable. You can enable or disable links to any of the 61 social networking systems listed and customize the label that will appear next to them.

To keep track of the number of times your blog posts were submitted to Digg or bookmarked in Delicious, you can install John Lawrence's free plugin called Socialist (**http://www.johnlawrence.net/index.php/2007/02/12/sociallist-for-wordpress/**). Once Socialist is installed it creates a new tab at the top of your admin control panel dashboard. From the Socialist tab you can see just how many people are bookmarking or Digging your site (see **FIGURE 5.11**).

del.icio.us	
Homepage	30
SXSW Panel Picker Open: Place Your Vote	19
Inside Designer's Sketchbooks	12
Blueprint: A Practical CSS Framework	22
Guest Talk on Findability at Macquarium	15
The Power of Contrast in Design	11

FIGURE 5.11 *Socialist is a free WordPress plugin created by John Lawrence that allows you to track the number of Digg submissions and Delicious bookmarks your blog is receiving.*

Displaying Related Posts

Showing related posts on individual blog pages is a great way to keep your users on your site longer and keep old posts from being lost in your archives. Although there are a number of good plugins that will automate the task, Rob Marsh has created an exceptionally good one called Similar Posts (**http://rmarsh.com/plugins/similar-posts/**).

Once you've installed the plugin just place this simple code in the `sidebar.php` file or your custom theme or anywhere else you'd like them displayed.

```
<ul><?php similar_posts(); ?></ul>
```

Go to Options and choose Similar Posts to define how many related posts you'd like to display. You can also fine-tune the way it generates its suggestions.

Automatically Generating an XML Sitemap

The major search engines including Yahoo!, Google, and MSN have recently cooperated on the development of a standard XML sitemap format (**http://sitemaps.org**) that allows webmasters to communicate the structure of their site to search engines for efficient and complete indexing. The sitemaps XML file gets created either manually or with a tool that can scan your site and build it for you. You then save the file as `sitemap.xml` in the web root directory of your server and let search engines know where to find it. We'll examine this topic further and how to submit your `sitemap.xml` file to search engines in the bonus chapter entitled "Free Search Engine Tools and Services" on the companion website **http://buildingfindablewebsites.com**.

Using the Google Sitemap Generator Plugin

Blogs tend to have very large structures, which makes creating an XML sitemap tedious without some tool to automate the process. Arne Brachhold has created a really useful WordPress plugin called Google Sitemap Generator (**http://www.arnebrachhold.de/2005/06/05/google-sitemaps-generator-v2-final**) that builds a `sitemap.xml` file for you each time you post to your blog. It even pings Google with the location of the file when it's been updated.

Dragon Design offers a great WordPress plugin (http://www.dragondesign.com/articles/sitemap-generator-plugin-for-wordpress/) that will generate a full-page link sitemap of all your blog posts.

Once you've installed the plugin it will create a preferences panel that you'll find when you go to Options and choose Sitemap. That's where you can configure it and manually rebuild the `sitemap.xml` file. You'll need to click the "Rebuild Sitemap" button once when you've first installed the plugin to generate the `sitemap.xml` file on your server. When you make future posts it will automatically append new URLs to the file for you.

It also lets you include in the `sitemap.xml` file other pages in your site that aren't part of your blog to create a comprehensive listing of your site's entire structure. By default the plugin will automatically ping Google when you write new posts to let them know the `sitemap.xml` file has changed, but you can disable this option if you like.

Other Handy SEO Plugins for WordPress

There are so many SEO plugins for WordPress that it's daunting to try to sift through them all. Most of the SEO plugins primarily manipulate your title tags or meta tags, and sometimes do both at the same time. The benefit of these plugins is that they can place the same content in your `<title>` that is in your post heading, which can create strong keyword prominence in your post pages.

Using the All in One SEO Plugin

One plugin seems to do all of the things the others do individually. It's aptly named All in One SEO (**http://wp.uberdose.com/2007/03/24/all-in-one-seo-pack/**). One of its nicest features is the ability to create unique `<title>` and meta tags for your home, archive, categories, and permalink pages.

When you've downloaded and installed the plugin you'll notice on the Write page where you author your posts three new fields added where you can manually define the text for the `<title>` tag, meta keywords, and a meta description for the post. When you're done writing, simply cull important keywords and phrases from your post and fill them in. It offers impressive control over getting your keywords into important places in your pages.

Meta keywords content is not such a huge SEO asset anymore as we saw in Chapter 2 in the section "The Myth of Meta: the Good, the Bad, and the Ugly." The major search engines do not view the meta keywords tag because of the very sketchy use of it in the past. The `<title>` tag is an exceptionally important place for keywords, and the meta description generates traffic by describing on search engines results pages what a page is about. A custom meta description for a post could better inform users about the content on the page and encourage them to visit your site.

You can control the structure of your `<title>` tags for categories, archives, home, and permalink pages very precisely when you go to Options and choose All in One SEO. In the preferences panel for All in One SEO you can also choose to have a `<meta name="robots" content="noindex,follow" />` automatically added to the head tag of your categories, and archive pages to prevent search engines from indexing duplicated content.

If you are using WordPress's pages feature to add additional pages to your site, you can modify the blog search feature to include all page content using the search pages plugin (http://www.internetofficer.com/wordpress/search-pages/).

The All in One SEO plugin really lives up to its name offering a lot of good SEO features for your WordPress blog.

Tagging Your Posts

As we discovered in Chapter 2 in the section "Tagging Content with rel-tag," a tag is a keyword that serves as meta data used to describe blog posts or other content on a website. The more descriptive information that is associated with your content, the better users and applications will be able to locate it. Though tags often link to other services like Technorati where related information that shares the same tag can be found, WordPress tags link to related posts within the blog.

Since the release of WordPress 2.3, tagging is a native feature. Directly under the text field where you write and edit blog posts you'll find a field where you can add a series of descriptive tags separated by commas. These tags will be displayed after each post, and will be added to a tag cloud. As **FIGURE 5.12** shows, a tag cloud is simply a collection of all tags throughout a site. The popularity of each tag is visible by the scale of its type. It's a convenient way for users to explore vast amounts of content by topic and get an overview of the type of content your blog contains.

FIGURE 5.12 *The popular photo-sharing Web application Flickr (**http://flickkr.com**) provides a tag cloud navigation system that illustrates the most popular tags applied to photos. It makes exploring photo collections convenient and easy.*

Displaying Post Tags

Although you can tag your posts directly as you write them, you'll need to make some minor modifications to your theme to display them. To display tags next to your posts use `the_tags()`. This template tag function receives three parameters. The first and last are where you can declare any HTML or text you'd like to have written into the page before and after the tags respectively. The second parameter is the character you'd like to use to separate tags. Here's a simple example you could add to your theme template files anywhere you want to show your tags:

```
<?php the_tags('Tags:', ',', '<br />'); ?>
```

You can see more code examples and learn a little more about `the_tags()` in the WordPress documentation (**http://codex.wordpress.org/Template_Tags/the_tags**).

Showing a tag cloud not only offers users a convenient way to browse your content by keywords, but it also communicates which tags are the most popular by the scale of the text. The size of each tag is determined by how many times that particular tag has been assigned to posts. You can display a tag cloud and configure the font sizes for the varying levels of tag popularity using the `wp_tag_cloud()` function.

```
<?php if ( function_exists('wp_tag_cloud') ) : ?>
<h2>Popular Tags</h2>
<ul>
    <?php wp_tag_cloud('smallest=10&largest=24'); ?>
</ul>
<?php endif; ?>
```

Notice that the sizes of the smallest and largest tags are defined within the function call. Because `wp_tag_cloud()` offers a great deal of display control, you could display a tag cloud on an entire page or scaled down to fit into smaller spaces. See the documentation on this function for more detailed display options (**http://codex.wordpress.org/Template_Tags/wp_tag_cloud**).

Optimizing Content Delivery with Caching

If your site gets Dugg and suddenly you've got thousands of people on your blog, caching your WordPress pages can help ensure that your site doesn't go down. Ricardo Galli has created a sophisticated caching plugin called WP-Cache (**http://mnm.uib.es/gallir/wp-cache-2/**) that handles the entire configuration for you.

Before installing WP-Cache, be sure to disable WordPress's Gzip Compression option by going to Options and choosing Reading. Upload and install the plugin, then go to Options and choose WP-Cache and the plugin will guide you through the setup process.

6

Adding Search to Your Site

Once your audience arrives at your site, will they be able to find the content they seek? By adding a search system to your site all of your content will be instantly more findable.

Search has become an indispensable means of navigation for most users. During usability test sessions I've watched users pass up very conspicuous, logical navigation systems in favor of search to complete every task. Search is more than an added convenience; it's an essential tool that users expect to find on sites.

There are three options for adding search to your site:

- Use one of many free search systems that offer advanced feature sets but display ads in search returns.
- Purchase a search system that doesn't display advertising.
- Build your own simple search to locate content within a database.

We'll explore a number of search system options in this chapter. With most of these search systems you can track the terms that your users are searching for, which can provide a glimpse into user behavior and your site's shortcomings.

If you find that users are searching for something that you thought was very obvious in your interface, then perhaps your design is not communicating as well as you'd hoped. You could make adjustments to your design, and continue to observe search patterns to see if the usability of your site has improved.

By observing search statistics you can identify patterns in the terms your audience is searching for. This data could help you identify what content you could add to your site to best serve your audience's interests, and perhaps build more traffic from the major search engines as well.

Once you've drawn your audience to your site it's important to help them find what they've come for. Adding a search system to your site is the easiest solution and will help make your content more findable.

Using Free Search Systems

There are a lot of free search systems with great features that you can easily integrate into your site. These systems are free because they generate money for the companies that create them by displaying ads on the search results page. Usually the ads aren't that distracting from your site's design. In some situations you can actually capture some of the ad revenue yourself. If you want to avoid displaying any ads on your search results page then you may want to skip to the next section, "Using Paid Search Systems," as these options are ad-free.

When researching the best free search tool for your site, look for these essential features:

- Customizable search results page template, so you can integrate your site's design
- Search term tracking, so you can identify what people are searching for the most
- Indexing of PDF, Word, PowerPoint, and other file types in addition to regular text
- Ad revenue sharing, so your site can make money when users click ads on the search results page

If possible, take each search system for a test drive to see how well the feature set will serve your needs.

Using Google Custom Search Engine (CSE)

It's no surprise that Google, the search giant of the Web, offers a brilliant search tool that is easy to integrate into your site. Google's Custom Search Engine (CSE) is a free search tool that harnesses the power of its search algorithm and content index, but can limit search results to just your site, or a series of related sites that you define.

Google CSE's feature set is impressive for a free search tool. It allows you to customize the search results to match your site's design, captures some basic data about searches performed on your site, indexes content within various file types, and offers money-making opportunities through the display of AdWords text ads–Google's advertising system. The only real downside of Google CSE is that you are required by the terms of service to display AdWords ads on the search results page and you must display Google branding in one of the predefined styles. Considering the amazing features it offers for free, it seems like a fair trade.

Setting Up Google CSE

Setting up Google CSE on your site is relatively easy. To get started visit **http://www.google.com/coop/cse/** and follow the directions to set up your custom search engine.

On the setup page (see **FIGURE 6.1**), define the sites to be included in search results. For our purposes we want the search engine to just search a single site, including all sections within.

List your domain name with an asterisk after it to include all subdirectories in the search index (such as example.com/*). The asterisk signifies a wildcard where any text could appear.

Of course you could list the URLs of individual pages in your site if you wanted to limit the scope of the search very specifically.

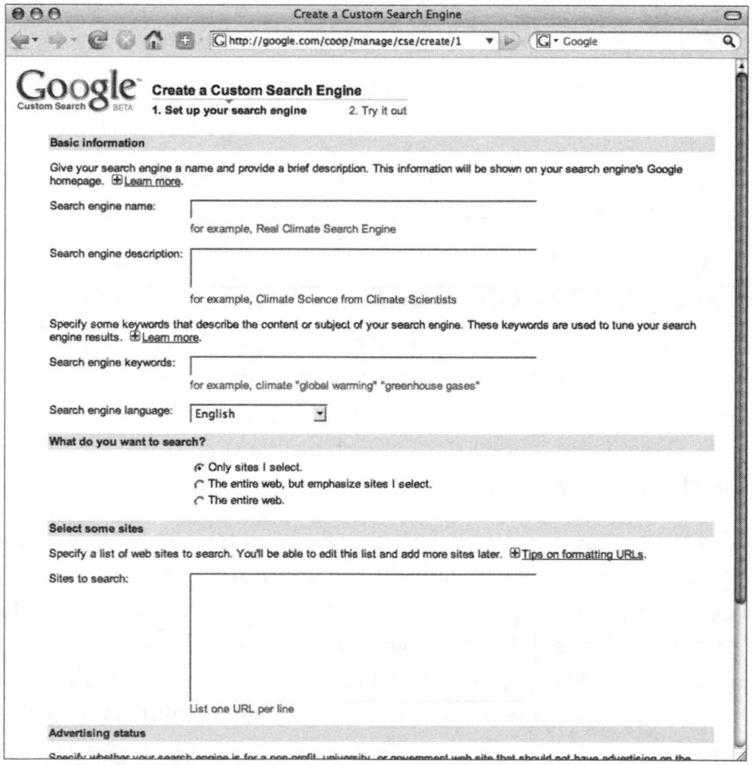

FIGURE 6.1 *On the setup page for Google's Custom Search Engine you can specify what sites should be included in search results. If your site is for a nonprofit organization or educational institution, you can choose to not display ads on the results page.*

The last option on the setup page is "Advertising Status." If you are building a site for an educational institution or a nonprofit organization, Google offers a version of CSE that has no advertising on the search results page. If you select the no-advertising option, Google will verify your nonprofit status.

Integrating the Search Box and Customizing the Results Page Once you've completed all of the steps in the setup process, you can begin to integrate the search box and the results page into your site. To get started, navigate to the control panel for your custom search engine and go to the section labeled "Code" (see **FIGURE 6.2**).

FIGURE 6.2 *In the Code section of your CSE control panel you can specify the search box style you'd like to use, then copy the code needed to integrate it into your site. Also provided is the code needed to show the search results in your site's template.*

The Code section provides code snippets to display just the search box, or the search box and results on your site. If you just show the search box on your site, users will be directed to Google, where they'll see the search results in their page template. To integrate the search results into your site, click the link labeled "Search box and search results code for your website."

Before adding the code to your site, choose the branding style for your search box. As part of the terms of service, Google requires that its branding be displayed along with the search box in one of the provided styles. Click "Save Changes" and the code snippet will update to reflect your branding style choice.

Next, specify the URL on your site where the search results will be displayed. This page currently doesn't exist, but we'll create it and upload it shortly. Choose where on the results page you'd like to have Google's text link ads displayed, then click "Save Changes."

Copy the search box code and paste it into your site's page template or any place you'd like the search tool to be displayed. Google's search box code should look something like this:

```
<!-- Google CSE Search Box Begins  -->
<form id="searchbox_011526365580152612345:eumeqg1p1ya"
action="http://example.com/search-results.html">
    <input type="hidden" name="cx" value="011526365580152612345:
eumeqg1p1ya" />
    <input type="hidden" name="cof" value="FORID:0" />
    <input name="q" type="text" size="40" />
    <input type="submit" name="sa" value="Search" />
    <img src="http://www.google.com/coop/images/google_custom_
search_smnar.gif" alt="Google Custom Search" />
</form>
<!-- Google CSE Search Box Ends -->
```

NOTE You can change the width of the text field by modifying the size attribute of its <input> tag.

The code that Google supplies for the search box has an inconspicuous but significant problem that we'll need to fix. We'll be creating a custom search results page shortly that will be hosted on your site and will match your design. Google's code to display search results in your custom page requires the use of JavaScript to dynamically write them into your page. If users have JavaScript disabled or are using a browser that doesn't support it, the results page will be blank.

To solve the problem, you can change the action attribute in your search box <form> tag to point to the default results page on Google at **http://google.com/cse**. This page will look like a typical Google search results page and will only be seen by users who don't have a browser that supports JavaScript.

Following your search box code you can add a little JavaScript that will change the action attribute to point to the custom results page on your site. If JavaScript is enabled, users will be directed to your custom results page when they search. If JavaScript is not enabled, they'll still see the search results on the default Google page. This approach is called *graceful degradation*.

Here's a revised version of the search box form rebuilt to support all users. The JavaScript that follows it will look for the `<form>` tag by the incredibly verbose `id` that Google assigned it. It will then change the value of the action attribute to point to the custom results page.

```
<!-- Google CSE Search Box Begins  -->
<form id="searchbox_011526365580152612345:eumeqg1p1ya"
action="http://google.com/cse">
    <input type="hidden" name="cx" value="011526365580152612345:
eumeqg1p1ya" />
    <input type="hidden" name="cof" value="FORID:0" />
    <input name="q" type="text" size="40" />
    <input type="submit" name="sa" value="Search" />
    <img src="http://www.google.com/coop/images/google_custom_
search_smnar.gif" alt="Google Custom Search" />
</form>
<!-- Google CSE Search Box Ends -->

<script type="text/javascript" charset="utf-8">
    document.getElementById('searchbox_011526365580152612345:
eumeqg1p1ya ').action = "http://example.com/search-results.html";
</script>
```

NOTE The very long id that Google assigns your <form> tag contains your search account number, and it will be different than the one displayed in this example.

Once you've successfully integrated the search box into your site, create a new page that matches your site's design and paste the search results code in the central content area. Name your file to match the URL you specified in the JavaScript following the search box. In this example, the custom results page is called `search-results.html`. Here's what the search results code looks like:

```
<!-- Google Search Result Snippet Begins -->
<div id="results_011526365580152612345:eumeqg1p1ya"></div>
```

```
<script type="text/javascript">
    var googleSearchIframeName = "results_011526365580152612345:
eumeqg1p1ya";
    var googleSearchFormName = "searchbox_011526365580152612345:
eumeqg1p1ya";
    var googleSearchFrameWidth = 600;
    var googleSearchFrameborder = 0;
    var googleSearchDomain = "google.com";
    var googleSearchPath = "/cse";
</script>

<script type="text/javascript" src="http://www.google.com/
afsonline/show_afs_search.js"></script>
<!-- Google Search Result Snippet Ends -->
```

The highlighted variable in this example called `googleSearchFrameWidth` is where you could define the width of the search results display area. Upload your file and test it out. By default the color of the text and links probably won't match your design, but you can customize the color palette in the control panel in the section labeled "Look and Feel."

Earning Money from Ads Also in the control panel is the option to earn money from the ads featured in the results page. In the section labeled "Make money" you can either use an existing AdWords account or create a new one. Once it's set up, when users click the text link ads in your search results page you'll share in some of the profits.

Reviewing Site Statistics Google CSE also provides some basic data about the queries users are performing in your search system. While still in the control panel click the "My search engines" link in the left column, then click the link labeled "statistics."

The data logged include popular search terms and frequency of searches on particular days. Knowing what terms are frequently searched for can help identify usability problems on your site. If you see the term "contact" searched for often, then you could infer that your users are having a tough time finding the link to your contact page. This type of information can help you refine your interface to make critical content more findable.

You can also observe popular search terms to determine what content your users find most desirable. Adding content to your site that relates to popular search terms can generate more traffic and keep users on your site longer.

TIP If you run into trouble setting up your Google CSE or want to explore some of the more advanced features, take a look at the documentation at **http://www.google.com/support/customsearch/**.

Using Google's Ajax Search API

The Google Ajax Search API (**http://code.google.com/apis/ajaxsearch/**) provides a more advanced search interface using JavaScript. Before examining ways to use it, let's take a look at the basic concepts of APIs and Ajax.

Understanding APIs

An *API (Application Programming Interface)* opens up the feature set of an application so developers can integrate its functionality into their applications. APIs save developers a lot of time because they don't have to build complex features from scratch. Instead they can simply harness the power of an existing application to create interesting new derivatives called *mashups*.

APIs are a smart move for the applications providing them too because they propagate their services to a wider audience and increase revenue-generating opportunities. In this case the service we'll be integrating is Google's search, which distributes AdWords text ads that generate revenue for Google.

Rather than going through a Web interface to provide Google your information and get the code needed to integrate its search feature, the API lets you use JavaScript to speak to the search system directly. This approach provides a great deal more control over the features of the search interface, and the degree to which it can be integrated into your site seamlessly. Using CSS, you'll be able to style the search interface and results created by the API with a great deal of precision.

Understanding Ajax

The Google Search API uses Ajax to communicate with other sites. Ajax is simply JavaScript communicating with a server to send or receive information. *Ajax* is a name created by Jesse James Garrett of Adaptive Path (**http://adaptivepath.com**) that was once an acronym for *Asynchronous JavaScript and XML*. The acronym fell out of favor in the developer community because not all JavaScript communication with servers is done through XML. The Ajax moniker is still used to describe interaction with servers through JavaScript.

Read Jesse James Garrett's famous article that gave Ajax its name and helped start a Web application revolution at http://www.adaptivepath.com/ideas/essays/archives/000385.php.

Ajax has become a bit of a sensation in the Web development world because it can be used to create very responsive Web applications that behave similarly to desktop applications. Because Google's search API uses Ajax to send search queries to the server and respond with results, users will instantly see search results in the page. No page refresh is needed because Ajax is handling the communication with the server behind the scenes. The result is a faster search system that doesn't take users away from the page they were browsing.

Getting an API Key

Before you can use the Google Ajax Search API you'll need to get an API *key* from **http://code.google.com/apis/ajaxsearch/signup.html**. Most APIs require that you get a key (a unique identifier a bit like an account number) in order to control system use. Each key is tied to a domain name so if someone is misusing the application service the key can be disabled to deny further access. Once you've obtained your API key, you're ready to start building your Ajax search system.

Understanding Content Search Options

Using the Google Ajax Search API you can create custom systems that search the entire Web, Google News, YouTube videos, Google Image, Google Maps, and Google Blogs. These services provide some exciting opportunities to create unique search utilities. You can see some examples at **http://code.google.com/apis/ajaxsearch/**.

We'll be using the Google Ajax Search API to search just your site. Like the Google Custom Search Engine created earlier in this chapter, the Ajax system will search content in PDFs, Word documents, PowerPoint, and text files. You can place the search box wherever you like in your interface, and the search results will by default display underneath. Using CSS positioning it is possible to show the search results anyplace in your interface. **FIGURES 6.3** and **6.4** illustrate what the search system we'll be building might look like.

As we saw earlier with the Google CSE, there are some pitfalls to using the Google Ajax Search API. If users don't have JavaScript enabled, your search system won't work for them. To mitigate the problem you'll need to have a backup in place that still allows your users to search your site, but may compromise some of the more advanced features.

Another pitfall to be aware of is that users on older browsers may experience problems with an Ajax-driven search system. Currently the Google Ajax Search API supports Firefox 1.5+, Internet Explorer 6+, Safari, and Opera 9+.

FIGURE 6.3 *Using the Google Ajax API, a simple search box is written into a <div> tag in your page wherever you like.*

FIGURE 6.4 *Search results will load into the page using Ajax, eliminating the need for a page refresh.*

Although support for these browsers is likely to cover most of your users, it is possible that some people may be using legacy browsers, and could run into trouble trying to search your site.

In order to manage the inbound API search traffic, the Google Ajax Search API limits the number of results you can display on your site. You can display up to 1000 results on your site per day, and just 10 results at a time. If a query returns more than 10 results or you exceed the daily maximum, users will still be able to view results on a typical Google search results page.

Building the Ajax Search System

To begin building the Ajax search system, create a new HTML page or open the page template you're using for your existing site. To use Google's Ajax Search API you'll need to connect to it and pass the API key you obtained earlier. Add the following `<script>` tag in the <head> tags of your page, replacing "your key here" with your API key:

```
<script src="http://www.google.com/uds/api?file=uds.
js&amp;v=1.0&key=your key here" type="text/javascript"></script>
```

The API will write in the search box and results into a <div> tag in your page. You can place it wherever you like, but you'll need to assign an id attribute to it so the API can find it in the page.

As mentioned earlier, if JavaScript is disabled in the user's browser the Ajax search system will not work. To solve the problem we'll make use of the Custom Search Engine created earlier in this chapter to provide a viable alternative. We'll place the HTML for the CSE inside the <div> tag where the API will write the Ajax search tool. When JavaScript is enabled, the HTML for the CSE will be overwritten with the Ajax search tool code. When JavaScript is disabled, the page will gracefully degrade to show the CSE and will still provide Google-powered search results from your site.

Your CSE HTML code can be obtained by logging into your control panel at **http://www.google.com/coop/cse/**. Navigate to the section labeled "Code" and click the link in the page labeled "Search box code for your website." If you've not yet set up a Custom Search Engine, see the section earlier in this chapter entitled "Using Google Custom Search Engine."

Here's what your HTML might look like for the search system:

```
<div id="searchcontrol">

    <!-- Google CSE Search Box Begins  -->
    <form id="searchbox_011526365580152612345:eumeqg1p1ya"
action="http://www.google.com/cse">
        <input type="hidden" name="cx" value="01152636558015261234
5:eumeqg1p1ya" />
        <input type="hidden" name="cof" value="FORID:1" />
        <input name="q" type="text" size="40" />
        <input type="submit" name="sa" value="Search" />
        <img src="http://www.google.com/coop/images/google_custom_
search_smwide.gif" alt="Google Custom Search" />
    </form>
<!-- Google CSE Search Box Ends -->

</div>
```

The Google CSE form code is placed inside of a <div> tag with the id searchcontrol. This id name will be used by the Ajax Search API to draw its search system into the page, overwriting the code within. Make sure your form code has your CSE id number rather than the example id highlighted in the example.

Now that you've made a connection to the Google Ajax Search API and have your HTML set up, you can begin to create and configure your Ajax search tool. Add another <script> tag in the <head> tag of your page and add the following:

```
<script type="text/javascript">
function OnLoad() {
  // Create a search control
  var searchControl = new GSearchControl();

}

// Build search when page has loaded
GSearch.setOnLoadCallback(OnLoad);
</script>
```

The first step is to create a function called `OnLoad()` that will contain the search building code, but will only be called once the entire page has finished loading. If called immediately as the page loads, it would attempt to draw into the page the search tool but the <div> tag where it should be placed would not yet exist. Waiting for the whole page to load ensures that the script can find the spot where it is supposed to draw the search tool. The `GSearch.setOnLoadCallback(OnLoad)` function built into the Google API calls `OnLoad()` when the page load completes.

Inside of the function a new search controller object is initialized with new `GSearchControl()`. The search controller is the heart of the search system and will be used to draw the search tool into the page.

Next we'll define the type of search functionality to be added to the search controller, specify what site should be searched, and create a label for the search results. Add the following code to your `OnLoad()` function after the search controller.

```
var siteSearch = new GwebSearch();
siteSearch.setSiteRestriction("mysite.com");
siteSearch.setUserDefinedLabel("Search Results from MySite.com");
```

The new `GwebSearch()` function creates a new Web search object that we'll add to the search controller shortly. If you recall, there are all sorts of different types of search systems that the Google Ajax Search API can create to search videos, images, blogs, and much more. We've opted for a basic Web search, but the `setSiteRestriction()` function limits the results to your site. Simply adding this one line causes the search controller to return results from just your site rather than the entire Web. The last line writes in a label above the search results identifying their source. If you decide not to define a label, the default text "Web" will be displayed.

If you look back at Figure 6.4, you can see the search results are displayed with these expansion controls.

By clicking these buttons users can show few or many search results. You can optionally define the default expansion mode when search results are displayed with the `GsearcherOptions()` function.

NOTE The expansion feature will only work if you link to Google's style sheet to define its presentation. To use this feature, add the following link tag to your page: `<link type="text/css" rel="stylesheet" href="http://www.google.com/uds/css/gsearch.css" />`

```
var options = new GsearcherOptions();
options.setExpandMode(GSearchControl.EXPAND_MODE_PARTIAL);
```

There are three expansion mode options:

- `OPEN`
- `CLOSED`
- `PARTIAL`

`OPEN` displays a long list of results. `CLOSED` collapses the results so none are visible initially, which probably won't be very intuitive for your users. `PARTIAL` shows a limited number of search results, and takes up a little less space in the page.

To change the default expansion mode, simply replace the highlighted code in the `setExpandMode()` function to the desired mode.

To complete the Ajax search system, add the Web search object to the search controller, then draw the search tool on the page in the `<div>` tag with the id `searchcontrol` created earlier:

```
searchControl.addSearcher(siteSearch, options);
searchControl.draw(document.getElementById("searchcontrol"));
```

Here's what the script looks like all together:

```
<script type="text/javascript">
function OnLoad() {
    var searchControl = new GSearchControl();
    var siteSearch = new GwebSearch();

    siteSearch.setSiteRestriction("aarronwalter.com");
    siteSearch.setUserDefinedLabel("AarronWalter.com");

    var options = new GsearcherOptions();
    options.setExpandMode(GSearchControl.EXPAND_MODE_PARTIAL);

    searchControl.addSearcher(siteSearch, options);
    searchControl.draw(document.getElementById("searchcontrol"));
}

GSearch.setOnLoadCallback(OnLoad);
</script>
```

That's it! When you test it in your browser you should see search results pulled from your website. It's surprisingly little code for the amount of functionality that it delivers. That's the benefit of using an API. Very quickly and easily you can build sophisticated tools for your site rather than building them from scratch.

TIP If you need help troubleshooting your Google Ajax Search system or want to discover further configuration possibilities consult the official documentation at **http://code.google.com/apis/ajaxsearch/documentation/**.

Using Rollyo

Rollyo (**http://rollyo.com**) is another popular search utility that you could add to your site. Rollyo's search can be limited to a single site, but it's intended to be used to search across multiple sites that you define. It's free and very easy to set up (see **FIGURE 6.5**). Simply create an account and follow the intuitive steps to build your custom search engine.

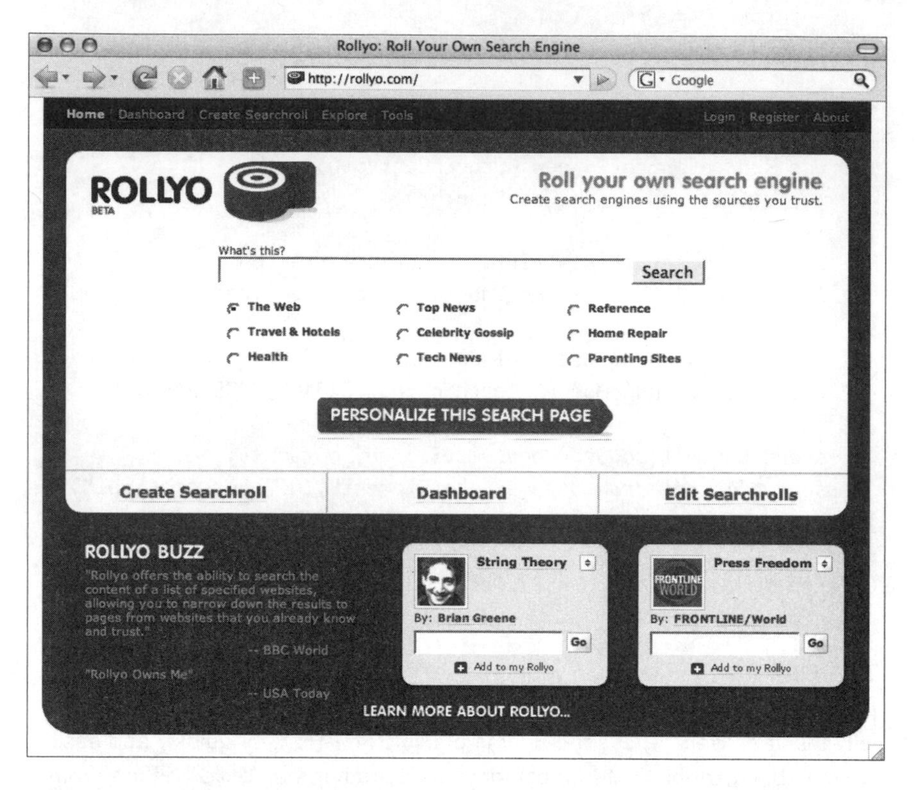

FIGURE 6.5 *Rollyo (**http://rollyo.com**) is a free search tool that is easy to set up and add to your site.*

Like Google's search services, Rollyo provides the HTML code you'll need to add its search system to your site. Its code comes with a lot of inline CSS scattered throughout, which is good for novices who want a quick way to copy and paste the search box into their page without worrying about the design. For developers who follow Web standards and like to keep their formatting separate from the page structure, removing all of the inline CSS can be a bit tedious. Here's an example of the search box HTML Rollyo provides with the CSS stripped out of the code:

```
<form action="http://www.rollyo.com/search.html" id="rollyo">
    <fieldset id="searchboxset">
        <input type="text" size="30" name="q" id="query"
value="" />
        <input type="image" src="http://rollyo.com/remote/
btn-togo-search-ph2.png" alt="Go" id="submit" /><br />

        <input type="hidden" name="sid" value="123456" />
        <input type="hidden" name="togo-v" value="1" />
```

```
    <div id="rollyo-branding">
      <div>Powered by <a href="http://www.rollyo.com/">Rollyo
</a></div>
    </div>
    </fieldset>
</form>
```

You'll need to place your Rollyo account id in the `<input>` tag where highlighted in this example. The `<div id="rollyo-branding">` tag includes the branding that Rollyo's terms of service require.

The biggest drawback of using Rollyo is that it doesn't provide any way to customize the results page. All search results will be displayed on their site.

Rollyo does index PDF, Word, and PowerPoint files on your site. More importantly, it offers some nice social networking features that can help people stumble across your search system and can build new traffic to your site. For the networking features alone it's worth considering.

Using Atomz

Atomz (**http://www.atomz.com/**) is a free search system that has been around for a long time. It offers many of the same features as Google Custom Search Engine, including a customizable search results page. Atomz uses a proprietary markup language to insert search results into your custom template file, which provides very granular control of each element that is dynamically written to the page. The default results page template it provides uses antiquated markup so you'll definitely want to build your own version.

Atomz highlights the user's search terms on the results page so they can more easily locate the content they're looking for. Atomz also doesn't require its logo to be displayed next to the search box like many other systems do.

You can control the indexing of your site and view statistics about searches run in the system's control panel. It also provides some basic settings for the type of content to be indexed, including PDF and text files. To access your control panel simply log in at **http://atomz.com** once you've created an account (see **FIGURE 6.6**).

Atomz offers its search system for free because it displays text link ads on the results page. The ads aren't terribly obtrusive, and considering the quality of the search system it's a reasonable trade.

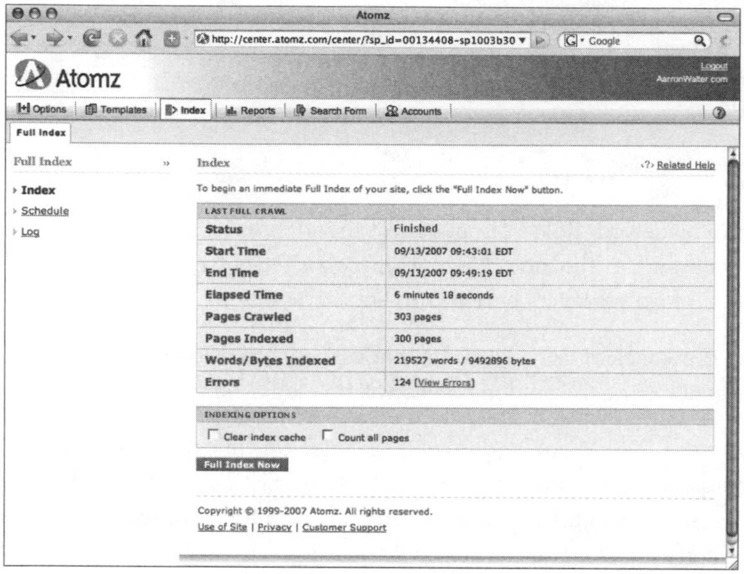

FIGURE 6.6 *Atomz has a nice control panel where you can view search statistics, initiate site indexing, and configure a few options for your search system.*

Using Yahoo! Search Builder

Yahoo! Search Builder (**http://builder.search.yahoo.com/**) is another nice search tool option to consider, although it's not as feature-rich as Google's Custom Search Engine. Like Google's CSE, Yahoo! Search Builder provides search statistics and the basic HTML code to place a search box on your site. But Yahoo!'s search results page is not nearly as customizable as Google CSE (see **FIGURE 6.7**).

Yahoo! Search Builder lets you place a logo and some text above the search results and change some colors, but that's about it. You can't create your own results page template. Like Google, Yahoo! displays text link ads on your search results page, but you can't choose where in the page you'd like them displayed.

Yahoo!'s search API, however, is in many ways superior to Google's. A free development kit can be downloaded at **http://developer.yahoo.com/search/** with examples of how to connect to and use the Yahoo! search API using PHP, Flash, Flex, Ruby, Java, C#, JavaScript, ColdFusion, VB.NET, and many other languages. You'll need to sign up for an API key before you can develop your own custom search tools with Yahoo!'s API. The great control that Yahoo!'s search API offers comes at the price of simplicity. You'll need to parse the XML results that it returns in order to display them on your page. If you're comfortable with a programming language already, though, this is probably not a significant deterrent.

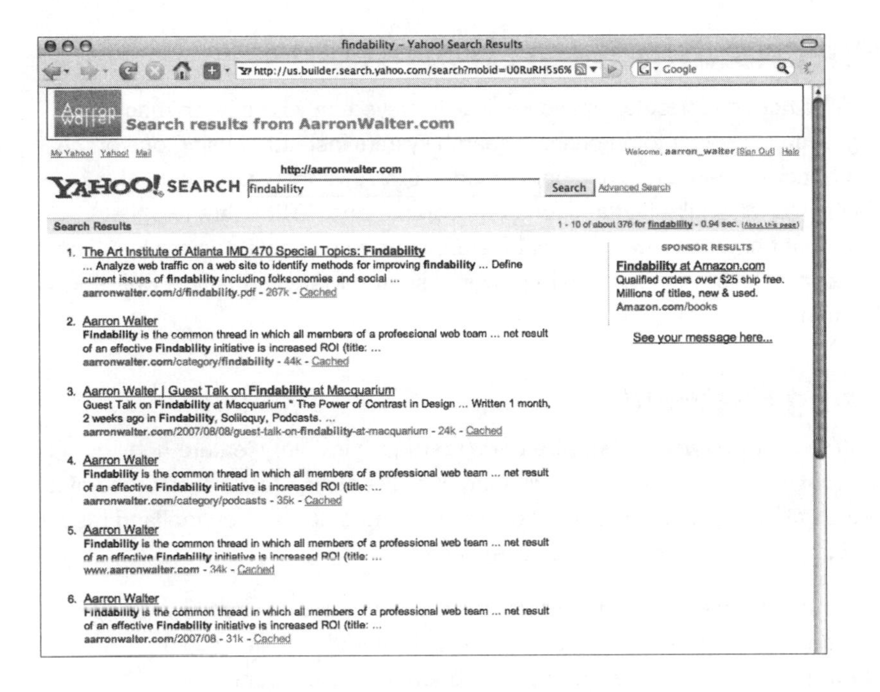

FIGURE 6.7 *The Yahoo! Search Builder provides good search results, but limited customization of the results page.*

Rather than being relegated to JavaScript to create your search tools, as is the case with Google Ajax Search API, you can work in the language with which you are most comfortable. The features and control that Yahoo! provides to developers via their API is really quite amazing.

For a comparison of free search systems, see **TABLE 6.1**.

TABLE 6.1 Free Search Systems Compared

	Results Page Customization	Search Stats	Keyword Highlighting	PDF, Word Document Indexing	Points of Interest
Google CSE	yes	yes	yes	yes	Make money with AdSense on results page; good search stats
Google Ajax Search API	yes	no	yes	yes	Seamless integration of results into page; more programmatic control
Rollyo	no	no	yes	yes	Social networking features; very easy to set up and use
Atomz	yes	yes	yes	yes	No logo required next to search box; good search stats
Yahoo! Search Builder	very limited	yes	yes	yes	Good search results

Purchasing Search Systems

If you're not comfortable with ads being displayed on your search results page, you may want to purchase a search system instead of using one of the free options. There are a number of paid search systems on the market, most of which offer similar features for a comparable price. There are two that stand out from the crowd for great features and reasonable pricing: FastFind and Zoom are both exceptionally powerful search systems that are well worth the money.

Using FastFind

FastFind (**http://www.interspire.com/fastfind/**) is a very feature-rich search tool that is worth the licensing price tag. It offers similar features to those of its free competitors, such as control over the styling of the search tool and results page, but also provides many unique features.

One such feature is the simple and advanced search that users can toggle between at will. Power searchers will enjoy having the ability to search your site with more control over the types of queries they can run.

FastFind lets you selectively prevent certain content on your site from being included in the search index. To hide content from the search spider, simply wrap it in some simple HTML comments and it will be passed over when indexing.

In FastFind's control panel you can choose the types of files it will index, initialize another complete indexing of your site when you've added new content, and view search statistics. The stats FastFind provides are exceptionally good—see **FIGURE 6.8**. It provides data about which terms are searched for most often, the number of results returned for each query, and the links users clicked in the search results.

A quality search tool is essential to the findability and usability of your site, so shelling out some cash for the one that best fits your needs is well worth it. FastFind provides a good feature-to-cost balance that makes it a worthy search tool candidate for your site.

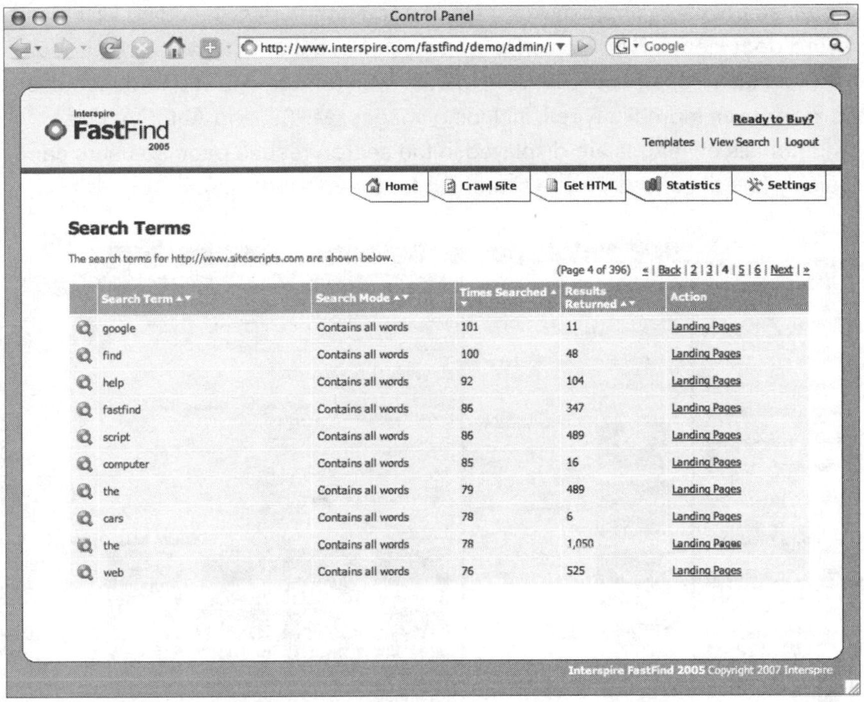

FIGURE 6.8 *FastFind (**http://www.interspire.com/fastfind/**) provides very useful statistics about search behaviors on your site, including popular search terms and pages users visited from the search results page.*

Using Zoom Search Engine

WrenSoft's Zoom Search Engine (**http://www.wrensoft.com/zoom/**) is a powerful paid search system with very reasonable pricing, and offers a number of features that FastFind doesn't. Zoom highlights the keywords the user has searched for in the results page, which makes it easier to locate the desired content.

Like Google, Zoom will spell check queries and even provide synonyms to the terms users search for. Most search systems will return a blank results page when keywords are misspelled. Users may not even realize they've made a spelling error, and might assume the content they're looking for doesn't exist. The spell check and synonym feature can significantly improve the findability of your content.

You can define certain pages as recommended links in your Zoom search results. A link to your frequently asked questions page or forum can be highlighted at the top of the results page when search terms match their content, to point your users to the pages that will most likely have answers to their questions.

Zoom searches an impressive variety of document types, including PDFs, Word documents, RTF, PowerPoint, Excel spreadsheets, WordPerfect documents, Flash Paper, and SWFs. Its plugin architecture lets you add modules to index even more file types, including images, MP3s, and AutoCAD files. Thumbnails of images are displayed in the search results page so users can quickly find the image they're searching for (see **FIGURE 6.9**).

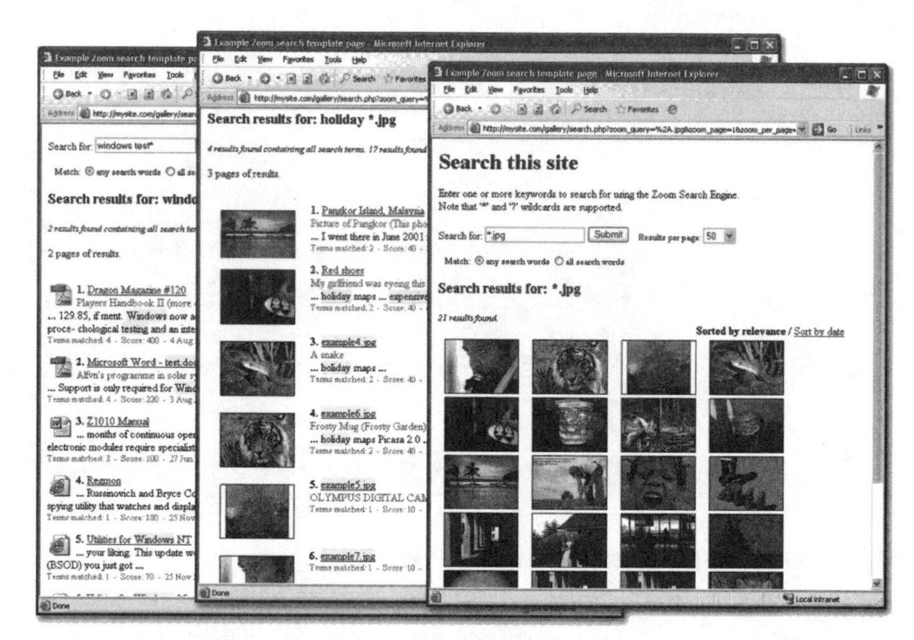

FIGURE 6.9 *Zoom indexes a wide variety of file types, including images, PDFs, and Word documents. Users can see thumbnails of images that match their search criteria on the search results page.*

Later in this chapter you'll learn about Amazon's search standard, simply named OpenSearch, which helps make search systems interoperable. With OpenSearch developers can easily build search systems that search multiple sites from a single system. Zoom publishes its search results following OpenSearch standards, which fosters the aggregation of your search results to other sites and can help you generate more traffic.

Zoom also has the typical search system features like search results page customization and query logging. Zoom is available in PHP, ASP, JavaScript, or CGI, so it will work with most any server. The Zoom setup and site indexing tool is a Windows-only application, however, so it may not be the best choice for Mac-only users. You can see a short video demonstrating the setup process at **http://www.wrensoft.com/videos/Zoom-Add-Search-Engine/**.

Building Your Own Simple Product Search System

If your search needs are relatively basic and your site's content is stored in a database, you could build your own search system using PHP and a MySQL database.

For this example, let's assume you have a table in your database with a series of products that you want your users to be able to search. The keywords that users enter in a search box will be checked against content in the `title` or `description` fields in the `products` table. Though the results won't be weighted in this example, users will still receive a list of products that contain the keywords they're looking for.

Creating a Custom Product Search Tool

To start your custom product search tool, add a search box to your site's page template or pages where your users will need to perform queries. Your HTML might look something like this:

```
<form action="search-results.php" method="get">
    <fieldset>
       <legend>Search</legend>
       <input type="text" name="q" id="search" />
       <input type="submit" value="Search" />
    </fieldset>
</form>
```

The queries will be sent from the search form to a search results page via the GET method, which will append the search terms to the URL in a query string. It's important to note that the name of the search field is `q`—short for query. The PHP script searching the database will need to access the contents of this GET variable.

Next, create a new PHP page called `search-results.php` to display the results. Add the basic HTML to make the layout match the rest of your site, then clear some space in your code where you'd like the search results to display. This is where the PHP search code will be built.

Before your script tries to run a query it's a good idea to confirm that search terms have been provided. It's possible for users to navigate to the search results page by typing in the URL into their browser. In this situation there would be no search terms to look up.

Start your search script with a conditional that checks for the presence of the q GET variable set by typing search terms in the search box, then submitting it. If none are detected, a descriptive error message will be displayed along with the search tool so the user can try the search again:

```
<?
if(!$_GET['q']){
    // Error: No query supplied ?>

    <p class="error">
        No results found because you forgot to enter search terms
    </p>

    <p>
        <form action="search-results.php" method="get">
            <fieldset>
                <legend>Search Again</legend>
                <input type="text" name="q" id="search" />
                <input type="submit" value="Search" />
            </fieldset>
        </form>
    </p>

    <? exit;
}
```

If there were search terms in the `$_GET['q']` variable, then the script would connect to the database and run a query looking for content matches. You'll need to define in your code the hostname, database name, username, and password for your MySQL database.

```
$con = mysql_connect('hostname','dbusername','dbpassword');
mysql_select_db('dbname',$con);

$query = mysql_real_escape_string($_GET['q']);
$sql = "SELECT * FROM products WHERE title LIKE '%$query%' OR
description LIKE '%$query%'";
$result = mysql_query($sql);
```

Communication with the database is done using SQL–Structured Query Language. To prevent dangerous SQL injection attacks, the query string is run through PHP's built in `mysql_real_escape_string()` function, which escapes special characters in the query. If special characters are permitted in user-authored content that is to be placed inside your SQL statements, anyone could hijack your query to delete content, expose passwords, or generally wreak havoc on your database.

To learn more about the dangers of SQL injection attacks and see how to prevent them visit http://en.wikipedia.org/wiki/SQL_injection.

The SQL statement is doing the most important part of the search script: It's attempting to select records from the products table that have text in the `title` or `description` field like what the user is looking for. The `%` on either side of the query variable are wildcards that indicate any text could precede or follow the search term to trigger a match.

After running the query, you'll need to confirm that some results were found then write them to the page. If none were found then an appropriate message should let the user know:

```
if(mysql_num_rows($result) > 0){
    while($row = mysql_fetch_array($result)){
        echo "<h3><a href=\"products/$row[id]\">$row[title]</a>
</h3> ";
        echo "<p>$row[description]</p>";
    }
}else{
?>
    <div class="message">
        Sorry, no results were found.
    </div>
<?
}
?>
```

The results page will display each record with the product title in an <h3> tag and provide a link to view the product followed by the product's description.

Searching with Other Databases

As you might guess, many other database servers provide similar search capabilities. SQL Server in particular uses FREETEXT to locate content that is similar to the keywords queried. Here's a quick example of how it might be used to query a products table:

```
SELECT * FROM products WHERE
FREETEXT(description, $query)
```

Check out Wyatt Barnett's two-part blog post on SitePoint for more info about doing full text searches on SQL Server.

http://www.sitepoint.com/blogs/2006/11/12/sql-server-full-text-search-protips-part-1-setup/

http://www.sitepoint.com/blogs/2006/12/06/sql-server-full-text-search-protips-part-2-contains-vs-freetext/

If you have a very large array of products, you'll probably need to use one of the more sophisticated search systems examined earlier in this chapter. But for a small site with a limited number of records in a database, this simple script might be exactly what you need.

Logging Local Searches To Understand Your Site's Shortcomings

You could extend this script very easily to log each product search so you could gain a better understanding of what your audience is interested in. At the very end of the script just add another database query that inserts some information about the user's search into a table called "search_log." Your table should have the following fields: query (text), date (integer).

The query field, as you might guess, stores the search terms for each search executed. The date field stores a date/time stamp indicating when each search was performed. Here's what your query might look like:

```
$sql = "INSERT INTO search_log SET query='$query', date='".
time()."'";
$result = mysql_query($sql);
```

You could record further information about each query too, if you like, such as the number of results displayed on the page. Logging search terms is easy to do and can give you interesting insight into the search behaviors on your site.

Adding OpenSearch To Your Site

If you're a Firefox 2 or Internet Explorer 7 user you've probably noticed the great search feature integrated into each browser that lets you search various sites directly (see **FIGURE 6.10**). Both of these browsers support a standard created by Amazon.com's A9 (**http://opensearch.a9.com/-/company/opensearch.jsp**) called OpenSearch (**http://www.opensearch.org**), which lets site owners syndicate the search functionality of their site to third party applications including browsers.

Users who visit a site that supports OpenSearch can add the search system to their browser so they can search its content without having to be on the site. Firefox 2 alerts users when an OpenSearch system is detected on a site by highlighting the search engine drop-down arrow (see **FIGURE 6.11**).

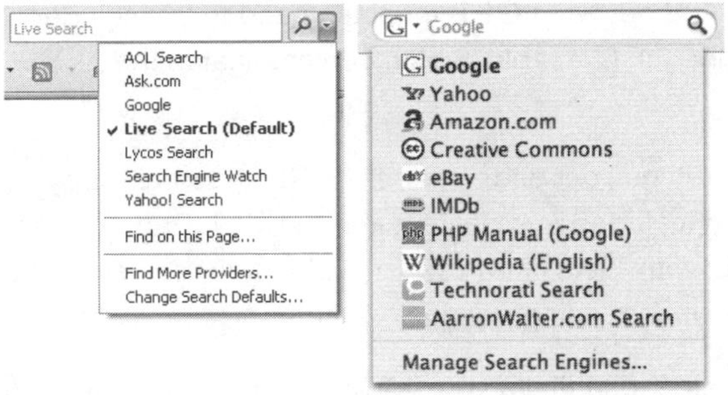

FIGURE 6.10 *Internet Explorer 7 and Firefox 2 support OpenSearch, which allows users to add search engines to their browsers.*

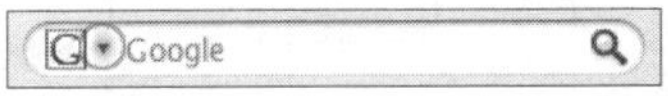

FIGURE 6.11 *Firefox 2 highlights the search engine drop-down arrow when an OpenSearch system is detected.*

Adding OpenSearch to your site can increase repeat traffic because your search engine is conveniently available to your users even when they're not browsing your site.

Setting Up OpenSearch on Your Site

To set up OpenSearch on your site you'll need to create an XML file that describes your search engine. Here's a short example of what it might look like:

```
<?xml version="1.0" encoding="UTF-8" ?>
<OpenSearchDescription xmlns="http://a9.com/-/spec/
opensearch/1.1/">
<ShortName>AarronWalter.com</ShortName>
<Description>Search Aarron's site</Description>
<Tags>web design development</Tags>
<Image width="16" height="16" type="image/png">http://aarronwalter.
com/favicon.ico</Image>
<Url type="text/html" template="http://aarronwalter.com/
?s={searchTerms}" />
</OpenSearchDescription>
```

Most of the structure of the file is self-explanatory. The document provides a short name for your search engine, a brief description, tags that further describe your content, and an icon to be shown when your search engine is selected in the browser. The `<Url>` tag is the most important part of the file, as it contains the URL structure for a query on your search engine. The query string structure tends to vary for different search engines so you'll need to do

Chris Fairbanks created a WordPress plugin that quickly adds OpenSearch to your blog: http://williamsburger.com/wb/archives/opensearch-v-1-1.

a test search on your site to find out what GET variables need to be included. In this example there's just one GET variable, which communicates the search terms.

Once you've done a test search on your site to see the URL structure, copy the URL with the query string included and paste it into the `<Url>` tag. Replace the search terms in your URL with `{searchTerms}` so the browser can send the terms to your search engine when running queries.

Upload your OpenSearch description file to your server, then add a `<link>` tag to the `<head>` tag of your pages or template to let the browser know where the file is located.

```
<link title="AarronWalter.com Search" type="application/opensea
rchdescription+xml" rel="search" href="http://aarronwalter.com/
search.xml" />
```

Now when users browse your site they'll be notified of your OpenSearch system that they can add to their browser. It's an amazingly simple setup process that adds searching convenience for your users and can generate more return traffic on your site.

To learn more about the content you can include in your OpenSearch description file visit **http://www.opensearch.org/Specifications/OpenSearch/1.1**.

7

Preventing Findability Roadblocks

Some types of content can be difficult or impossible for search engines to index. JavaScript, Ajax, Flash, audio, and video all pose unique findability challenges. But if you build intelligently you can create sophisticated interfaces with rich content without compromising search engine visibility.

Several content formats and interface scenarios might enhance the user experience, but create serious roadblocks for search engines spiders. Sites that are built entirely in Flash, though richly interactive, are often opaque to search engines. Like Flash, JavaScript-dependent interfaces often incorporate animation and sophisticated interactivity, but may make search engine indexing difficult or impossible if built improperly. Audio and video content also present huge roadblocks for search engine spiders.

With a little knowledge and forethought you can build websites that incorporate all of these great technologies without sacrificing the findability of your site. In this chapter we'll identify the specific challenges these technologies pose for search engines, and examine practical solutions that will unlock your content for indexing. As we discovered in Chapter 2, "Markup Strategies," search engine optimization and accessibility go hand in hand. The SEO strategies we'll explore in this chapter will also make your content more accessible for users with disabilities and those using alternate platforms, thus broadening your potential audience.

Avoiding JavaScript Pitfalls

There's been a boom recently in highly interactive interface design as dozens of JavaScript libraries have been released that make creating animation and various effects easy. MooTools (**http://mootools.net/**), Scriptaculous (**http://script.aculo.us/**), YUI (**http://developer.yahoo.com/yui/**), and Prototype (**http://www.prototypejs.org/**), to name just a few of the most popular libraries, have made the JavaScript that drives these systems more accessible to novice and intermediate scripters without extensive knowledge of the language.

Ironically, though JavaScript libraries have helped fuel innovations in interface design, they've also helped make it easier for front-end Web developers to degrade the findability of their site. It's easy to be seduced by the bells and whistles JavaScript libraries offer, but don't forget to be mindful of how search engines will view your site.

Search engine spiders are unable to read and execute JavaScript. If the content of your site is not accessible without the use of JavaScript it won't be properly indexed. It's easy to find out if your site has indexing pitfalls: Simply disable JavaScript in your browser and try to access all content. You can disable JavaScript in most modern browsers using the preferences panel. If you discover any content you cannot navigate to or view, then you'll need to make some changes to help search engines do their job and ensure your content is accessible to your users.

The most common situations where JavaScript might pose a hindrance to indexing is in scripted navigation systems, scripted CSS styles that are by default set to `display:none`, and content that is loaded via Ajax—see the section in Chapter 6 entitled "Using the Google Search Ajax API" for an explanation of Ajax. Each of these scenarios can be easily resolved by progressively enhancing your interface.

To get up to speed on JavaScript and Ajax, read Jeremy Keith's books on *Dom Scripting* (http://domscripting.com/), published by Friends of Ed, and *Bulletproof Ajax* (http://bulletproofajax.com/), published by New Riders.

Progressive Enhancement

Progressive enhancement is a layered approach to interface development that helps ensure all users can navigate and read the content on a website regardless of browser or device limitations. The key to progressive enhancement is keeping the structure, presentation, and behavior separate (see **FIGURE 7.1**).

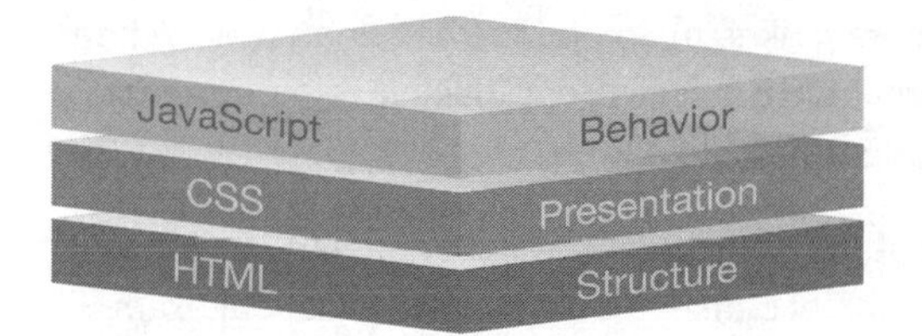

FIGURE 7.1 *By keeping the structure (HTML), presentation (CSS), and behavior (JavaScript) separate when you build websites, content remains accessible to search engine spiders.*

Before creating intricate JavaScript behaviors for your interface, begin with a semantically meaningful HTML document that communicates the information hierarchy of your page. Use heading, strong emphasis, emphasis, lists, and other semantic tags to mark up your document so search engines can understand your content (see Chapter 2 for further details).

Next, add a presentational layer using an external CSS file that creates the design of the document without altering the HTML code. Then add a behavior layer of JavaScript that enhances the interactions of the page. The JavaScript is also kept external in a separate file, and can easily take control of elements in the page without mixing in with the HTML structure, as we'll see in some examples in this chapter.

Building your documents with this additive approach keeps them functional with each step. Without CSS and JavaScript enabled, the user can still see the content and understand the information hierarchy as it's communicated through your semantic markup. When CSS is enabled, the interface design is enhanced. When JavaScript is enabled, the interactions of the document are enhanced.

When search engines encounter sites built using progressive enhancement they'll be able to index all of the content because JavaScript will no longer be a roadblock. Externalizing CSS and JavaScript also improves the speed at which search engines can index your page. If the three layers were integrated, search engines would be required to download JavaScript with HTML even though they can't read it. When it's separate, it can be ignored. CSS can be downloaded once by search engine spiders and cached for faster reference with each additional page crawl.

As Chapter 3 explained, you can configure your server to tell search engine spiders to cache your external CSS and JavaScript files. This can greatly increase the speed at which spiders can index your site. It's just one more reason why keeping structure, presentation, and behavior separate is good for SEO.

Of course, keeping things separate makes maintenance easier as well. When you make a change in your external CSS or JavaScript files, every page that links to them will inherit the update automatically.

Now that you are privy to the benefits of progressive enhancement and how it will serve the findability of your site, let's take a look at some practical examples of how you can prevent problems with your navigation, scripted styles, and content loaded with Ajax.

Solving JavaScript Navigation Problems

Navigation systems that require JavaScript to function and don't gracefully degrade into a viable alternative when JavaScript is disabled should be avoided at all costs. When search engines encounter such systems they are unable to index all pages and much of the hard work that went into creating engaging content will be lost. It's perhaps the fastest way to destroy all search engine referrals to your site. Disable JavaScript and browse your site; if you can't get around, then you've got problems to resolve.

Dropdown menu systems are a popular navigation approach that let users dig down into subsections of a site without requiring a lot of clicks. If you're using this type of navigation system on your site, make sure it's accessible without JavaScript enabled. Legacy dropdown menu systems significantly hinder navigation when JavaScript support is unavailable.

James Edwards–known on the Web as Brothercake–has created an accessible version of the classic dropdown navigation system called Ultimate Dropdown Menu (**http://www.brothercake.com/dropdown/**). It uses progressive enhancement to deliver usable versions of the system regardless of whether JavaScript is supported (see **FIGURE 7.2**).

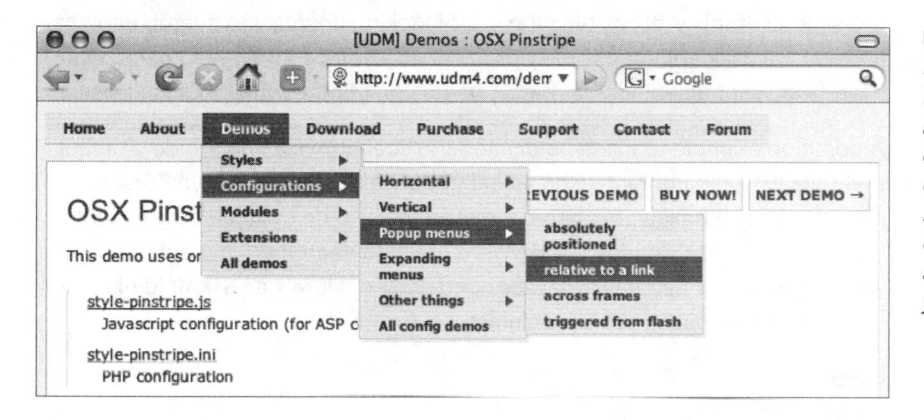

FIGURE 7.2 *James Edwards' Ultimate Dropdown Menu (**http://brothercake.com/dropdown/**) is a search engine friendly, accessible navigation system that is easy to integrate into a site, and can be styled to match your design.*

Edwards' menu passes both the U.S. government's Section 508 accessibility guidelines and the W3C's Web Content Accessibility Guidelines (WCAG), which means it's highly accessible to disabled users and search engines. It's a good replacement option for JavaScript-dependent systems.

Alternatively, you can create your own search engine friendly navigation system using CSS instead of JavaScript. Rachel Andrew has written a great article on SitePoint called "Nifty Navigation Using CSS" (**http://www.sitepoint.com/article/navigation-using-css**), which provides a number of practical examples of dropdown menu systems. Although the navigation systems are a bit simpler than Ultimate Dropdown Menu, they're still quite accessible and search engine friendly.

Solving Scripted Style Problems

Web pages that use JavaScript to manipulate the style of a page pose a potential problem for search engines and users. If JavaScript is disabled, your CSS should still display all of the content on the page so users can still see it and search engines can index it without mistaking it for dishonestly cloaked content.

In order to dishonestly achieve higher search rankings, some sites stuff their pages with keywords. This black-hat SEO trick is often accomplished by hiding keywords from users with the `display:none` CSS property. Search engines are wise to these sorts of tricks, and sometimes ban sites from their listings when they see dishonest content cloaking.

JavaScript interfaces sometimes need content hidden by default so it can be revealed when the user requests it. Any element that is by default styled by your CSS with `display:none` and is shown when a JavaScript event changes the style to `display:block` runs the risk of looking spammy to search engines. It's also a significant accessibility problem as it will be invisible to users who have JavaScript disabled. Of course, users can't find content that isn't visible.

A common example of this type of interface scenario is a show/hide element that reveals some content when a user chooses to expand it. If you create a series of such boxes on a page and style them to be collapsed by default using CSS they could look like keyword spam to search engine spiders, and will be invisible to users with JavaScript disabled. Here's an example of some code that could cause such problems:

CSS

```
. hide {display:none;}
```

XHTML

```
<div class="display-box">
    <a href="#" onclick="showText();">Expand</a>
    <div class="hide">This text is inaccessible to users without
JavaScript support, and might look like dishonest cloaking to
search engines.</div>
</div>
```

The text inside `<div class="hide">` is by default hidden using `display:none`. Because JavaScript would be required to change the style of this `<div>` tag to be visible, it's inaccessible when JavaScript is unsupported and search engines might mistake it for cloaked content. A better approach to this common problem is to style the `<div>` to be visible by default and then, if JavaScript support is available, collapse the box.

The above example mixes the JavaScript behavior into the HTML structure. It's preferable to keep them separate so search engines don't have to waste time downloading JavaScript code that is of no use to them. In the example that follows, the JavaScript onclick behavior will be attached to the expand/collapse link from an external file instead of mixing behavior and structure.

FIGURE 7.3 illustrates a progressive enhancement approach to a series of expand/collapse boxes in which content is visible without CSS or JavaScript support. The page is progressively enhanced with style and behavior as support is available.

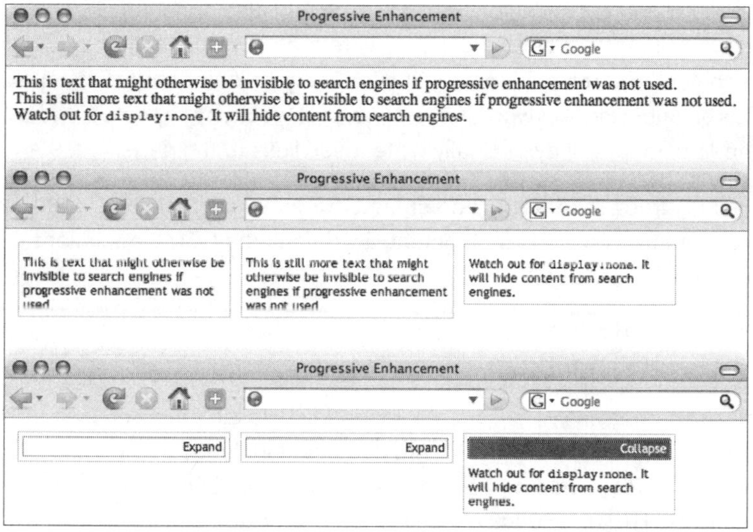

FIGURE 7.3 *The same document can be progressively enhanced from basic HTML, to a styled design, to an interactive interface. When CSS or JavaScript are disabled, the content is still accessible and search engines won't mistake it for cloaked content.*

To build a more accessible, search engine friendly version of the page, start by creating an HTML document that keeps JavaScript and CSS external and uses some logical class names to identify the <div> tags to be manipulated. This example has three collapsible boxes, but the JavaScript we'll write for the page behavior will be intelligent enough to accommodate as many or as few of these elements as you like.

```
    ...
    <div class="display-box">
        <div class="expand">This text will be accessible to users
with or without JavaScript support, and won't look like cloaked
content to search engines.</div>
    </div>

    <div class="display-box">
       <div class="expand">This is still more text that will be
accessible to users with or without JavaScript support, and won't
look like cloaked content to search engines.</div>
    </div>
```

```
    <div class="display-box">
        <div class="expand">Watch out for <code>display:none</
code>. It sends the wrong message to search engines.</div>
    </div>
...
```

Notice that there are no links in the page to make the boxes expand and collapse. This is because they are only relevant when JavaScript is enabled, so they shouldn't be present if it's not. These links would also unnecessarily pollute the keyword density of the page if they were present when search engines spider the content. Search engines could mistakenly perceive the link label "Expand" as an important keyword in the page as it would be repeated often. Instead, the JavaScript will dynamically write these links to the page.

With the HTML structure in place, add some CSS in an external file. Create a class to expand and collapse the content. By default the HTML document shows the content expanded.

```
.expand {display:block;}
.collapse {display:none;}
```

The last step in a progressive enhancement workflow is the behavior layer defined by JavaScript. Because the HTML document includes a few class names, the JavaScript should be able to walk the page and manipulate the desired elements. The JavaScript will be placed in an external file called `expand-collapse.js`.

Inside the external JavaScript file a function is created so the page behavior can be invoked easily when the page is done loading. This function first checks to see if the browser supports JavaScript sufficiently to find the elements in the page by tag name. If it can't, then we want to stop the script from proceeding, to avoid errors.

```
function expandCollapseBoxes(){
    if(!document.getElementsByTagName){return;}

};
```

The function will find all of the `<div>` tags in the page with the class `expand` and run a loop to change them to `collapse`. This will close all of the content boxes, which are left open for search engines by default.

```
function expandCollapseBoxes(){
    if(!document.getElementsByTagName){return;}
```

```
    var divs = document.getElementsByTagName("div");
    for (var i=0; i < divs.length; i++){
        if(divs[i].className == "expand"){
            divs[i].className ="collapse";

        }
    };
};
```

Next, inside the loop the link tags that toggle the expand/collapse functionality are dynamically added to each display box. When each link is created it's assigned a class so it can be styled. Though the link won't navigate to another page, it's given an href attribute so it will look and behave like an interactive link in the browser. A label is added to the link, then it's drawn into the page.

```
var closeLink = document.createElement("a");
closeLink.className = "close-box";
closeLink.href = "#";
closeLink.innerHTML = "Expand";
divs[i].parentNode.insertBefore(closeLink,divs[i]);
```

Following the dynamic link-generation code inside the loop, the link behavior is added. Inside the onclick function a variable is created to capture a reference to the <div> tag that is to be manipulated when the link is clicked. Then a conditional is used to toggle between expanding and collapsing the target <div>. If the text in the link is "Expand," then the function should expand the box and change the link label to "Collapse."

```
closeLink.onclick = function(){
    var displayBox = this.parentNode.getElementsByTagName("div")[0
];
    if(this.innerHTML == "Expand"){
        this.innerHTML = "Collapse";
        displayBox.className ="expand";
    }else{
        this.innerHTML = "Expand";
        displayBox.className ="collapse";
    }
};
```

Here's what the function looks like when it's completed:

```
function expandCollapseBoxes(){
    if(!document.getElementsByTagName){return;}
```

```
    var divs = document.getElementsByTagName("div");
    for (var i=0; i < divs.length; i++){
        if(divs[i].className == "expand"){
        divs[i].className ="collapse";

        // Build close link
        var closeLink = document.createElement("a");
        closeLink.className = "close-box";
        closeLink.href = "#";
        closeLink.innerHTML = "Expand";
        divs[i].parentNode.insertBefore(closeLink,divs[i]);

        // Create link behavior
        closeLink.onclick = function(){
            var displayBox = this.parentNode.getElementsByTagName(
"div")[0];
            if(this.innerHTML == "Expand"){
                this.innerHTML = "Collapse";
                displayBox.className ="expand";
            }else{
                this.innerHTML = "Expand";
                displayBox.className ="collapse";
            }
        };
    }
    };
};
```

All that's left to do is link the HTML page to the external JavaScript file. To do this, add a script tag before the close </body> tag in the HTML page. You can call the `expandCollapseBoxes()` function with an `onload` event listener to make sure the JavaScript doesn't attempt to manipulate the page until all elements are loaded into the browser.

```
<script type="text/javascript" src="js/expand-collapse.js"></
script>
<script type="text/javascript" charset="utf-8">
    window.onload = expandCollapseBoxes;
</script>
```

Another benefit of using this sort of progressive enhancement approach is that it makes it very easy to add to any page. Now that you have this expand/collapse interface behavior built, in future projects all you need to do to use it is create elements in the page with the appropriate class names and link to the JavaScript. It's instant interface functionality that preserves the findability of your content.

Handling JavaScript Events Properly

For the sake of brevity the `expandCollapseBoxes` function is attached to the page using the `window.onload` event. Although this works fine, it doesn't allow you to attach any additional events to the `onload` event.

You might want to use one of the many event attachment functions freely available on the Web to keep your code flexible. Popular JavaScript libraries like Prototype (**http://www.prototypejs.org/**) and Yahoo!'s YUI (**http://developer.yahoo.com/yui/**) have event attachment functions built in. JavaScript gurus Dustin Diaz (**http://www.dustindiaz.com/rock-solid-addevent/**) and John Resig (**http://ejohn.org/projects/flexible-javascript-events/**) have both published functions to simplify event attachment. Their functions could be added to your own JavaScript library file so you can easily add event listeners in any project.

Using an event attachment function you can ensure your pages can be progressively enhanced with new functionality in the future.

Solving Ajax Problems

Web pages that use Ajax to access and display content pose yet another search engine visibility problem. Ajax is simply JavaScript that can pass information to and from a server. It's a bit like a dumbwaiter that can connect a client-side interface to server-side scripts. It's is often used in Web applications to speed up basic data manipulation tasks like reordering user input or editing text inline. Since no page refresh is required to store the user's changes, the interface behaves very much like a desktop application with nearly instantaneous reactions.

Because only humans perform these types of information storage tasks, they typically have no adverse affect on search engine optimization. Ajax creates SEO problems when it is used to load content into the page. Because search engine spiders can't run JavaScript, any content loaded by Ajax won't be indexed.

There are two solutions to the Ajax content indexing problem: First, if your site's use of Ajax is not essential to the user experience, consider eliminating it. If you're using the technology for the cool factor rather than to speed up interface reaction time, then it's probably not worth risking search engine visibility.

It is possible, though, to use Ajax in a search engine friendly way. If it is important for your site to load content via Ajax, you can progressively enhance your interface to work with or without JavaScript support, so search engines can still index it.

A Progressively Enhanced Ajax Catalog System

Let's take a look at a progressively enhanced example that uses Ajax to create a single-page products catalog that users can browse quickly without a page refresh (see **FIGURE 7.4**). With a little bit of tweaking, this catalog example could be converted into a full ecommerce system.

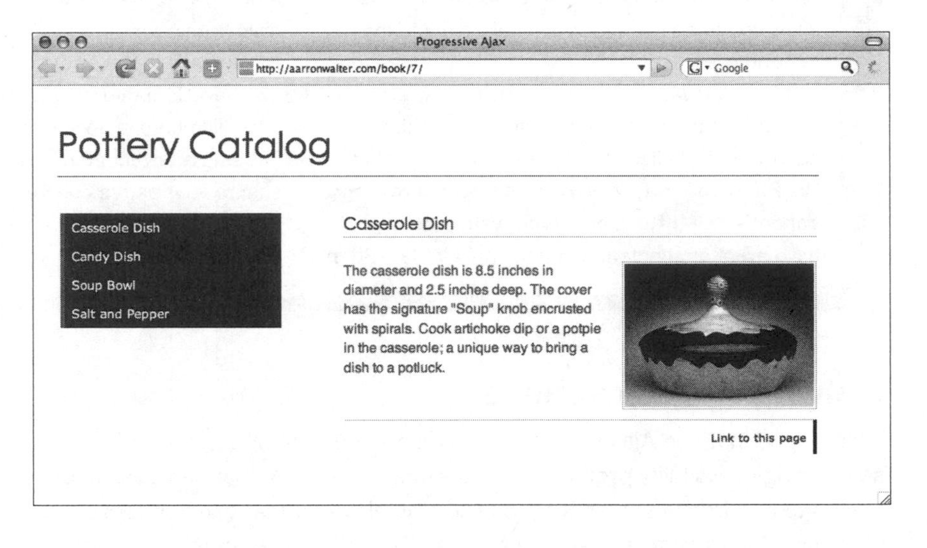

FIGURE 7.4 *This simple products catalog uses Ajax to load information without refreshing the page. If the browser doesn't support JavaScript, the progressively enhanced interface will instead take the user to a separate product page where the content is loaded with a page refresh required.*

This interface will let users browse a catalog of an artist's pottery showing the title, a description, and a product image. When JavaScript is enabled, the links in the navigation that would normally go to another page are disabled. An Ajax content loading behavior is then attached to each link to make the browsing experience very fast. Using Ajax, no page refresh is required to view any of the products.

If JavaScript is not supported, as would be the case during search engine indexing, the links would simply navigate to a separate products page where the user could browse the catalog but the page would need to refresh for each product. **FIGURE 7.5** illustrates the basic workflow the system will follow.

Both of the browsing scenarios in this example will use the same PHP script to grab content from a database. It's never any fun to double your development efforts to support different browsing situations. With a little forethought you can make your PHP script do double duty for you, which also simplifies maintenance.

To start, create a database on your server called `ajax_products` with the following fields: `prodid` (INT, auto increment, primary key), `title` (TEXT), `description` (TEXT), `image` (TEXT). Add a few product records to your database to work with.

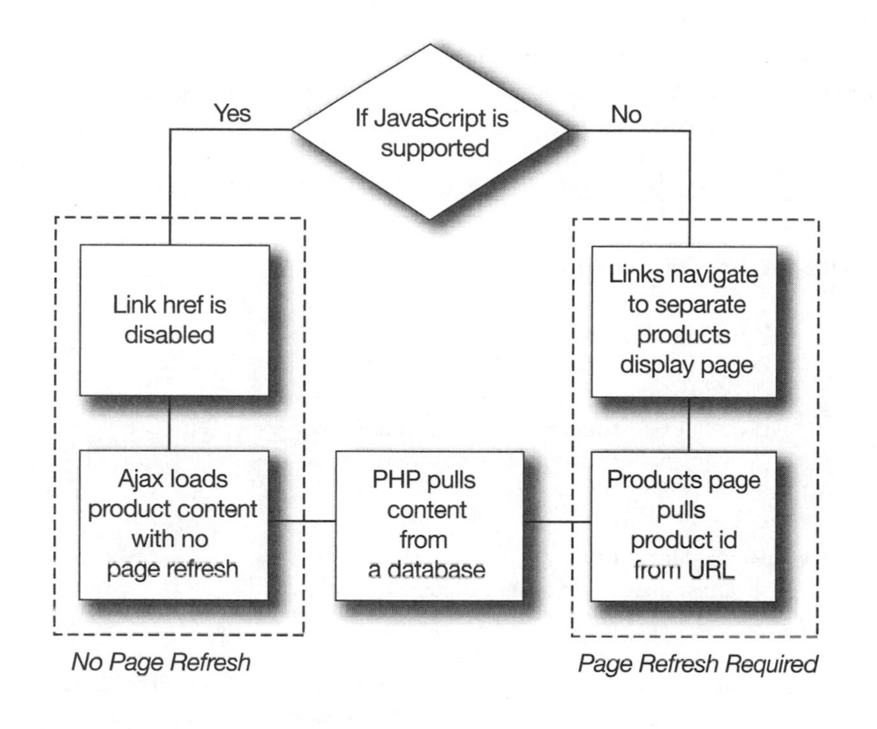

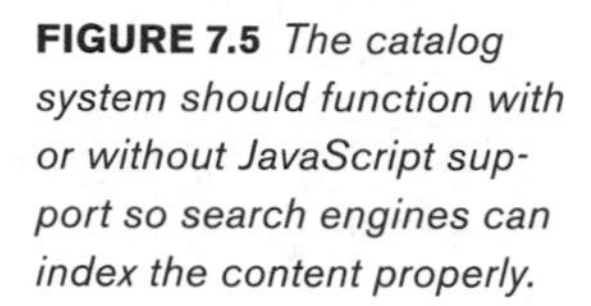

FIGURE 7.5 *The catalog system should function with or without JavaScript support so search engines can index the content properly.*

FIGURE 7.6 *To begin building the search engine friendly Ajax catalog, create a directory structure as shown.*

You'll also need to set up a directory structure that matches the one shown in **FIGURE 7.6**. To simplify the Ajax interactions we'll use the popular JavaScript framework Prototype (**http://www.prototypejs.org/**), so you'll need to download it and place it in the `js` folder.

Building the Catalog's HTML Structure

Following the same progressive enhancement workflow shown earlier, in the section "Solving Scripted Style Problems," we'll start the catalog with a well-structured HTML page. This document connects to an external style sheet inside <head>, and two external JavaScript files at the bottom of the page before the close </body> tag. Placing the JavaScript at the bottom of the document will make it render faster for users and search engines. The page can't begin to render when it's waiting for external JavaScript linked within the <head> tag to load. Putting your script tags in the bottom of the page is a simple technique that can speed up the user experience and help search engines index your pages faster.

Here's the basic structure of the index.html page of the catalog:

```
...
<h1>Pottery Catalog</h1>

    <ul id="ajax-catalog">
    <li><a href="products/1">Casserole Dish</a></li>
    <li><a href="products/2">Candy Dish</a></li>
    <li><a href="products/3">Salt and Pepper</a></li>
    <li><a href="products/4">Soup Bowl</a></li>
</ul>

<div id="product-display">
    Some introductory content would go here.
</div>

<script type="text/javascript" src="js/prototype.js"></script>
<script type="text/javascript" src="js/progressive-ajax.js">
</script>
...
```

All of the navigation will link to a single products.php page that will load different product information—no Ajax required—based on the product id it's passed. But notice that the path in the anchor tag doesn't seem to be pointing to a file called products.php. As we learned in Chapter 3 in the section "Building Search Engine Friendly URLs," a URL like http://example.com/products.php?prodid=3 can create search engine indexing problems. This example will use the URL rewriting techniques covered in Chapter 3 to make the URLs more search engine friendly.

If you decide to convert this example into a real catalog for your site, you'll want to have PHP generate the navigation for you with a query to the database and a loop. As it stands now, when a new product is added you'd need to manually update the navigation system.

The next step in a progressive enhancement workflow would be to create a presentation layer of CSS for the page. Since you're probably already a CSS guru, I'll skip this step and let you style your catalog as you like.

Content Retrieval with PHP

Following a progressive enhancement philosophy, let's first make the catalog work without JavaScript by creating the products.php file alluded to earlier. Save a copy of the index.html page as products.php. You can remove the two script tags from the new products page. No need for JavaScript here as this is the fallback solution if the user's browser doesn't support it.

Replace the default text inside <div id="product-display"> with the following PHP that will separate the product id from the URL then pass it over to a PHP script that fetches product information.

```
<div id="product-display">
    <?php
    require_once('inc/getProduct.php');
    echo getProduct($_GET['prodid']);
    ?>
</div>
```

Remember, we're not using a query string in the navigation links to pass the product id, but this script is still accessing a mysterious GET variable called prodid. Using the Apache server module mod_rewrite we'll direct URLs like this products/1 to URLs like this products.php?prodid=1. Although users and search engines will see the simpler URL structure, the PHP script will be able to access $_GET variables in an invisible query string. We'll build the getProduct.php file referenced in this script and the getProduct() function it will contain shortly.

To correctly remap the search engine friendly URLs to the products.php file with a trailing query string, create a .htaccess file with the following rewrite rule and place it in the directory on your server where your catalog system is stored.

```
RewriteEngine On
# Catches URL with or without a trailing slash
RewriteRule ^products/([0-9]+)\/? products.php?prodid=$1
```

This rewrite rule, which is very similar to those covered in Chapter 3, should now successfully route your navigation system to the products.php page.

All of the database interactions for the JavaScript-enabled and -disabled versions of the catalog system will be handled by a file called getProduct.php stored in the include folder called inc. It contains a single function called getProduct() that receives a product id in order to retrieve the desired record. Here's how it starts:

```
<?php
function getProduct($prodid){
    if(!$prodid){
      echo "Oops! We ran into some trouble getting info about this
product.";
      exit;
    }

    $con = mysql_connect('db host', 'your username', 'your
password');
    mysql_select_db('db name', $con);

    $prodid = mysql_real_escape_string($prodid);
    $result = mysql_query("SELECT * FROM ajax_products WHERE
prodid='$prodid'");
}
```

Be sure to change the host, username, password, and database name to reflect your database's access information.

If no product id is supplied, the function will display an error message, and halt the script's progress. If a product id has been supplied, it's cleaned up using mysql_real_escape_string() to prevent SQL injection attacks on the database (see **http://us3.php.net/manual/en/security.database.sql-injection.php** to learn more about SQL injection attacks). Once the potentially dangerous characters in the product id are escaped it can be used in a query to pull the record.

After the query is run, you'll need to make sure a result is returned before trying to write it to the page.

```
if(mysql_num_rows($result) == 0){
echo "Sorry, we couldn't find any information about this
product.";
}

while($row = mysql_fetch_array($result)) {
$content = '
<h3>'.$row['title'].'</h3>
<p>
<img src="i/'.$row['image'].'" alt="'.$row['title'].'" />
```

```
'.$row['description'].'
</p>
<p>
<a href="products/'.$row['id'].'" title="Right click or control
click to copy URL">Link to this page</a>
</p>';
}

return $content;
```

The conditional and loop are pretty basic, but notice the link highlighted at the bottom of the `$content` variable. Ajax interfaces that load content into a single page only use one URL for all content. This makes it difficult for users to bookmark or email links that preserve the state of the page, and degrade a site's findability. Google Maps, a paragon of Ajax-powered interfaces, attempts to solve the problem by providing a direct link to search results that preserve the state of the page. Because we've already set up the `products.php` page to show individual records based on the parameters in the URL, it's pretty easy to add a similar feature to this interface. In Figure 7.4 you can see at the bottom of the page a link labeled "Link to this page" that will make it easier for users to share or bookmark content.

When all of the content has been retrieved and assembled into a basic HTML structure, it's returned to the place where the `getProduct()` function was called. When an Ajax request is made to this script, there's actually no way to trigger the function. In `products.php` the `getProduct()` function is called and the results are written to the page. The `getProduct.php` script will need to be smart enough to detect when an Ajax request is being made so it can trigger the function automatically. All it takes is a simple conditional at the very end of the script:

```
if($_GET['ajax']=='true'){ echo getProduct($_GET['prodid']); }
```

We'll set the `$_GET['ajax']` variable when we build the Ajax call. That's it for the PHP. The catalog should now work perfectly for search engines without support for JavaScript. The last piece of the system is to use JavaScript to disable the navigation links and use Ajax to load content into the page for a super-fast browsing experience.

Adding Ajax to the Catalog

Create an external JavaScript file called `progressive-ajax.js` and save it in the `js` folder. Inside this file create two functions: one to initialize the page behaviors, and another to handle the Ajax communication with the server:

```
window.onload = init;

function init(){

};

function loadProduct(prodId){

}
```

The init() function will be called automatically when the page loads. It will deactivate all of the links in the navigation and assign the alternate Ajax behavior. The loadProduct() function must receive a product id so it can in turn pass this number on to the getProduct.php script.

The init function will first determine to what degree the browser supports JavaScript. If it doesn't support the getElementsByTagName or the getElementById methods, then the script will have to terminate. If sufficient JavaScript support is detected, the init() function will find all of the links in the navigation system and attach the Ajax loading behavior. JavaScript can locate the navigation system by its catalog-nav id:

```
function init(){
   if(!document.getElementsByTagName || !document.
getElementById){return;}

   var nav = document.getElementById("catalog-nav");
   var navlinks = nav.getElementsByTagName("a");

   for (var i=0; i < navlinks.length; i++){
      navlinks[i].onclick = function() {
         urlarray = this.href.split("/");
         loadProduct(urlarray[urlarray.length-1]);
         return false;
      };
   };
};
```

Inside the loop each link is assigned an onclick event listener. When a link is clicked the script grabs the href attribute value and splits it into an array with values created each time a / is detected. The URLs in each href look something like this: products/1. The last value in the array will be the product id. To access this value, the script finds the number of elements it contains using the

JavaScript keyword length, and subtracts 1 from it, since arrays begin indexing at 0. So urlarray[urlarray.length-1] will contain the product id we need to pass to the loadProduct() function.

The return false in the last part of the loop disables the links from navigating away from the page. All that remains to make the Ajax catalog complete is the loadProduct() function, which will handle the Ajax communication with the getProduct.php script on the server. Here's what it will look like:

```
function loadProduct(prodId){
    var display = document.getElementById('product-display');
    display.innerHTML = 'Loading ...';
    var url = 'inc/getProduct.php';
    var pars = 'prodid='+escape(prodId)+'&ajax=true';
    var myAjax = new Ajax.Updater(display, url, {method:'get',
parameters:pars});
}
```

The function starts by defining which tag will display the results of the Ajax request. In the HTML document a <div> tag with the id product-display has already been created just for this purpose. If the user's network connection is slow, a loading message will be written to the display <div> while the page is waiting to receive the results from the database query.

Next, a few variables are defined. The url variable identifies the path to the PHP script that will receive the Ajax request. The pars variable defines the parameters that will be passed in a query string to the getProduct.php script. Notice that one of the parameters is ajax=true. At the end of the getProduct.php script a conditional was added to see if the request made was from the Ajax script so the getProduct() function could be triggered automatically. The ajax=true variable is what the PHP script will be looking for.

The JavaScript framework Prototype, to which the HTML page already links, simplifies the Ajax communication to a single line of code. The last line of this function creates a new Ajax object that will send a request to the PHP script using the get method to transmit the variables. The data that is returned will automatically be written to the <div id="product-display"> tag.

The Ajax catalog is now all set and ready for fast browsing. Search engines will appreciate the simple URLs that include no messy query strings and the graceful way the JavaScript will degrade to facilitate indexing of the site. Users will appreciate how quickly they can navigate through content without pesky page loads that can slow down their browsing experience.

Is Ajax Worth the Trouble?

Is adding Ajax to your site worth the potential findability pitfalls? Ultimately, you'll need to evaluate your project and your users' needs to decide for yourself. But with progressively enhanced Ajax there's no reason you can't support the needs of your users and search engines simultaneously.

This example doesn't sacrifice search engine visibility. All of the content is accessible to search engine spiders and can be thoroughly indexed. Although the lack of unique URLs in Ajax systems is a potential findability pitfall, this system compensates by providing users with a link for each product page so they can bookmark it or email it to a friend. Inbound links that users create build your search engine page ranking, but you're not likely to receive many if you don't provide unique URLs for your content.

If the speed that Ajax can bring to your user interface is important to the objectives of your site, then don't shy away from it because of fears of ruining your site's search engine optimization. It is possible to have your cake and eat it too.

Findable Flash

Flash is often demonized as an SEO death sentence for websites. In reality it's not the tool that should be receiving the criticism so much as the way it is improperly used. Flash is no worse for search engine visibility than Ajax. When used with no consideration for how search engines view content, both Flash and Ajax can, in fact, significantly hinder search engine indexing. But just as we saw with Ajax, if you use your noodle and follow a few best practices when building Flash sites, you won't sacrifice search engine traffic.

After receiving some criticism a few years ago for Flash's poor search engine support, Macromedia–now Adobe–released a software development kit (**http://www.adobe.com/licensing/developer/**) that converts SWFs to HTML documents in an effort to make Flash content more search engine friendly. Macromedia's goal was to provide the major search engines with some helpful tools to be incorporated in page indexing systems to make reading Flash content easier.

To some degree their efforts have paid off. Today, Google actually does index Flash content but with its own proprietary sytem. To get a sense of what the Google spider sees when it reads a SWF file, simply do a Google search for any keywords followed by the operator `filetype:swf`. This will limit your search returns to keywords found inside SWF files. **FIGURE 7.7** illustrates some typical search results for content in Flash files.

Some of the search results in Figure 7.7 contain consistent yet poorly written HTML that suggest it was generated by some SWF-to-HTML translation system, probably part of Google's search spider. When you compare the text shown in Google's results page to the content within the SWF files you'll discover that there's not always parity between the two. This is probably because Google also reads meta data stored in the SWF if the developer has included any.

You can add descriptive meta data to your Flash files by simply modifying the document settings before publishing. In Flash, go to Modify > Document and enter a title and description as shown in **FIGURE 7.8**.

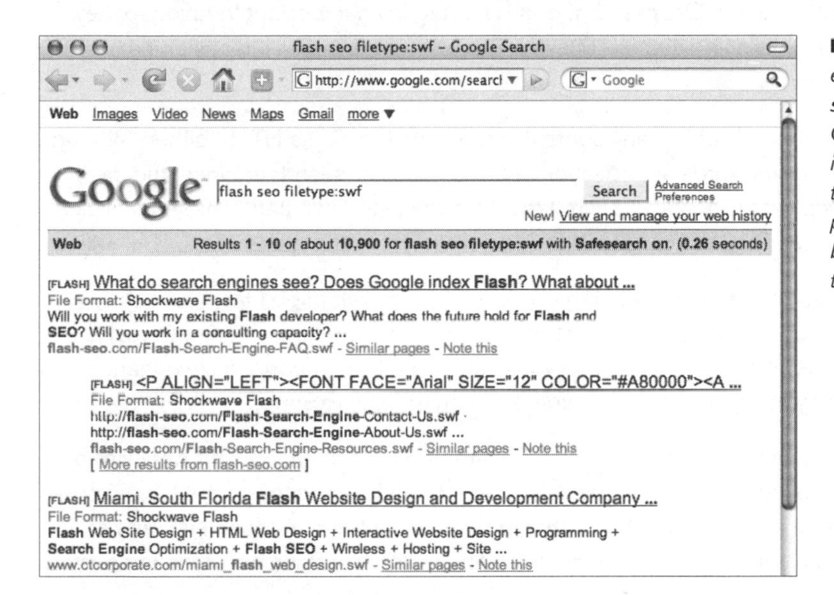

FIGURE 7.7 *This search, executed using the `filetype:swf` operator, illustrates that Google can see the content inside SWF files. Some of the files appear to have been poorly translated into HTML by Google's mysterious SWF translation engine.*

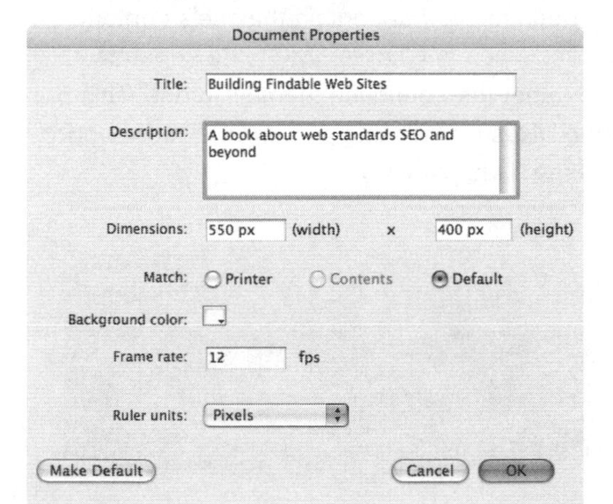

FIGURE 7.8 *You can add meta data to your Flash content by navigating to the document settings in Modify > Document and entering a title and description.*

Although Google can read content within Flash, the information hierarchy is often ambiguous to its search spider. This makes achieving good SEO results from Flash content alone difficult. When competing against HTML sites that use semantic tags to communicate information hierarchy Flash files will consistently rank lower in search results. For a Flash site to achieve high search rankings it needs to use HTML effectively.

Though HTML can make Flash content much more findable it's usually an afterthought for most Flash designers. Often SWFs are embedded in pages directly from Flash, then published to the Web without modification to the HTML. By default Flash writes the file name of the FLA into the `<title>` tag. As discussed in Chapter 2, the `<title>` tag is an important location for keywords. Publishing your HTML with Flash's default text in it is a significant SEO opportunity missed.

Flash doesn't publish any content in the meta tags in its HTML either. Although meta tag keywords are no longer viewed by major search engines, the meta description is shown on search results pages, and can entice users to click to visit your site. It's another missed opportunity to generate traffic to your site.

Adding `<title>` and meta tag content to the HTML page Flash publishes will help SEO but it's still not quite enough to be competitive. To create real keyword density and prominence you'll need to follow a progressive enhancement strategy much like the one discussed earlier for JavaScript.

Rather than thinking of Flash as the structure, presentation, and behavior of a site rolled into one file, consider it the fourth layer on top of the typical progressive enhancement trinity that creates rich interaction (see **FIGURE 7.9**). It enhances the user experience much like JavaScript does when it's supported.

Start your Flash site with HTML documents that contain the site's content marked up using the strategies discussed in Chapter 2. Create separate SWFs for each page in your site rather than bundling them all in one. This provides search engines with unique URLs for indexing and creates more opportunity to embed your content in the HTML pages.

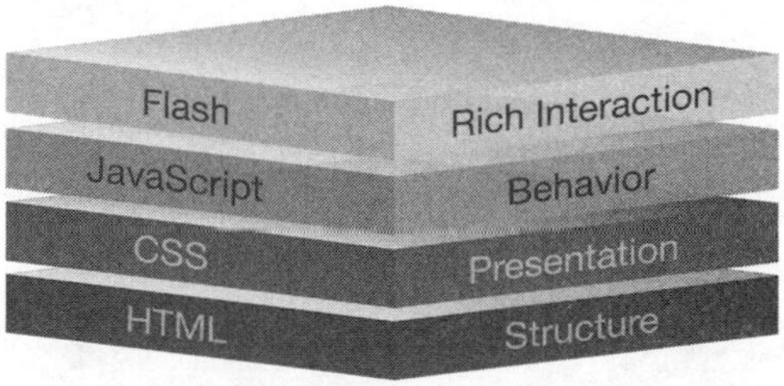

FIGURE 7.9 *Flash is a rich interaction layer that should by delivered on top of the typical structure, presentation, and behavior layers of a progressively enhanced website or application.*

With the HTML structure built to best communicate your content, you can add CSS to refine the presentation of the page in which your Flash movie will sit. Flash will be the crowning layer that will sit on top of the HTML structure embedded in the page using a simple JavaScript file called SWFObject.

Using SWFObject for Flash Progressive Enhancement

Geoff Sterns created `SWFObject` to offer a better way of embedding Flash content into HTML pages. Sterns' simple JavaScript file detects the Flash plugin before embedding SWF files within a `<div>` tag or other element you define. The target tag can contain search engine friendly alternative content that will make your site more competitive in search results, but will be replaced when users view the page with the correct plugin. `SWFObject` progressively enhances the page with Flash content but gracefully degrades to HTML content for search engines. You can use `SWFObject` to embed smaller Flash movies into your site to create a hybrid of HTML and SWF content, or embed a single SWF that occupies the entire page.

Bobby Van Der Sluis has written a brilliant article on the Adobe site about Progressive Enhancement and Flash http://www.adobe.com/devnet/flash/articles/progressive_enhancement_03.html

Let's take a look at it in action.

Hybrid Sites

This example will examine a common scenario in which a Flash slideshow is embedded on the home page of a site to catch the audience's attention by cycling through a series of product promotions and sales (see **FIGURE 7.10**). The slideshow is intended as a complement to other HTML content on the page.

FIGURE 7.10 *Hybrid sites use Flash in select areas to capture the user's attention or enhance the interface. In this example Flash is used to cycle through sales and promotions in a slideshow that can present more information than a static image.*

Once the general HTML structure is built, a <div> tag needs to be added to the page to define where the Flash content will be displayed. Add an id to the tag to make it easy for SWFObject to target.

```
<div id="flash-promo">
    <a href="promos/" title="See our latest promotions">
        <img src="images/promo.jpg" alt="Save 10% on the Berry
Bowl" longdesc="#slideshow" />
    </a>
</div>
```

Users who don't have the Flash player will see the content within <div id="flash-promo">. To make the slideshow gracefully degrade for users, an <img /> tag is added to show the first promo slide and will link to a page where all of the promos can be seen. The full text of the slideshow can be accessed via the longdesc attribute. In Chapter 2's "Making Images Visible" you saw how the longdesc attribute could link to an area on a page that further describes content within images that would otherwise be invisible to search engines. The same thing happens here with the image substitute for the Flash movie.

Add the full text from the Flash slideshow in a div at the bottom of the page:

```
<a name="slideshow"></a>
<dl id="slideshow">
    <dt><a href="promos/1/" title="Buy the berry bowl">Slide 1:
Berry Bowl Sale</a></dt>
    <dd>Save 10% on the berry bowl April 7-21</dd>
    [...]
</dl>
```

A definition list lends itself well to communicating each slide's title and content, but you could use any number of markup techniques here. The important part is that a text equivalent is provided for the slides, and markup is used to communicate the information hierarchy.

As the example in Chapter 2 illustrates, you can use some simple CSS to remove the slideshow text from view of sighted users, but it will stay visible to search engines.

```
#slideshow {text-indent:-9999px; position:absolute;}
```

To add the Flash layer to the page using SWFObject, first link to the external JavaScript file, then create a new object that will replace the text within the <div id="flash-promo"> tag:

```
<script type="text/javascript" src="js/swfobject.js"></script>
<script type="text/javascript">
    var so = new SWFObject("slideshow.swf","myswf","600","400","8"
,"#ffffff");
    so.write("flash-promo");
</script>
```

The instantiation of `SWFObject` includes six parameters to define how it will embed the SWF in your page. Here's an explanation of each one:

- `slideshow.swf`: path to the SWF to be embedded
- `myswf`: name for the JavaScript object
- `600`: width of the SWF
- `400`: height of SWF
- `8`: version of Flash player to be detected
- `#ffffff`: base color for the SWF

Once `SWFObject` is instantiated, call the object's `write()` function, passing the id of the target tag where the SWF should be embedded.

Voila! The search engine friendly HTML will now be replaced with a SWF when Flash is supported. Search engines will never see the SWF because JavaScript is used to write it to the page. There's no SEO compromise with this Flash embedding solution.

To see how SWFObject stacks up to the other Flash embedding techniques, visit http://blog.deconcept.com/swfobject/#whyitsbetter. Bobby Van Der Sluis's article, entitled "Flash Embedding Cage Match," provides further detail: http://www.alistapart.com/articles/flashembedcagematch/

Entirely Flash Sites

As mentioned earlier, it's not a good idea to create one giant SWF for your entire site. Instead it's smarter to create separate SWFs, each with its own HTML page. There are many reasons why separate SWFs are more desirable, but here are a few of the more compelling ones.

Single SWF sites

- Can be significantly harder for search engines to index
- Break the browser's back button
- Don't provide unique URLs for bookmarking and sharing
- Require all alternative content for the entire site to be embedded in one HTML page
- Prevent direct navigation to content
- May take longer to load if the main SWF doesn't load other SWF files

It's OK to have an entirely Flash site, but be sure to use separate HTML pages to circumvent these issues.

The previous example of using SWFObject for hybrid sites isn't very practical for an entirely Flash site. It would require you to write all of your content in HTML, then do it again in Flash. If you need to make a content change for any reason you'll have twice as much work. It would be smarter to consolidate your content in one place and let some code do the work for you. There are two ways to accomplish this.

The first option would be to put all of your content into a database. Using PHP or another server-side scripting language you could write content into the HTML pages where the Flash files are embedded. Another server-side script could generate an XML page of the same content that Flash can easily link to and consume. The XML source Flash would link to would actually be a PHP file that outputs XML content. Although this approach requires a little extra work to create the XML generation script, it would be a one-time buildout that would certainly simplify maintenance.

Putting all of the site's content into a database would also make it easier to tie in a Content Management System (CMS) such as Joomla (**http://joomla.com/**), Drupal (**http://drupal.org/**), Expression Engine (**http://expressionengine.com**), or one that you create yourself. Using a CMS makes keeping your content current much easier, and can allow clients to manage the site themselves. **FIGURE 7.11** illustrates the relationship between a CMS, the database where all content would be stored, and the front end that would deliver the same content in HTML and Flash formats.

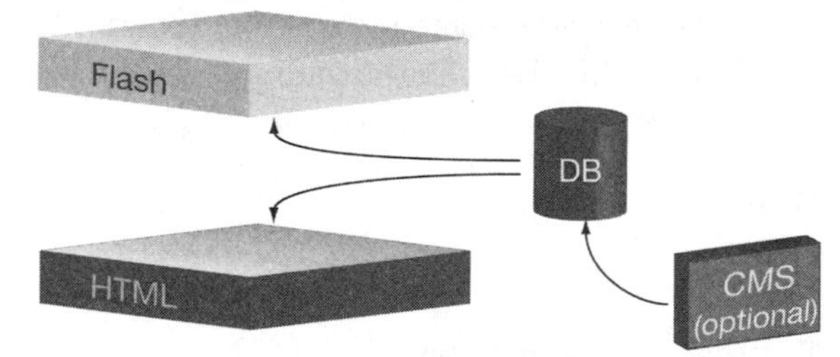

FIGURE 7.11 *When all content is stored in a database it can be sent to multiple delivery platforms using server-side scripting. A CMS could be connected to the database to make content management easier.*

If the prospect of creating a PHP script to write XML is too daunting, you may find this next option more attractive.

Once you've built the structure of your site with HTML and have integrated all of your content, you can pass it into Flash along with the markup using `SWFObject`. Since the Flash layer gets its content from the HTML structure, any change you make to the text in the HTML will also automatically update your SWF too.

Once SWFObject is instantiated you can use its addVariable() function to send in the text from the HTML page. In this example we'll create a <div> tag containing all of the text to be passed to Flash. Here's how it might look:

```
<div id="content">
    <h1>Findable Flash</h1>
    <p>This text will be passed into a SWF using SWFObject. Once
the content is in Flash, you will need to do a little XML parsing
to grab nodes and manipulate the content as you like.</p>
</div>
```

Just like the previous SWFObject example we'll instantiate it, but before writing the SWF to the page we'll use addVariable() to pass in the HTML text. I've highlighted the code that will pass the content into the SWF:

```
<script type="text/javascript" src="js/swfobject.js"></script>
<script type="text/javascript">
    var so = new SWFObject("flash-content.swf", "passdata", "800",
"500", "8", "#ffffff");

    var content = document.getElementById('content').innerHTML;
    so.addVariable('xmlData', encodeURIComponent(content));
    so.write("content");
</script>
```

Using some JavaScript, we first grab the text inside <div id="content">. Inside the addVariable() function a variable called xmlData is defined to contain the content and will automatically be created inside the SWF. Next, all of the content that is to be passed into the SWF is URL-encoded so special characters in the text don't cause trouble as Flash imports it.

Flash will view the HTML content we're passing it as XML. This makes a lot of sense, as both are markup languages that use tags to wrap text, and the HTML we're using in this book is actually **X**HTML, a dialect of XML. With the content wrapped in HTML tags, Flash will be better able to access individual nodes of text.

In a Flash file named flash-content.fla create a new actions layer and a text field layer. In the text field layer add a dynamic text field to the stage and name the instance "display." In the actions layer on the first frame, open the Actions window and add the following:

```
var xml = new XML();
xml.ignoreWhite = true;
xml.parseXML(unescape(_root.xmlData));

display.text = xml.toString();
```

This simple ActionScript starts by creating a new XML parsing object. After indicating that all white space in the content should be ignored, the script parses the content as XML. The highlighted code `_root.xmlData` is the variable just passed to Flash via the `SWFObject` JavaScript. The last line writes the content to the text field named display.

Once the SWF is published it will automatically display the content from your HTML page. You may want to manipulate the imported content further using Flash's various XML parsing functions. To learn more about how to parse XML with Flash and ActionScript, check out Jesse Stratford's article on ActionScript.org entitled "XML 101" (**http://www.actionscript.org/resources/articles/9/1/XML-101/**).

Now that both the Flash and HTML layers share the same content you'll only need to make text changes in one place. This solution will provide search engines and users without Flash support the same content users with the Flash plugin will enjoy.

> **TIP** You can get help if you run into trouble working with SWFObject in the support forum at **http://blog.deconcept.com/swfobject/forum/**.

You Don't Have To Compromise

Often Flash is written off as a technology to be avoided if SEO is at all a concern, but eliminating Flash from every site is not an acceptable compromise. Flash is a powerful, compelling technology that can deliver an enhanced user experience. When used properly, you don't have to sacrifice Flash in the name of search engine visibility.

If you progressively enhance your interfaces and add Flash as the crowning layer, search engines can fall back to the HTML structure to discern the content and information hierarchy of the page.

The progressive enhancement examples explored in this chapter also improve Accessibility. Guideline 6 of the W3C's Web Content Accessibility Guidelines states that pages featuring new technologies should gracefully degrade (**http://www.w3.org/TR/WAI-WEBCONTENT/#gl-new-technologies**). Although Flash is hardly a new technology these days, it is one that can pose accessibility issues to the disabled and users of alternate devices. Using Flash as the top layer in a progressively enhanced interface ensures all users can enjoy the content.

Claus Wahler has created another search engine visibility solution for Flash called SEFFS (Search Engine Friendly Flash Site) http://wahlers.com.br/claus/blog/seffs-to-flash-or-not-to-flash/.

Findable Audio and Video

The content trapped within audio and video files is inherently invisible to most search engines. Currently, there is no mechanism built into Google, Yahoo!, MSN Live Search, or other major search engines to transcribe speech to text so the content can be indexed and searched.

Audio and video are very desirable for users. These formats have the potential to explain some topics better than plain text because they're closer to human-to-human communication. They also provide a passive content consumption experience that people tend to enjoy, especially when transferred to a portable device like an iPod.

Audio and video content are far too attractive to users to remain un-findable. Though content in these formats is arguably the most invisible to search engines of the various technologies discussed in this chapter, it is also the easiest to transform into search engine friendly formats.

EveryZing

EveryZing–formerly PodZinger–(**http://www.everyzing.com/**) is a unique search tool that can transcribe the spoken word in MP3s, video, and other rich media file types to text so the content can be searched. Like YouTube, EveryZing is a central repository for video content on a wide variety of topics, but also hosts podcasts and other audio content as well. See **FIGURE 7.12**.

You can post your content on EveryZing for free and it will use its proprietary audio-to-speech technology to create a text transcript of your video or audio file. When users search on EveryZing they can discover your video or audio files via keywords in the text transcript. It's also possible for users to find your files on EveryZing via queries on major search engines too.

The content you post on EveryZing can be pulled onto your site using RSS, but the text transcript stays on its site. You can also provide EveryZing your RSS feed containing links to your audio and video files, and it will automatically transcribe and post it when you publish new content.

FIGURE 7.12 *EveryZing (**http://everyzing.com**) is a media search tool that creates text transcripts of audio and video posted by users. It's free to use and will automatically create searchable transcripts of your media files linked to within your RSS feed.*

It's a free and easy way to expose your content to search engines and a broader audience. Any of the thousands of users who search EveryZing daily could potentially stumble across your content and visit your site via a link that will be automatically displayed with it.

When you sign up with EveryZing you can choose to display ads with your content. Revenue earned from these ads gets shared with you directly via a PayPal account.

Creating Text Transcripts

The surest way to make your audio and video content visible to all search engines is with a simple text transcript. Although EveryZing creates transcripts automatically, it would be preferable to host the text on your site to draw direct search referrals.

You can create your own transcripts, but it's a tedious job. There are a number of inexpensive services that will do the dirty work for you in a relatively short turnaround time. All of the services discussed here use humans rather than software to create transcripts, which results in more accurate transcripts.

CastingWords

If you're a podcaster, CastingWords (**http://castingwords.com**) is a great way to get transcripts made (see **FIGURE 7.13**). Simply choose the desired turnaround time, then upload your audio file, and you'll receive your transcript in plain text, HTML, and RTF formats. They also provide an RSS feed of all of your transcripts so your podcast listeners can subscribe to the full text if they like.

You can provide CastingWords with a podcast RSS feed to request transcripts automatically each time you release a new podcast. This will save you the time and hassle of having to visit the site repeatedly to place orders.

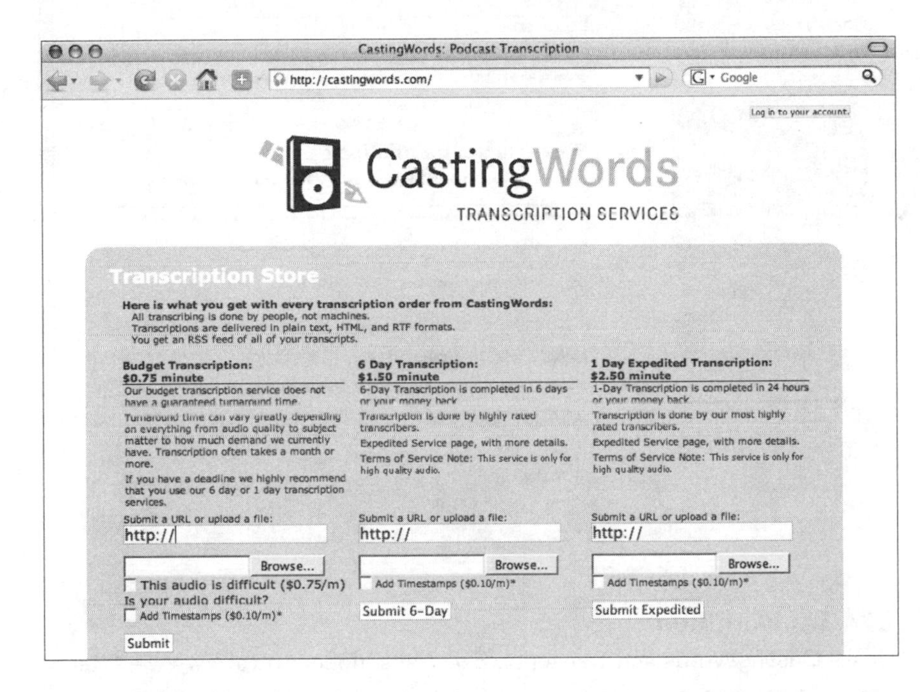

FIGURE 7.13 *CastingWords (**http://castingwords.com**) provides high-quality transcripts of podcasts and other audio files at reasonable prices.*

Transcribr

Enablr has an audio transcription service called Transcribr (**http://enablr.com/transcribr.php**) similar to CastingWords (see **FIGURE 7.14**). Like CastingWords, Transcribr lets you provide your podcast RSS feed URL to automatically create transcripts for you a few days after publication.

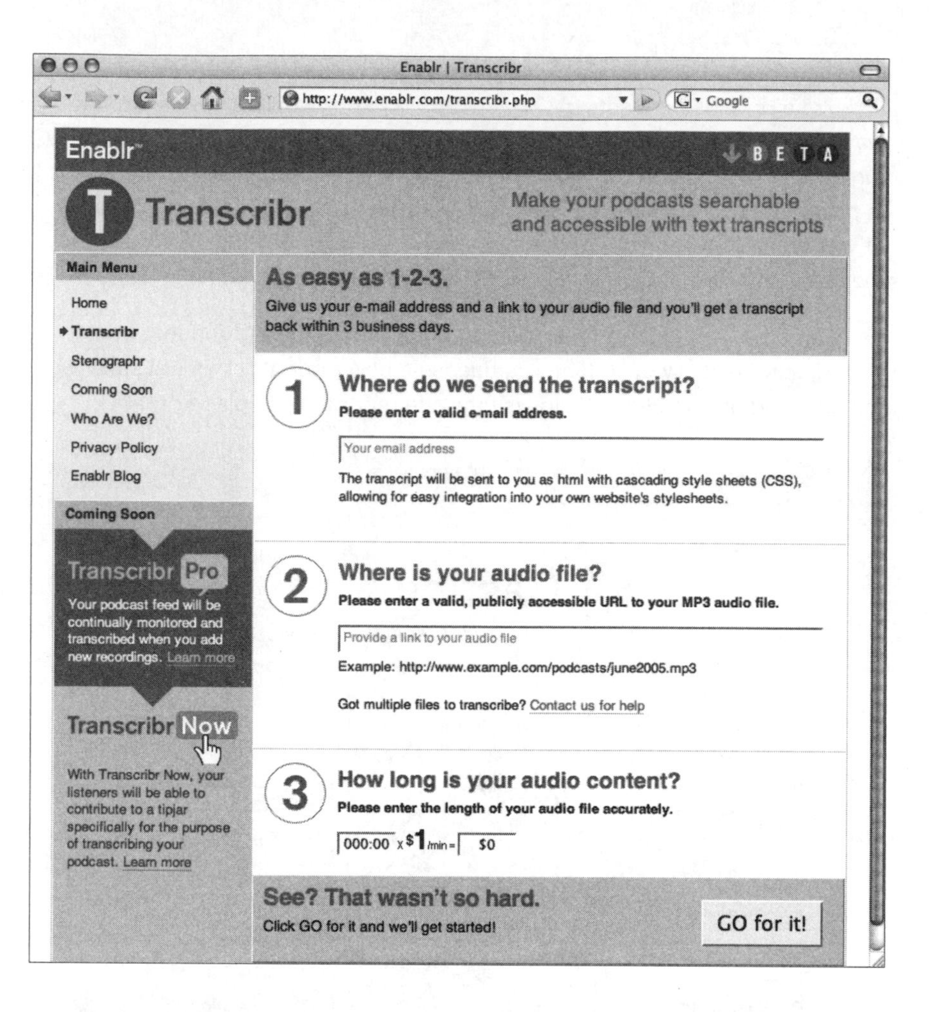

FIGURE 7.14 *Transcribr (**http://enablr.com/transcribr.php**) is another great audio transcription service worth considering.*

E24 Transcription

Unlike CastingWords and Transcribr, E24 Transcription (**http://www.e24tech.com**) creates transcripts of both audio and video files. See **FIGURE 7.15**.

It's exceptionally inexpensive, but only provides transcripts in Word document format and has no RSS auto-generation service. If you're looking for economy and don't care much about advanced features and alternate transcript formats, then this might be the right option for you.

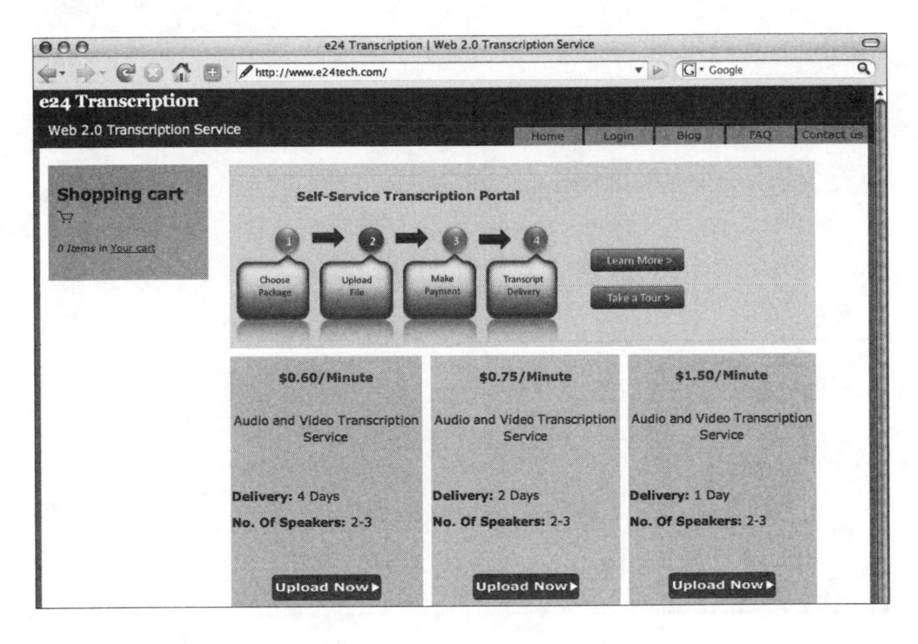

FIGURE 7.15 *E24 Transcription (**http://www.e24tech.com**) creates audio and video transcriptions at exceptionally low prices.*

Text Transcripts Make Your Content Accessible

Like so many other SEO techniques discussed throughout this book, text transcripts for video and audio also make your content accessible. Users with hearing impairments would miss out on audio or video content if a text transcript weren't included.

Users who don't speak English fluently will also appreciate the transcripts as they can follow along while listening to catch words and phrases that might be obfuscated by an unfamiliar accent.

The more users you include in your audience, the more likely you are to achieve the business and communication goals of your site. Text transcripts require little effort yet pay big dividends in search traffic and reaching a broader audience.

8

Bring Traffic Back With a Mailing List

Findability is more than just getting people to your site. You can convert your new visitors into repeat visitors with a mailing list subscription system.

A mailing list is an exceptionally valuable tool as it allows you to stay in touch with your audience and keep your website on their radar. When you publish new content, update features on your Web app, or just have something to share with your audience, a mailing list is the most direct way to get the word out and generate immediate traffic to your site.

Users who sign up for your mailing list are your superfans. They trust you enough to give you their email address, and enjoy your content so much they're requesting more via email.

A mailing list is a relationship builder that, if used properly, will cultivate a closer connection between you and your audience. It can turn one-time visitors into repeat visitors, and can get your audience more invested in the content your site provides.

This chapter will introduce some best practices and strategies to help you build your mailing list. It will also teach you how to build an Ajax-powered subscription system that will tie directly into a popular mailing list management Web app to help you manage your list, build email campaigns, and track the success of your messages.

Encouraging Subscriptions

There are a number of factors that can inhibit mailing list subscriptions. Keep these best practices in mind when you present your subscription form to improve your signup rate.

Earn Their Trust

When people sign up for your mailing list they place trust in you that you won't pester them with spam messages or, worse, sell their email address to those who would. People receive way too much spam email these days to voluntarily put themselves in harm's way. That's why it's imperative that you make it clear to your audience that their email address is safe with you when they subscribe to your mailing list.

To earn your audience's trust, provide the following reassurance:

- Provide a reassuring message near the email address field indicating that their email address is safe with you. See **FIGURE 8.1**.
- Let your audience know they can unsubscribe whenever they like, and provide a link to the unsubscribe page.
- Let your audience know how frequently you'll be sending them email, and stick to your word. Sending messages too often might cause a mass exodus from your mailing list, so err on the side of caution.
- Create a privacy policy page that states that you will never share your audience's email address, and their email address will be stored on a secure server.
- Never automatically sign people up for your mailing list. Let them opt in of their own accord.

FIGURE 8.1 *Reassure users that their email addresses will not be abused.*

Users are reluctant to share their email addresses, and rightly so. When you make it clear to your audience that their email addresses are safe with you, you'll have better luck getting people to subscribe. Of course, it goes without saying that the promises you make to your audience regarding your mailing list must be kept if you hope to maintain a healthy list of subscribers.

Make It Obvious

You don't want your users to overlook your signup form, so be sure to make it obvious that they have the option. Your subscription form's location and design are critical to a good signup rate. Make it one of the most prominent elements on your page in order to capture your users' attention and call them to join the mailing list with a clear heading.

Your home page is a smart place to include the form, and you'll likely get the best results if you place it in the top third of the page where it will be most visible. There's no need for blinking images or gaudy colors to capture attention. In fact, this will probably deter subscriptions, as it will look like a sleazy marketing ploy.

Learn to direct a user's attention by reading "Contrast and Meaning" by Andy Rutledge http://www.alistapart.com/articles/contrastandmeaning

Simply use the power of visual contrast to direct the user's gaze to the signup form. An accent color, prominent typography, or a unique texture will do the job without making your page look like something from the Las Vegas strip.

Make It Quick

If it looks like it will take too long to sign up for your mailing list users probably won't bother. Your mailing list should only collect information from the user that's absolutely essential in order to expedite the signup process.

The simplest subscription form would only ask for an email address. Because it takes so little time to fill out a single field and submit a form, you're likely to improve your signup rate—especially when the form is placed in a high-traffic place like the home page.

However, it can be advantageous in some situations to request more information from your users. Geographic information such as a home state or zip code or topics the user is interested in can help you send more targeted messages to segments of your mailing list. You could use this information to let people know about an event that is happening near them, or send emails that only contain information of interest to the user.

Be sure to let potential subscribers know why you are requesting this information so they know it can help improve the quality of content they'll receive. Otherwise, some might be suspicious as to why their zip code is required to receive your emails.

More verbose subscription systems like this may not comfortably fit on a home page, and might need to be placed on a page of their own. You could also take a hybrid approach, providing an email-only subscription form on the home page for speed and a more detailed subscription form on a separate page for users willing to spend a little more time in order to get more targeted messages.

The subscription system that we'll construct later in this chapter will use Ajax to store subscriptions so no page refresh is required. This will make signing up almost instantaneous.

Tell Them What To Expect and Make It Valuable

You can encourage subscriptions by simply letting your audience know what to expect in your emails. What's in it for them?

Entice subscriptions by providing content that's valuable to your audience. Content such as short articles, news, updates about new content on your site, or discounts on products you sell make it worthwhile for users to subscribe to the mailing list.

SitePoint (see **FIGURE 8.2**) does a brilliant job of providing valuable content in their email newsletters (**http://www.sitepoint.com/newsletter/**). Each newsletter contains short articles on topics relevant to their audience, along with links to related discussion threads, blog posts, and articles on their site. It works as a miniature digest of their site.

By culling a portion of their newsletter materials from their website they decrease some of the time it takes to author each message, direct loyal readers to the latest content, and make it easy for their audience to stay abreast of their offerings.

Each email message you send is an opportunity for your subscribers to become disenchanted with your mailing list. You can keep your subscribers around by making sure each message contains something of use.

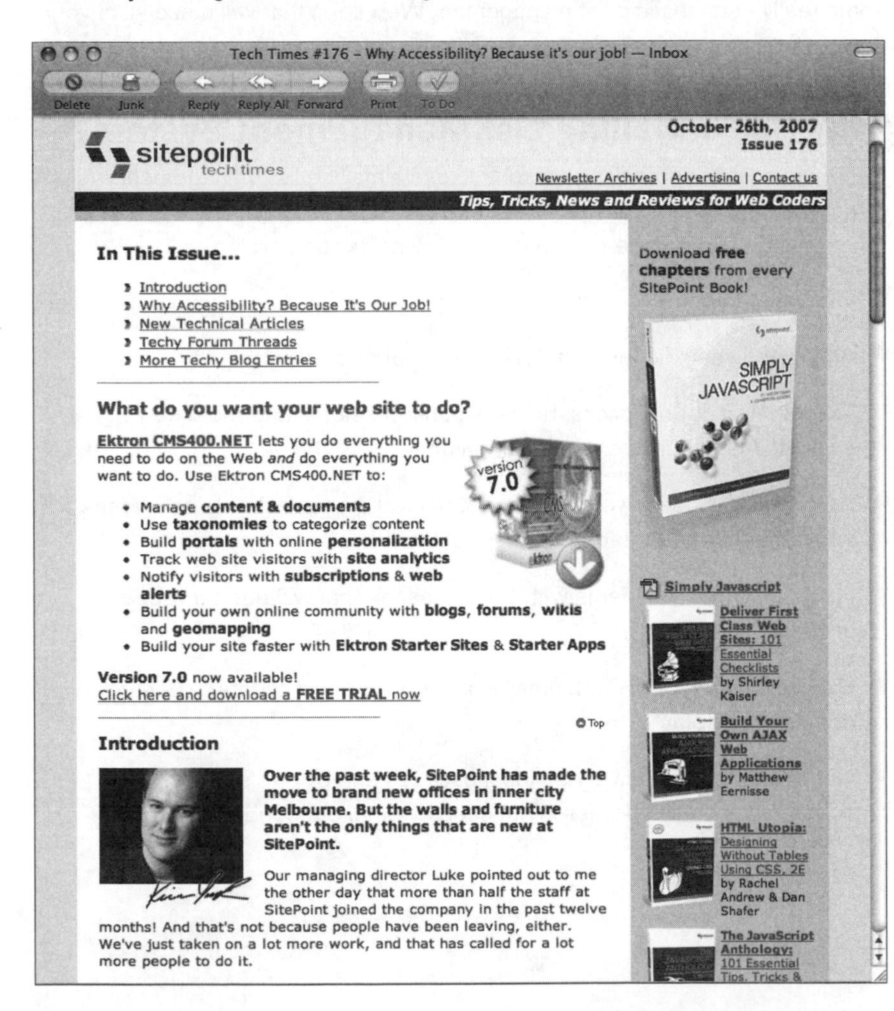

FIGURE 8.2 *SitePoint's Tech Times email newsletter always includes useful information, which keeps their audience subscribed.*

Using a Mailing List Management System

Managing a mailing list has its challenges. You'll need to store your subscribers' email addresses securely so they don't fall into the hands of spammers. You have to provide a convenient way for your audience to unsubscribe from your mailing list. And of course you'll also need to construct, send, and track your email campaigns. The biggest challenge of building your own mailing list system is handling the incremental email deliveries for large lists, and keeping your server from being blacklisted as a source of spam.

Although it would be possible to tackle these challenges and build all of this functionality from scratch, you'd be reinventing the wheel. Luckily there are some really great mailing list management Web apps that will make all of your mailing list tasks quick and easy.

Why Use a Mailing List Management System?

There are a lot of compelling reasons to use a mailing list management system rather than trying to build your own. Here's an abbreviated list of some of the functionality at your fingertips when you use an existing system:

- Secure storage of your list, which will preserve the trust of your subscribers
- Quick and easy design and development of email campaigns
- Tracks email opens, clicks, bounces, unsubscribes, and more so you can evaluate the success of each campaign to make the next one even better
- Automatically cleans your mailing list of invalid or out-of-date addresses when they're encountered
- Helps diagnose problems with your message that will get it trapped in spam filters
- Easy testing of your HTML email in all popular email clients to ensure consistent display
- Incremental email delivery sends messages one by one so each subscriber's email address is not seen by other subscribers
- Scheduled delivery

- Mailing list segmentation to communicate better with targeted portions of your list
- Can help keep your mailing list communication compliant with spam laws
- APIs make it easy to integrate mailing list management system features into your Web apps

Building your own app that does all of this is probably not how you want to spend your time. By using a mailing management system you can stay focused on building your mailing list, and staying in contact with your audience.

It's free to store your list in a mailing list management system, but sending emails to your subscribers does require payment. The prices are generally very reasonable, and usually get cheaper the more emails you send per campaign.

There are a few mailing list management Web apps to choose from, each offering many of the previously mentioned features. **TABLE 8.1** gives you a quick overview of three popular options on the market.

TABLE 8.1 Mailing List Management Systems Compared

	MailChimp	Campaign Monitor	Constant Contact
URL	http://mailchimp.com	http://campaignmonitor.com	http://constantcontact.com
Features of Note	• A/B split testing identifies most effective subject lines and design • Preview layout in all popular mail clients before sending • Create interest groups to help tailor messages to subscriber interests • Advanced campaign statistics • Automatically cleans bad email addresses from list • Template builder • Forward to friend feature can be added to your message • Spam checker identifies problems that will get your message caught in junk mail filters	• Preview layout in all popular mail clients before sending • Advanced campaign statistics • Automatically cleans bad email addresses from list • Template builder • Spam checker identifies problems that will get your message caught in junk mail filters • Forward to friend feature can be added to your message • Client report access • Display sent campaigns on your site	• Template builder • Create interest groups to help tailor messages to subscriber interests • Image hosting • Advanced campaign statistics • Automatically cleans bad email addresses from list • Forward to friend feature can be added to your message

Each of these mailing list management systems provides exceptional functionality and good pricing. All three have an API that makes creating your own subscription forms on your site easy. You could also use a subscription API to integrate mailing list subscriptions into your ecommerce checkout process or any other Web application.

Although a subscription API provides a great deal of flexibility, it's not required to receive new subscriptions. MailChimp, Campaign Monitor, and Constant Contact will host your signup forms for you if you're looking for a quick solution. The drawback of hosted forms is that the integration into your site is not quite as seamless.

You can try each system for free first before committing to one. Simply create an account and take each for a spin. You can even create a sample campaign and send it to get a sense for the workflow of each application.

Building an Ajax-Powered Subscription System

The subscription system we'll build will be flexible enough to be quickly dropped into any page on your site, and will tie directly into a mailing list management system so you can take advantage of the useful features described earlier. Though all three mailing list management systems have their merits, this system will store subscriptions using MailChimp using its handy API. It could easily be adapted to work with any mailing list management system that provides an API.

The subscription form will use Ajax to send email addresses to the server when JavaScript is supported. This eliminates the need for a page refresh, making the signup process exceptionally fast. When JavaScript isn't supported the system will still be able to store email addresses but will require a page refresh.

Before building the subscription system you'll first need to set up a free MailChimp account, and create a list to receive your subscriptions.

Monkeying Around with MailChimp

To get started using MailChimp, visit **http://mailchimp.com** and click the "Free Trial" button to set up an account. It will walk you through a brief setup process, after which you'll be sent an email with a link to activate your account.

NOTE In the back of this book you'll find a special code that will get you a discount on MailChimp's service so you can check it out without significant investment. New accounts get 30 free credits for test driving purposes.

Once your MailChimp account is active, log in and click the "Lists" tab to create your mailing list (see **FIGURE 8.3**).

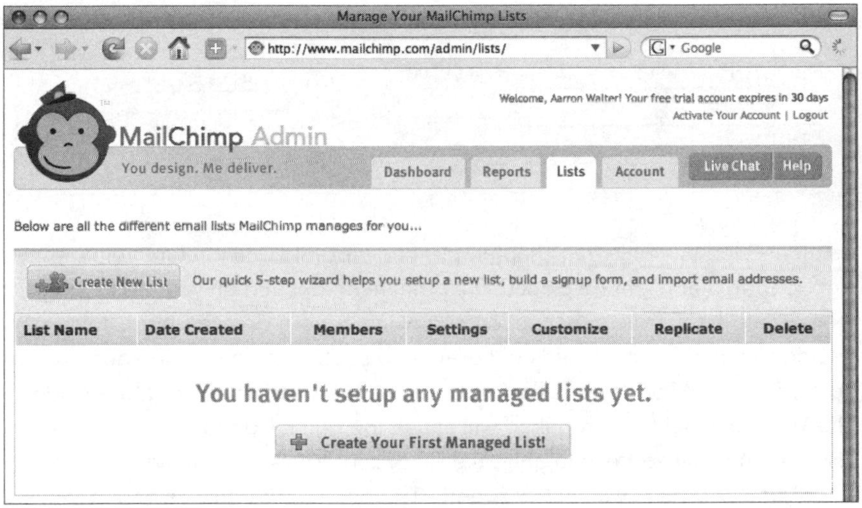

FIGURE 8.3 *In the Lists section of MailChimp, you can create as many managed mailing lists as you like.*

Setting Up Your Mailing List

The list setup process is pretty simple. You start by naming the list and providing a default reply-to email address and subject line. You can choose to receive email notifications when users subscribe and unsubscribe if you like.

Next, you'll need to provide some information about your list that will remind users why they're receiving your messages, and some contact info in case they want to get in touch. This will help make your list compliant with the United States CAN-SPAM Act, which requires you to include your contact info in every email campaign.

In the next step you can define as many or as few fields as you wish to be included in your subscription form (see **FIGURE 8.4**). This step is primarily for people who want to host their subscription form on MailChimp and just link to it from their site. We'll be building our own custom form that will connect to MailChimp using its API, and will only ask for the user's email address. This will allow the subscription form to be more seamlessly integrated into your site.

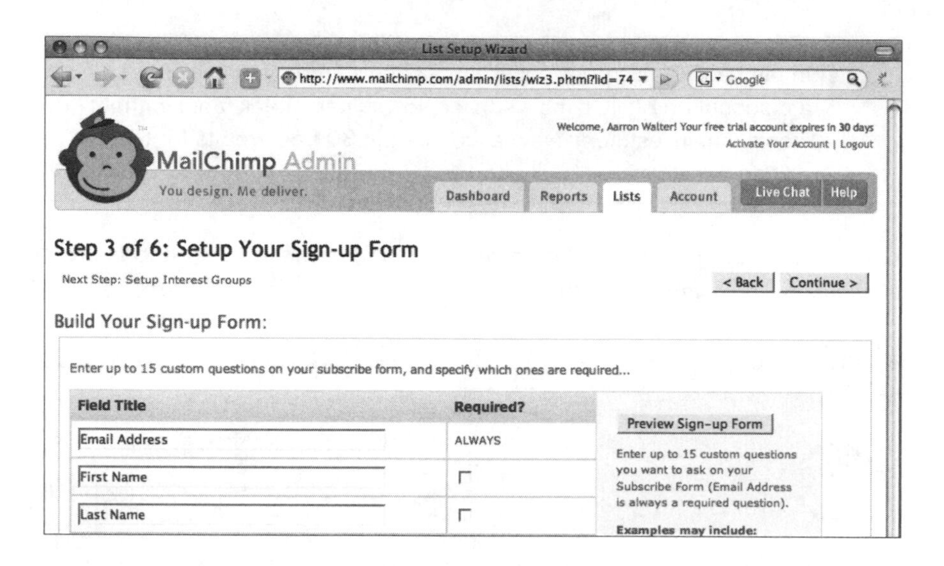

FIGURE 8.4 *You can include as many fields in your signup form as you like and even define which are required. Our signup system will only collect an email address, so don't make any additional fields required.*

As mentioned earlier in this chapter, you could create one custom quick signup form that might be placed in a prominent location on your home page, then create a separate subscription page with a more detailed form. If you decide to add additional fields to collect info such as a name and address, be sure the email address is the only one that the user is required to provide. Making additional fields required will cause the quick signup form that only asks for an email address to generate validation errors like "Name was not provided" and "Address was not provided." The point of the quick signup form is to avoid requiring the user to provide extensive information.

If you have an existing mailing list, you can import it into MailChimp as a tab-delimited text file exported from your database or an Excel spreadsheet. If you don't have an existing mailing list–which is the case with this example–you can skip this step and start from scratch.

Your list should now be set up and ready to receive subscriptions.

Sign Me Up! The Big Picture of the System

Now that your MailChimp account is all set to receive subscriptions, let's get a bird's-eye view of the Ajax subscription system. It will consist of three key components:

1. An HTML form receives the visitor's email address.
2. JavaScript will listen for the form submission, then make the Ajax call to the server with the email address.

3. PHP on the server will receive the address, check for errors, then store the address in your MailChimp account using their API. A success or error message will be sent back to the HTML page via Ajax to provide user feedback.

To simplify the Ajax coding in our system we'll use the popular JavaScript framework Prototype (**http://www.prototypejs.org/**) to listen for an email submission, and handle the Ajax messages. You'll need to download Prototype before getting started on the subscription system.

The reason that Ajax will be used to store the email address in your mailing list is that it requires no page refresh, which makes the signup process incredibly fast. The progressive enhancement concepts discussed in Chapter 7 will be employed here to make the subscription system work even when JavaScript is disabled or unsupported. When JavaScript isn't supported the page will have to refresh in order to store the address.

The folks at MailChimp have created a handy API class built with PHP that will make integrating their services into your app pretty easy. You can find the API class, code examples, and documentation of the API at **http://mailchimp.com/api/**. Be sure to download the API class before getting started.

Create a folder for the project. Inside make a folder called `js`, and another called `inc`. Place `prototype.js` downloaded earlier from **http://www.prototypejs.org/** in the `js` folder. Place the MailChimp API class called `MCAPI.class.php` in the `inc` folder.

With all the preliminary setup complete, we can begin development starting with the subscription form.

Creating the Subscription Form

The subscription form is very simple. It has just one field to receive an email address and a button to submit it. As mentioned earlier in this chapter, it's important to let potential subscribers know that you don't send spam, or share your mailing list with anyone. Also, give them a quick synopsis of what content they can expect to receive in your emails, and how often they'll be sent. **FIGURE 8.5** shows the signup form we'll be building.

When the form is submitted, user feedback will be displayed adjacent to the email address label where it will be clearly visible. Here's the HTML for the form marked up with ids so it can be easily styled with CSS and the behavior enhanced with JavaScript:

```
<p id="description">
     Monthly news and updates plus discounts on all our products.
</p>

<form id="signup" action="<?=$_SERVER['PHP_SELF']?>" method="get">
    <fieldset>
        <legend>Join Our Mailing List</legend>
        <label for="email" id="address-label">Email Address
            <span id="response">
            <? require_once('inc/store-address.php');
            if($_GET['submit']){ echo storeAddress(); }?>
            </span>
        </label>
        <input type="text" name="email" id="email" />
        <input type="image" src="i/join.jpg" name="submit"
value="Join" alt="Join" />

        <div id="no-spam">We'll never spam or give this address
away</div>
    </fieldset>
</form>
```

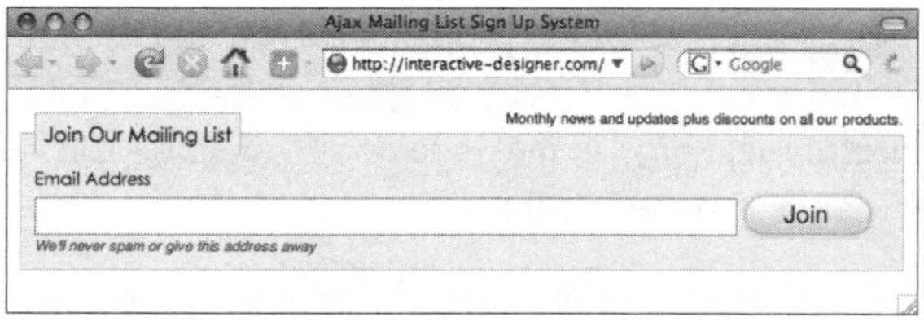

FIGURE 8.5 *The signup form asks only for an email address*

The highlighted code points out a couple areas of interest in the form. The action attribute is populated with the `$_SERVER['PHP_SELF']` superglobal variable to make this form submit to itself. By having PHP write in the name of the page rather than hard coding it, the form will work regardless of the filename of the page to which it is added. This will make it easier to drop into any project.

The second highlighted bit of code is what makes this form work when JavaScript is not supported or is disabled. Inside of the response <span> tag a PHP file that will contain a function called `storeAddress()` is included into the page. The function is then called and its results are written to the page. This file and its function don't currently exist, but we'll create it next.

The storeAddress() function will only run when the form has been submitted. Because the submit button has a name and value attribute it will automatically create a variable called $_GET['submit'] in PHP's memory when the form is submitted. By looking to see if the variable exists, PHP can determine when to store the address.

This form uses the GET method to transmit the information it gathers to the server. This is because Ajax will be sending information to the server via GET. Keeping the two consistent makes it easier for the PHP script to receive and process the form submission without having to switch between GET and POST methods depending on whether the form was submitted via Ajax or a regular page refresh submission. A consistent submission method keeps things simple.

I'll skip the CSS for the form here since the primary focus for this example is its functionality. You can download the style sheet used for this example from the companion website at **http://buildingfindablewebsites.com**.

Building the storeAddress() Function

Before starting the storeAddress() function referenced in the HTML form, create a file for it in the inc folder called store-address.php. This function will perform the following tasks:

1. Validate the email address provided, checking first for an empty submission, and then making sure it appears to be a valid email address.

2. Use the MailChimp API class to save the email address to the mailing list.

3. Return a response to the HTML form indicating an error if the address is invalid or the user is already signed up, or a success message letting the user know they should check their email for a signup confirmation.

There's one other trick to this function. If JavaScript is not supported it will still be called within the HTML page when the form is submitted, but if Ajax is used to submit the address it will need to be smart enough to run automatically.

Start the function by defining its basic structure and setting up the validation:

```
function storeAddress(){

    // Validation
    if(!$_GET['email']){ return "No email address provided"; }
```

```
    if(!preg_match("/^[_a-z0-9-]+(\.[_a-z0-9-]+)*@[a-z0-9-]+(\.[a-
z0-9-]+)*$/i", $_GET['email'])) {
        return "Email address is invalid";
    }


    // Store subscriptions in MailChimp managed list

}
```

The first part of the validation is simple. If no email address is provided then it returns a message to let the user know a problem was encountered.

The second validation conditional is a little daunting at first glance. It evaluates the email address provided to see if it looks like a real email address. The long strange string of characters is a regular expression, which was introduced in Chapter 3. In case you missed the earlier explanation, a regular expression searches strings for patterns.

Email addresses follow a very standard pattern that makes them relatively easy to recognize. They start with some letters and numbers followed by an @. More letters and numbers follow, and they wrap up with an extension like .com. This is what the regular expression is looking for, and it will return an error if it doesn't find it.

Just because the correct pattern is identified doesn't ensure that it's a valid email address. Regular expressions can't sniff out bogus email addresses, just the ones that don't match the pattern.

Now that the input has been validated, the function needs to send the email address to MailChimp to add it to the mailing list created earlier. We'll be using MailChimp's API and their PHP class to tie into the list.

Using this class requires some knowledge of object-oriented programming (OOP), which was discussed briefly in Chapter 4. OOP lets you create discrete, autonomous instances of functionality built from a reusable code block called a class. A class is sort of like the blueprint for these new instances of code—called objects. It defines what the object can do, and what properties it has.

The MailChimp API class will create an object that can perform tasks like add a subscriber or get error/success messages generated from a subscription attempt. The nice thing about using a class is you really don't have to know what's going on inside of it; you just have to know how to use it. It's a bit like driving a car. You may not know how to rebuild the transmission, but you might know how to push the gas pedal and turn the steering wheel.

Before the class can be used it needs to be included into the page. Creating new instances or objects from a class is done using the keyword `new`. When instantiating the MailChimp class you'll need to provide your username and password for your account. Replace the highlighted text in the following code example with your credentials.

```
require_once('MCAPI.class.php');
$api = new MCAPI('username','password');
```

Now that we have created a MailChimp subscriber object, we can use some of its built-in capabilities (called methods) to handle the subscription. Because MailChimp lets you create multiple mailing lists in one account you'll need to specify to which list you want to add the new subscription. The API has a handy method called `lists()` that helps you retrieve the list id for each list in your account.

In the following example, the first line of code grabs all lists, which are returned as an array. The second line stores the id of the first list–and in our case the only list–in a variable for use when storing the subscription.

```
$lists = $api->lists();
$list_id = $lists[0]['id'];
```

Now that the list id has been retrieved, the email address can be sent to MailChimp using the `listSubscribe()` method. This method requires three parameters:

1. The list id
2. The email address to be subscribed
3. Additional fields such as the subscriber's name, address, interest groups, or other information you might have gathered. Because this signup form only asks for an email address, this parameter is left blank.

To check for problems with the signup process the `listSubscribe()` method is run inside a conditional, which will return a success or error message to provide the user feedback about the process. If a problem is encountered, MailChimp will return a descriptive error message to let the user know what went wrong:

```
if($api->listSubscribe($list_id, $_GET['email'], '') === true) {
    'Success! Check your email to confirm signup.';
}else{
      // An error ocurred, return an error message
      return 'Error: ' . $api->errorMessage;
}
```

Notice that the success message tells the user to check their email to confirm the subscription. MailChimp automatically sends a confirmation message to the subscriber. This is called a double–opt in process, and it helps prevent accidental or unwanted subscriptions. You can customize the design and language of this email message in your MailChimp admin by navigating to Lists and choosing Customize Designs.

That closes out the function. There is still one small thing that needs to be added to the file outside of the function.

If you recall from the earlier description of the functionality of `storeAddress()`, I mentioned that the function should be able to run itself automatically when the address is submitted via Ajax. Although Ajax can pass information to the file, it won't be able to invoke the function without a little help.

After the function, add a very simple conditional that looks for the presence of a `GET` variable called `$_GET['ajax']`. This variable will be defined within the URL passed to the `store-address.php` page from the Ajax script we'll create next. If the variable is set, then the `storeAddress()` function will run automatically, writing out the response message to the page. The response string will be grabbed by the Ajax script and written into the HTML page inside the response <span> tag.

```
// If being called via Ajax, autorun the function
if($_GET['ajax']){ echo storeAddress(); }
```

This one extra line of code lets this script serve the progressively enhanced and JavaScript disabled state of the subscription system. Here's what the `store-address.php` file looks like when completed:

```
<?
function storeAddress(){

    // Validation
    if(!$_GET['email']){ return "No email address provided"; }

    if(!preg_match("/^[_a-z0-9-]+(\.[_a-z0-9-]+)*@[a-z0-9-]+(\.[a-
z0-9-]+)*$/i", $_GET['email'])) {
```

```
            return "Email address is invalid";
    }

        require_once('MCAPI.class.php');
        $api = new MCAPI('username','password');

        // Fetch mailing list id
        $lists = $api->lists();
        $list_id = $lists[0]['id'];

        if($api->listSubscribe($list_id, $_GET['email'], '') ===
true) {
              // It worked!
              return 'Success! Check your email to confirm signup.';
        }else{
              // An error ocurred, return an error message
              return 'Error: ' . $api->errorMessage;
    }
}

// If being called via Ajax, autorun the function
if($_GET['ajax']){ echo storeAddress(); }
?>
```

The Ajax Layer

The Ajax layer is the only remaining piece of the subscription system to be completed. It's made surprisingly simple by the Prototype JavaScript framework, which will help us attach an event to the form, and handle the communication with the server.

When JavaScript is enabled the form shouldn't actually submit because Ajax will be handling the submission process instead. Prototype will also help out by stopping the form submission event.

To start the construction of the Ajax layer, create a file called `mailing-list.js` and save it in the `js` folder.

The script begins by attaching an event to the window object that fires an initialization function when the page has loaded. The initialization function—called `init()`—attaches an event to the form listening to see if it's been submitted. When the form is submitted a function called `storeAddress()` is invoked, which will do all of the Ajax kung fu for us.

Here's what the basic setup looks like so far:

```
Event.observe(window, 'load', init, false);

function init(){
      Event.observe('signup','submit',storeAddress);
}


function storeAddress(event) {

}
```

You might be wondering why the script doesn't just skip the `init()` function and instead call `storeAddress()` directly when the window loads. Better yet, why not just skip the event listener for the window altogether and define the listener for the form immediately?

Because the browser will execute code immediately as it encounters it in a file, attaching an event to the form before the page has loaded would generate an error stating that the form doesn't exist. The browser can't attach the form event listener until the whole page has loaded.

The `init()` function makes this script scalable. It's not uncommon for modern Web pages to execute a series of JavaScript functions immediately when the page loads to set up the page's behavior. Using an initialization function allows you to run all sorts of script behaviors simultaneously when the window loads, keeping the script flexible and scalable.

The `storeAddress()` function is passed a reference to the event that triggers it via a parameter aptly named `event`. This will be used at the end of the function to disable the form submission.

The `storeAddress()` function will perform three simple tasks:

1. Update the HTML interface to let the user know their email address is being saved
2. Assemble some variables to be passed to the PHP script then do the Ajax request/response handling
3. Prevent the form from submitting and refreshing the page

Here's what's inside the function to make all this happen:

```
$('response').innerHTML = 'Adding email address...';

var pars = 'ajax=true&email=' + escape($F('email'));
var myAjax = new Ajax.Updater('response', 'inc/store-address.php',
{method: 'get', parameters: pars});

Event.stop(event); // Stop form from submitting when JS is enabled
```

Prototype has greatly simplified the tasks of this function starting with the way it accesses elements within the HTML document. Prototype lets you replace the verbose `document.getElementById('response')` with the much more succinct `$('response')`. This shorthand element access method is used to display user feedback inside `<span id="response">` within the subscription form while the Ajax communication is taking place.

The next line assembles two `GET` variables to be passed to the PHP script. The first one is the `$_GET['ajax']` variable referenced at the very end of the `store-address.php` script outside of the function. Its presence will trigger the PHP script to automatically run its function when Ajax communicates with it.

Another shorthand method is used when grabbing the email address typed into the form. The `$F('email')` shorthand function accesses the email field and is the same as `document.getElementById('email').value`. As you can see, the Prototype approach is much shorter. The special characters that might be within the address are encoded using `escape()` for safe transmission to the PHP script on the server.

Next, Prototype's `Ajax.Updater` object is used to send the variables in a query string to the PHP script. It will automatically display the response inside the `<span id="response">` tag in the form.

The very last line of the function uses Prototype's `Event.stop()` function to prevent the form from submitting. The argument within this function is the one passed earlier to the parent function `storeAddress()`.

Here's what the `mailing-list.js` file looks like when fully assembled:

```
Event.observe(window, 'load', init, false);

function init(){
    Event.observe('signup','submit',storeAddress);
}
```

```
function storeAddress(event) {
    // Update user interface
    $('response').innerHTML = 'Adding email address...';
    // Prepare query string and send AJAX request
    var pars = 'ajax=true&email=' + escape($F('email'));
    var myAjax = new Ajax.Updater('response', 'inc/store-address.
php', {method: 'get', parameters: pars});
    Event.stop(event); // Stop form from submitting when JS is
enabled
}
```

Now that the Ajax layer is complete, all that's left to finish up the subscription system is to link the form page to the external `prototype.js` and `mailing-list.js` scripts. Add the following script tags to the form page, then try it out.

```
<script type="text/javascript" src="js/prototype.js"></script>
<script type="text/javascript" src="js/mailing-list.js"></script>
```

Once you've got this subscription system up and running, you should notice that when JavaScript is supported, the Ajax layer makes the signup process almost instantaneous.

9

Putting Findability Into Practice

Now that you've got a host of findability techniques in your toolbox how will you assemble them into a cohesive strategy? By creating a prioritized list you can devise a clear path to findability bliss.

Each of the findability techniques introduced in this book addresses one or more of these primary goals:

- Help people find your website.
- Once your audience arrives, help them find what they seek on your site.
- Encourage return visits to your site.

You could certainly apply all of these techniques to every project, but one size does not fit all in the Web industry. You'll need to evaluate each project's unique goals and devise a findability game plan that will work best to reach the audience you're targeting.

Prioritizing each technique into a multi-tiered strategy will also help you remain focused on the things that will have the most significant impact on the findability of your site.

A Prioritized Approach

Since each project's scale, goals, and audience are different, your findability strategy will need to adapt accordingly. You will find there are a few findability techniques that can serve the needs of every project, while others aren't always a good fit.

It's a good idea to define a multi-tiered priority list of techniques to develop an overarching strategy to reach your target audience. Although you'll need to define a strategy that works best for your site, here's an abbreviated example of how you might define your priorities.

Priority 1

- Create well-written, original content that fills a niche and is relevant to your audience.
- Research target keywords and place them in strategic locations within your markup (keyword density should not exceed seven percent).
- Use semantic, standards compliant code.
- Meet accessibility guidelines to ensure content is legible to search engines.
- Create predictable, search engine friendly URLs.
- Create inbound links where possible and promote your site on other sites.

- Publish `robots.txt` and `sitemap.xml`, then notify major search engines of your sitemap file (see the bonus chapter entitled "Free Search Services" on the companion site **http://buildingfindablewebsites.com** for info on creating `sitemap.xml` files).
- Create custom 404 pages to get users back on track.
- Create an HTML sitemap page to help users and search engines navigate your site.
- Ensure JavaScript, and Flash content do not present roadblocks to search engine indexing.
- Diligently analyze your traffic for successes and failures (see the bonus chapter entitled "Analyzing Your Traffic" on the companion site **http://buildingfindablewebsites.com**).

Priority 2

- Add a local search engine to your site.
- Use microformats to make content such as events and contact info portable.
- Create a blog that notifies major ping services of new content.
- Syndicate content with RSS feeds where possible.
- Promote viral exchanges of your content (see the bonus chapter entitled "Viral Marketing" on the companion site **http://buildingfindablewebsites.com**).
- Optimize site performance for efficient indexing.

Priority 3

- Build and utilize a mailing list.
- Consider creating a Google AdWords campaign to create immediate traffic.
- Promote your site offline with print, television, and radio advertising (see the bonus chapter entitled "Places to Promote Your Site" on the companion site **http://buildingfindablewebsites.com**).

Discovering Problems on Your Site

After building your site to be findable, it's prudent to run a few tests to confirm it's as findable and search engine friendly as you think it is. Fortunately, there are some very helpful tools that simplify the testing process.

Sitening SEO Tools

Sitening–a search engine marketing and Internet strategy company based in Nashville, Tennessee–has a suite of powerful tools (**http://sitening.com/seo-tools/**) that can provide insight into the findability of your site. Use the SEO Analyzer tool to evaluate your search engine optimization efforts. The SEO Analyzer provides coding advice from an enlightened Web standards perspective, and displays your site in a text-only browser so you can get a sense of what search engines will see when indexing your site.

The Search Engine Ranking Page (SERP) tracker will watch all keywords you've targeted and let you know how you rank on the major search engines.

The Backlink Analyzer creates a quick view list of all sites that are currently linking to your site.

Spam Detector

As the name suggests, the spam detector (**http://tool.motoricerca.info/spam-detector/**) evaluates your site for spammy-looking techniques that could potentially cause search engines to penalize your rankings.

Semantics Extractor

The W3C has a nice semantics extractor (**http://www.w3.org/2003/12/semantic-extractor.html**) that evaluates your markup to show you how well you're communicating the information hierarchy of your page. When you run the semantics extractor you should see the keywords you're targeting and the root of your message visible in the results.

Keyword Priority and Density Evaluation

Be sure to evaluate your pages to discern their keyword density and keyword priority using the handy tools at **http://www.ranks.nl/cgi-bin/ranksnl/spider/spider.cgi**. Keyword priority should be high, but density should not exceed seven percent or it runs the risk of looking like the page has been dishonestly stuffed with keywords.

Watch Your Stats

Of course, you can also spot all sorts of problems by keeping a close eye on your statistics. Be sure to analyze your traffic stats on a regular basis so you can make immediate changes when problems are discovered.

When Will You See Results?

After investing much time and effort to make your sites more findable, you'll probably be anxious to see some results. You'll see improved traffic at different times depending on the techniques you're employing.

The time it takes to achieve top search rankings with target keywords depends on how stiff the competition is, how often people search for the target terms, and how well you've optimized your pages to highlight those terms. If you're competing against very popular sites for your keywords it could take a long time to raise your site's credibility in the eyes of the major search engines to outrank your competition.

Search engines will often index a site within approximately a week after being notified of the location of a `sitemap.xml` file. Once your site is indexed you may begin to see some referral traffic from search engines, with volume increasing over time as your ranking improves.

As your domain name ages you'll see improved rankings. Of course, more inbound links to your site from reputable sources will cause the biggest boost in your rankings and create immediate referral traffic as well.

One of the best ways to get immediate traffic results is to set up a blog, write often about topics of interest to your audience, and configure your blog software to notify all major ping services when you publish. Because search engines index blogs often, and services like Technorati (**http://technorati.com**) help users keep tabs on the blogosphere, blogging is one of the most immediate ways to reach your audience.

If your budget can accommodate, consider creating a Google AdWords (**http://adwords.google.com**) campaign after launching your site to generate immediate traffic. It's not the best fit for all situations, but for commercial websites it can jump start traffic and sales.

If you're providing exceptionally good content as Chapter 4 advises and implementing a comprehensive findability strategy, the word will get out about your site and your traffic will increase.

There's no short answer as to when you can expect to see the fruits of your findability labors. If you plan and build your sites intelligently from the start then continue to evaluate and improve their findability, you can bank on greatly improving your traffic and reaching a much larger segment of your target audience.

Final Notes: The Day Findability Saved the World

There are millions of websites vying for our attention like a cacophony of raised voices in which few are heard. If you hope to rise above the noise so your voice can be heard, you need to communicate more intelligently.

It's self-apparent that by improving findability you can make your business or your clients' businesses more successful, and you certainly can broadcast a message to a larger audience. These are the easy-to-comprehend, compelling truths of the value of findability in our projects, which can serve our immediate, individual needs.

I'd like to leave you with a story of how findability has already changed our world, and could someday do even more if we strive for distant long-term dividends as fervently as we seek the immediate short-term returns.

The Global Public Health Intelligence Network–GPHIN for short (**http://www.phac-aspc.gc.ca/media/nr-rp/2004/2004_gphin-rmispbk_e.html**), created by the Public Health Agency of Canada–monitors select areas of the Web for early signs and symptoms of dangerous epidemics that could wipe out humanity. It works like a search engine, crawling and cataloging data in order to identify signs of potential pandemics early so health authorities can quarantine and stop them from spreading.

If you've kept abreast of current events in recent years perhaps you recall the very scary news reports of the outbreak of the SARS virus (Severe Acute Respiratory Syndrome) in 2002 and 2003 in China. It was a very aggressive virus that threatened to spread across the globe and kill millions if it weren't discovered very early by GPHIN.

By crawling important sites on the Web, GPHIN was able to detect SARS *three months before* the World Health Organization announced it. The world escaped this brush with death because the early warning signs of the pandemic hidden in public content on the Web were findable by a software application. It's very unlikely that humans could have spotted the pattern of symptoms quite so fast. GPHIN's early detection led to an early response that squashed the outbreak and saved millions of lives.

Imagine how broader adoption of Web standards, microformats, and other findability techniques could dramatically improve GPHIN's ability to more intelligently index and find meaning in content published on the Web to immediately spot epidemics that threaten our survival. We empower our software to solve complex problems that are beyond our scope of vision when we publish our content using standards compliant, accessible, and findable practices.

Larry Brilliant's 2006 TED conference presentation on stopping pandemics http://www.ted.com/index.php/talks/view/id/58

GPHIN is just one of many Web crawlers that we need to communicate with more effectively. Whether we're searching for products or pandemics, findable content improves our Web user experience and our world. Although the content you're publishing might not help eradicate the next global disease, the stakes are still high for our websites.

No one publishes a website hoping to remain an unnoticed voice among the many. Obscurity won't do for our content, our clients' content, and for the future of our Web. It's time to integrate findability best practices into our project lifecycle and build all of our websites to be found.

NOTE If you'd like to continue the findability conversation, get in touch with me at **http://aarronwalter.com**.

Index

31Three, 130
301 redirects, 52–53, 58–60
404 error pages, 60–63, 76–77, 134, 144, 235

A

A List Apart
- accessibility article, 30
- "Contrast and Meaning" article, 95, 215
- CSS maps article, 33
- CSS sprites article, 74
- "Flash Embedding Cage Match" article, 203
- home page goals article, 93
- user research article, 89

A9 search standard, Amazon, 176
AarronWalter.com, 239
abbreviations, 36–37
accessibility
- guidelines, 29, 183, 206
- and images, 30–35
- standards, 5, 17
- and table-based layouts, 35
- and text transcripts, 211

accessible content, 29–30. *See also* accessibility
acronyms, 36–37
Adaptive Path, 159
Adobe, 198, 201
AdWords, Google, 104, 153, 158, 235, 237
Ajax
- catalog system, 190–197
- and Charles, 65
- and findability, 189, 198
- naming of, 159, 160
- purpose of, 159–160
- recommended book on, 181
- search system, 162
- subscription system, 220–232

Ajax Search API, Google, 159–165
algorithms, search engine, 19, 20, 47, 84, 153
All in One SEO, 147
Allsopp, John, 37, 43
AllTheWeb, 77
`alt` attribute, 5, 30
Amazon, 99, 172, 176
Ambient Findability, 2
anchor tags, 23
Andrew, Rachel, 183
animation tools, 180
Apache
- `.htaccess` files, 53, 55, 60, 66
- `mod_deflate` module, 73
- `mod_expires` module, 66
- `mod_gzip` module, 73
- `mod_headers` module, 67
- `mod_rewrite` module, 52–54, 57, 138

API keys, 160, 161, 168
APIs, 121, 159, 168, 219, 220
Application Programming Interface. *See* APIs
`array_slice( )` function, 111
articles, writing, 94–95
AskJeeves, 77
Atomz, 167–168
audio files, 180, 207–211
Authentic Jobs, 116
`author` meta tags, 26

B

Backlink Analyzer, 236
Barnett, Wyatt, 175
Bartelme Design, 45, 131
Bennett-Chamberlain, Jesse, 130
Berners-Lee, Tim, 12
.biz domain names, 51
Bjorkoy, Olav Frihagen, 82–83, 84
black hat SEO techniques, 9, 20, 133, 184
blog headlines, 126–127
blog pings, 136
Blog Search, Google, 136
blog templates, 125–126
blog tracking services, 98
blog update services, 136–137
blogging platforms, 134, 135
Bloglines, 93, 127
blogs, 124–149. *See also* WordPress
- adding OpenSearch to, 178
- adding popular posts section to, 129, 141–142
- adding recent posts section to, 129, 143–144
- analyzing traffic for, 124
- archiving options for, 127, 140
- automatic publication between, 94
- best practices for, 124–133, 134
- boosting site traffic with, 237
- comment spam in, 9, 125
- as content delivery platforms, 93–94
- creating post titles for, 126–127
- creating sense of trust in, 130
- creating sitemap for, 146
- creating your own template for, 126–127
- directing users to related posts in, 132
- duplicate content in, 132–133
- encouraging others to share posts from, 131–132, 144–145
- explaining purpose of, 130
- findability of, 134, 136
- including links in, 125, 131

including personal photo in, 130
linking to other, 125
promoting RSS feeds in, 130–131
SEO for, 125
summarizing posts in, 128, 140–141
tagging posts in, 147–149
time-consuming nature of, 94
as tool for discovering niche issues, 124
trackback feature, 94, 125
Blueprint CSS framework, 82–83, 84
BMW site, blacklisting of, 9
book reviews, 97–98
bookmark management systems, 117
bookmarklets, 117
Boulton, Mark, 82
Box.net, 117
Brachhold, Arne, 146
Brett, Matt, 130
Brilliant, Larry, 239
broken links, 60, 61
Brothercake, 183
browsers. *See also* specific browsers
adding OpenSearch to, 176–177
disabling JavaScript in, 181, 182
and Google Ajax Search API, 160–161
search features integrated into, 176
Bulletproof Ajax, 181

C

cache-control, 67, 68
caching, 64–68, 149
Campaign Monitor, 219, 220
CAN-SPAM Act, 221
<caption> tags, 36
Carr, Norm, 89
case studies, 94–95
CastingWords, 209
catalog system, 190–197
Cederholm, Dan, 63
<channel> tags, 108, 112
Charles program, 65
Chevy Tahoe user-generated ad campaign, 100
Child, Dave, 54
cite attribute, 87
clients, caching files for, 64–68
CLOSED expansion mode, 164
coding practices, CSS, 90
collapsible boxes, 185–186
color contrast checker, Snook's, 96–97
.com domains, 51
combine.php file, 73
Common Craft, 93
compressing files, 71–73
Constant Contact, 219, 220
contact information, 42–43
contact pages, 42–43
content, 80–121
accessible, 29–30. *See also* accessibility
alternatives to authoring your own, 107–121
in audio/video files, 207–211
blocking indexing of, 26–28, 133
examples of exceptional
AndyRutledge.com, 95
Blueprint CSS framework, 82–83
cartoon site, 91
e-commerce site, 80–82
Smashing Magazine, 89–90
Snook.ca, 96–97
Terra Incognita, 97–98
and findability, 80–82
funneling traffic to specific, 91–93
getting feedback on, 89
helping users find specific, 91–93
hiding, 184
indexing of duplicate, 132–133
licensing, 46, 47, 84
open *vs.* restrictive, 83–84
organizing, 7
originality of, 89–90
placing keywords in, 105–107
setting expiration date headers for, 68
stuffing with keywords, 7, 9, 184
syndicating, 93, 98
tagging, 7, 43–44
targeting keywords in, 100–105
traits of quality, 84–91
trustworthiness of, 86–88
types of, 93–100
typos/misspellings in, 87
updating, 90–91
user-generated, 98–100
using appropriate voice for, 90
content development strategies, 107–121
content karma, 82–84
Content-Language meta tags, 26
content-to-code ratio, 28
Content-Type meta tags, 26
"Contrast and Meaning" article, 95, 215
copyright meta tags, 26
copyright restrictions, 83–84
copywriters, 7
Creative Commons licensing, 46, 47, 84
Croft, Jeff, 82
CSE, Google, 153–159
CSS
and abbreviations, 37
background images, 30–31
benefits of, 28
coding practices, 90
compressing, 71–73
for expanding/collapsing content, 186
externalizing, 69, 182
folder names, 69
for hiding content, 184
for image replacement, 34
minifying, 71
navigation systems, 183
positioning, 32

and progressive enhancement, 181–182, 192
for showing microformat icons/links, 45–46
sprites technique, 74
for subscription form, 225
and Web standards, 16
CSS-based layout systems, 35
CSS Drive, 71, 72
CSS framework, Blueprint, 82–83, 84
CSS Zen Garden, 13
Custom Search Engine, Google, 153–159
Cutts, Matt, 125

D

database servers, 175
`datetime` attribute, 87
Davidson, Mike, 19, 20, 35
`<del>` tags, 87–88
Delicious
API, 121
bookmarklets, 117
browser extensions, 117
examples of RSS feed URLs, 119
link library, 119
researching keywords via, 101
RSS features, 116
sharing blog posts in, 131–132
syndicating bookmarks via, 117–118
and `<title>` tags, 22
deprecated elements, findability and, 28
`description` meta tags, 24, 25
designers, 7
Designing with Web Standards, 5, 13
Diaz, Dustin, 189
Digg, 131–132, 144–145
Dimon, Garrett, 62
directhit, 77
disabilities, accommodating users with, 29–30, 183. *See also* accessibility
`disallow` statement, 133
`display:none` property, 184
`<div>` tags, 111, 162, 185
DMXZone, 114
DOM Scripting, 69, 181
domain names
choosing/managing, 51–54
.com *vs.* other extensions, 51
including hyphens in, 51
including keywords in, 51
moving to new, 58–60
Dragon Design, 146
Dreamweaver microformats extension, 38
dropdown menu systems, 183
Duffy, Seth, 33
duplicate content, indexing of, 132–133
dynamic content, setting expiration date headers for, 68

E

E24 Transcription, 210–211
ecommerce system, 190
Edwards, Dean, 70, 71
Edwards, James, 183
`<em>` tags, 22–23
email addresses. *See also* mailing lists
collecting, 214–217
managing, 218–219
validating, 225
email newsletters, 216–217
Enablr, 209–210
error pages. *See* 404 error pages
event attachment functions, 189
EveryZing, 207–208
`expandCollapseBoxes( )` function, 186–189
expansion mode options, 164
`ExpiresDefault`, 66, 67, 68
Expression Engine, 135
Extensible Markup Language, 13. *See also* XML

F

Fahrner Image Replacement, 35
Fairbanks, Chris, 178
"fast" spider user-agent, 77
FastFind, 170–171
FeedBurner, 137, 144
FeedSmith plugin, 144
Fetch, 138
`fetch_rss( )` function, 110–111, 112
file storage site, 117
files
caching, 64–68
compressing, 71–73
managing size of, 69–71
minifying, 70
naming, 50–51
setting expiration of, 67
`FilesMatch` condition, 67–68
findability
and 301 redirects, 58–60
and 404 error pages, 60–63
and acronyms/abbreviations, 36–37
and Ajax, 189, 198
and audio/video content, 180, 207–211
of blogs, 134, 136
defined, 2
and deprecated elements, 28
developers' impact on, 3–4
and domain names, 51–54
and file/folder names, 50–51
and Flash, 180, 198–207
and frames, 28
goals, 234
honest *vs.* dishonest techniques for improving, 8–9
importance of, 238–239
iterative nature of, 6
and JavaScript, 180–198
and microformats, 37–38
and pop-up windows, 29
prioritized approach to, 234–235
retrofitting website for, 8
roadblocks, 180

server-side strategies, 50–77
tags that promote, 20–23
team members' roles in, 6–7
testing, 235–236
and URL design, 54–58
and Web project lifecycle, 2–3, 8
and Web standards, 5–6, 16–17
and website content, 80–82
FIR, 35
Firebug, 75
Firefox
and acronyms/abbreviations, 37
Firebug add-on, 75
and Google Ajax Search API, 160
integrated search feature, 176
and OpenSearch, 176
Operator add-on, 40
YSlow add-on, 75–76
Flash, 37, 180, 198–207
Flickr, 43, 116, 148
folders, naming, 50–51, 69
folksonomy, 7
`foreach` loop, 112
`<form>` tags, 156, 157
formatting tags, 28
forums, 99
frames, 28
FREETEXT, 175
FTP clients, 138
`function header( )`, 68

G

Galli, Ricardo, 149
Garrett, Jesse James, 159, 160
geo tags, 26
`GET` method, 225
GET variables, 54–57, 173–174, 178
Global Public Health Intelligence Network, 238–239
Google
accessibility guidelines, 29
Ajax Search API, 159–165
boosting page rank in, 23
canonical problem, 52–54
Custom Search Engine (CSE), 153–159
and duplicate content, 133
getting banned from, 9, 51
Image Search, 77
and keyword positioning, 25
keyword tool, 104
and link exchanges, 23
and microformats, 46
and multilingual sites, 24
search algorithm, 84
spider user-agent, 77
Google AdWords, 104, 153, 158, 235, 237
Google Analytics, 21
Google Blog Search, 136
Google Calendar, 40
Google Maps, 40, 46
Google PageRank, 51–52, 59, 106, 125
Google Reader, 93, 127
Google Sitemap Generator, 146
Google Toolbar, 52
Google Web Master tools, 54
googlebot, 77
Googlebot-Image, 77
GPHIN, 238–239
graceful degradation, 157
`GsearcherOptions( )` function, 164
`GwebSearch( )` function, 163
Gzip, 71–73, 149

H

`<h1>` tags, 17–18, 19, 105, 126
Happy Cog, 92
hCalendar microformat, 38–41, 46
hCard microformat, 39, 42–43, 46
`<head>` tags, 161, 163
heading tags, 17–18. *See also* `<h1>` tags
headlines, limiting number of characters in, 113
home page design, 91, 93
hResume microformat, 45
hReview microformat, 45, 97
`.htaccess` files, 53, 55, 60, 66
HTML
for Ajax search system, 162
converting RSS content into, 111–113
for custom search tool, 173
embedding Flash content in, 201
revamping of, 13
for Rollyo search box, 166–167
.html file extension, 51
HTTP
compression, 71
headers, 64–65
meaning of acronym, 64
monitoring program, 65
HTTP requests, reducing, 74
Huskisson, Jamie, 62
Hypertext Transfer Protocol. *See* HTTP
hyphens
in domain names, 51
in file/folder names, 50

I

icon development kit, 45
`If-Last-Modified` request header, 65
IIRF, 53
IIS, 53, 61, 138
image maps, 32–33
image replacement, 18, 33–35
images
accessibility techniques, 30–32
blinking, 215
combining in single file, 74
and file size, 69
naming folders for, 69
providing text descriptions for, 30–32
in search results, 172
in syndicated content, 98
inbound links
and blog posts, 94, 125
and Creative Commons licenses, 84

encouraging/generating, 23, 58, 82–84, 94, 124
and Google canonical problem, 52
and link libraries, 96, 121
placing keywords in labels of, 20
and search engines, 5, 198
as signals of quality, 19, 23
indexing. *See also* search engines
controlling with robots.txt, 76–77, 133
of duplicate content, 132–133
encouraging search engines to skip, 65–66
optimizing performance for efficient, 64–76
of PDF files, 169, 172
of scripted navigation systems, 181
of Word documents, 169, 172
information architects, 7, 88, 89
init( ) function, 196, 229–230
Inktomi, 77
Inman, Shaun, 128
<input> tags, 156
<ins> tags, 87–88
Internet Explorer, 37, 160, 176
Internet Information Services. *See* IIS
Internet Services Application Programming Interface, 53
Ionic's IIS Rewrite Filter, 53
ISAPI, 53
<item> tags, 108, 111

J

JavaScript
and accessibility, 37
for advanced search interface, 159
and Ajax, 159. *See also* Ajax
avoiding bloated, 69
benefits of unobtrusive, 69
compressing, 71–73
disabling in browsers, 181, 182
externalizing, 69
and findability, 180–198
handling events properly in, 189
libraries, 180, 189
minifiers, 70, 71
minifying, 70–71
navigation problems, 182–183
for progressive enhancement, 185–188
recommended book on, 181
for syndicating bookmarks, 117–118
job listing site, 116
Jordan, Miraz, 134

K

Kallestad, Steve, 71
karma, content, 82–84
KEI, 103
Keith, Jeremy, 69, 181
keyword analyzer, 106–107
keyword density, 7, 50, 106–107, 236
Keyword Effectiveness Index, 103
keyword meta tags, 24
keyword optimization, 106
keyword priority, 236
keyword research services, 101–105
keywords
in anchor tags, 23
in blog post titles, 126–127
calculating effectiveness of, 103
creating master list of, 7
including in domain names, 51
including in file/folder names, 50–51
placing, 105–107
researching/selecting, 100–105
stuffing pages with, 7, 9, 184
in <title> tags, 21–22
King, Alex, 141
Koch, Peter Paul, 69

L

lang attribute, 24–25
Langer, Maria, 134
Last.fm, 43, 115
Lawrence, John, 145
Leenheer, Niels, 72–73, 74
licensing content, 46, 47, 84
link exchanges, 23
link-farm sites, 51
link libraries, 86, 96, 117–121
link validation tool, 60
linkrolls, 117–118
links
exchanging, 23
finding/fixing broken, 60, 61
inbound. *See* inbound links
including in blogs, 125, 131
text labels for, 23
listSubscribe( ) method, 227
loadProduct( ) function, 196, 197
logo image files, 18
longdesc attribute, 31
Lycos, 77

M

Macromedia, 198
Magnolia
API, 121
bookmarklets, 117
examples of RSS feed URLs, 119–120
link library, 120
researching keywords via, 101
RSS features, 116
sharing blog posts in, 131–132
syndicating bookmarks via, 117–118
Magpie, 109, 110, 111
MailChimp, 219, 220–229
mailing list management systems, 218–220
mailing lists, 214–232
building storeAddress( ) function for, 225–229
constructing Ajax layer for, 229–232

- encouraging subscriptions to, 214–217
- managing, 218–220
- as relationship builders, 214
- setting up, 221–222
- signup forms for, 215–216, 220, 221–225
- validating email addresses for, 225–226

Marsh, Rob, 145
mashups, 159
media search tool, 207–208
Meehan, Tim, 89
meta tags, 24–26, 27
Mezzoblue, 129, 143
microformat extension, Dreamweaver, 38
microformat search engine, 45, 47, 97
microformat translation service, 40, 42
microformats, 37–47
- articles/books on, 37
- cheat sheets, 38
- defined, 37
- detecting, 40
- findability benefits of, 37–38
- for making event data portable, 38–41
- for marking up contact information, 42–43
- for marking up resumes, 45
- and search engines, 46–47
- standard icons for, 45–46
- for tagging content, 43–44
- wiki, 45
- for writing reviews, 45, 97

minifying files, 70
Mint, 21, 22
MIT open source license, 84
`mod_deflate` module, 73
`mod_expires` module, 66
`mod_gzip` module, 73
`mod_headers` module, 67
`mod_rewrite` module, 52–54, 57, 138
Moll, Cameron, 116
MooTools, 71, 180
Morville, Peter, 2
Movable Type, 135
movie rental service, 116–117
MP3 files, 207
MSN, 47
MSN Live Search, 77
msnbot, 77
multilingual websites, 24
music site, 115
MySQL, 173

N

naming files/folders, 50–51
National Federation for the Blind, 29
navigation systems, 182–183
nested tables, 20
.net domain names, 51
Net Results, 127–128
Netflix, 116–117
Netvibes, 93
newsletters, email, 216–217
niche websites, 85–86
`nofollow, noindex` meta tags, 27
`noindex, nofollow` meta tags, 27

O

object-oriented programming, 109, 226
`OnLoad( )` function, 163
OOP, 109, 226
open content, 83–84
OPEN expansion mode, 164
OpenSearch, 172, 176–178
Opera, 160
Operator Firefox add-on, 40
optimizing performance, 64–76
- caching files, 64–68
- compressing files, 71–73
- diagnosing problems, 75–76
- managing file size, 69–71
- reducing HTTP requests, 74

organic search terms, 104
originality, 89–90

P

Packer, 70, 71
page rank
- and duplicate content, 132–133
- and Google canonical problem, 52
- and link exchanges, 23
- tracking, 236

PageRank, Google, 51–52, 59, 106, 125
paid search terms, 104
pandemics, 239
`parseRSS( )` function, 109–110, 115
`parseRSS.php` file, 109, 114–115, 117
PARTIAL expansion mode, 164
PDF files, indexing, 169, 172
performance optimization, 64–76
- caching files, 64–68
- compressing files, 71–73
- diagnosing problems, 75–76
- managing files size, 69–71
- reducing HTTP requests, 74

performance problems, diagnosing, 75–76
permalinks, 138–139
Phark, 33
photo-sharing site, 116
PHP, 173, 193–195
.php file extension, 51
PHP function `header( )`, 68
PHPBB, 99
PHPDelicious, 121
Pierzchala, Stephen, 73
Pingerati.net, 47, 97
pings, blog, 136
PingShot, 137
pixel shims, 30
podcasts
- and EveryZing, 207
- and FeedBurner, 137
- on open content, 84
- providing transcripts of, 209
- on Web standards, 20

PodZinger, 207

pop-up windows, 29
Popularity Contest plugin, 141–142
Powazek, Derek, 93
privacy policies, 8, 215
Problogger, 129, 132
progressive enhancement, 181–188, 190, 201–207
project managers, 6
promotion, website, 235
Prototype
  built-in event attachment functions, 189, 229, 231
  and interactive interface design, 180
  minifying, 71
  simplifying Ajax interactions with, 191, 197, 223
Public Health Agency of Canada, 238

R

Ranks.nl keyword analyzer, 106–107
reading levels, 90
`<refresh>` meta tags, 25–26
regular expressions, 53
rel-license microformat, 46, 47
rel-tag microformat, 43–44, 147
`rel="nofollow"` attribute, 27–28
Resig, John, 189
resource websites, 86, 89, 96. *See also* link libraries
reviews
  user-authored, 99
  writing, 96–98
`<robots>` meta tags, 25, 27
`robots-nocontent` attribute, 27
`robots.txt` file, 27, 76–77, 133
Rollyo, 165–167
RSS
  aggregators, 93
  distributing content via, 98
  icons, 130–131
  introductory video on, 93
  meaning of acronym, 93
  parsing, 109–115
  syndication, 98
RSS feeds
  customizing icons for, 130–131
  promoting in blogs, 130–131
  publishing, 137
  subscribing to, 93
  tracking subscriptions to, 144
Rundle, Mike, 33
Rutledge, Andy, 95, 215

S

Safari, 160
SARS virus, 238
Scalable Inman Flash Replacement, 34
`<script>` tags, 161, 163
Scriptaculous, 180
Search Builder, Yahoo!, 168–169
search engine algorithms, 19, 20, 47, 84, 153
search engine optimization. *See* SEO
Search Engine Ranking Page tracker, 236
search engines. *See also* search systems
  and accessible content, 29
  and Ajax, 189
  and audio/video files, 180, 207
  controlling with `robots.txt`, 76–77
  and duplicate content, 132–133
  getting banned from, 9
  how they “think,” 19
  and image maps, 32–33
  and JavaScript, 180–181, 183–184
  and meta tags, 24–26, 27
  and microformat content, 46–47
  and nested tables, 20
  optimizing content delivery for, 64
  preventing content indexing by, 26–28
  and progressive enhancement, 182
  and semantic markup, 17, 28
  and table-based layouts, 35
  and update frequency, 91
  and URL design, 54–58
  and Web standards, 19–20
  what they like, 4–5
search spider user-agents, 76–77
search statistics, 152, 171
search systems, 152–178. *See also* search engines
  as alternative to navigation systems, 152
  browser-integrated, 176–178
  building custom, 173–176
  importance of, 152
  purchasing, 170–172
  using free, 153–169
search terms, organic *vs.* paid, 104
SearchEngineWatch.com, 105
Section 508 accessibility guidelines, 183
SEFFS, 207
semantic markup, 17–18, 19, 20, 28
semantics extractor, 236
SEO
  and accessibility, 29–30
  black hat techniques. *See* black hat SEO techniques
  complementary techniques, 6
  importance of, 4
  in-house *vs.* outsourcing, 8
  meaning of acronym, 2
SEO Analyzer tool, 236
SEO plugins, WordPress, 146–147
SERP tracker, 236
server-side findability strategies, 50–77
  building search-engine friendly URLs, 54–58
  choosing/managing domain names, 51–54
  controlling indexing with `robots.txt`, 76–77
  naming files, 50–51

optimizing for efficient indexing, 64–78
serving custom 404 pages, 60–63
using 301 redirects, 58–60
setExpandMode( ) function, 164
setSiteRestriction( ) function, 163
Shea, Dave, 13, 33, 74, 129, 143
Shull, Ed, 127
SIFR, 34
signup forms, mailing list, 215–216, 220, 221–225
Similar Posts plugin, 145
sitemaps, 146
Sitening, 236
SitePoint, 73, 175, 183, 217
Slurp, 77
Smashing Magazine, 89–90
Smith, Steve, 144
Snook, Jonathan, 96–97
Sociable plugin, 145
social bookmarking sites, 22, 101, 116. *See also* specific sites
social music site, 115
social news sites, 132
social tagging, 43. *See also* social bookmarking sites
Socialist plugin, 145
spam detector, 236
spam email, 214
spammers, 9, 99, 218
spider user-agents, 76–77
SQL, 174–175
SQL Server, 175
standards, Web. *See* Web standards
statistics, traffic. *See* traffic analysis tools
stats applications, 21
StephenGrote.com, 91–92
Sterns, Geoff, 201
storeAddress( ) function, 224–229, 230
strikethrough text, 87
strip_tags( ) function, 112
strlen( ) function, 113
<strong> tags, 22–23
Structured Query Language. *See* SQL
subscription APIs, 219, 220
subscription forms, mailing list, 215–216, 221–225
subscription system, Ajax-powered, 220–232
Suda, Brian, 37
summary attribute, 36
SWF files, 198, 203. *See also* Flash
SWObject, 201–206
syndicated content, 98

T

table-based layouts, 35–36
<table> tags, 36
tabular data, 35–36
tag clouds, 148–149
tagging content, 7, 43–44, 147–149
Target.com, 29
Tech Times newsletter, 217
Technorati
blog tracking service, 136, 237
and hResume microformat, 45
microformat conversion service, 40, 42
microformat search engine, 47, 97
and rel-tag microformat, 44
TED conference, 239
teomaagent1, 77
Terra Incognita, 97–98
text transcripts, 208–211
Textpattern, 135
<th> tags, 36
Threadless, 63
title attributes, 5, 36
<title> tags, 21–22
tool tips, 30
trackbacks, 94, 125
traffic analysis tools, 7, 21, 235, 236
Transcribr, 209–210
transcripts, text, 208–211
transparent GIFs, 30
truncation, 113
trustworthiness, 86–88, 130, 214–215
Type Pad, 135

U

UGC, 98–100
Ultimate Dropdown Menu, 183
underscores, in file/folder names, 50
UNIT Interactive, 95
Upcoming.org, 116
updating content, 90–91
<Url> tags, 177, 178
URLs
building search-engine friendly, 54–58
defining preferences for use of www in, 54
forcing www in, 53
general guidelines for designing, 58
with GET variables, 54–57
and Google canonical problem, 52–54
remapping permalink, 138–139
removing www from, 54
with session IDs, 54–55
usability experts, 7
user-agents, search spider, 76–77
user forums, 99
user-generated ad campaign, 100
user-generated content, 98–100
user research, 88–89

V

Van Der Sluis, Bobby, 201, 203
vBulletin, 99
video files, 180, 207–211
Vinh, Khoi, 82, 83
viral marketing, 235
VoteLinks, 45

W

W3C
- creation of, 12
- link validation tool, 60
- meaning of acronym, 12
- semantics extractor, 236
- Web Content Accessibility Guidelines, 183, 206
- and Web standards, 12

Wahler, Claus, 207
Walter, Aarron, 239
WCAG, 183, 206
Web browsers. *See* browsers
Web Content Accessibility Guidelines, 183, 206
Web pages. *See also* websites
- diagnosing performance problems of, 75–76
- evaluating keyword density in, 106–107
- moving with 301 redirects, 58–60
- signals of quality in, 19
- stuffing with keywords, 7, 9, 184

Web standards, 12–17
- benefits of, 5–6, 15–16
- and findability, 5–6, 16–17
- history of, 13
- podcasts, 20
- purpose of, 12–13
- and search engines, 19–20

Web Standards Project, 12–13
website content. *See* content
websites
- adding search to, 152. *See also* search systems
- blacklisting of, 9
- creating quality content for, 84–91
- findability of, 3–4. *See also* findability
- finding broken links in, 60
- generating traffic to, 214
- naming sections of, 7
- preventing content indexing of, 26–28
- promoting, 235
- standards-compliant, 15–16, 19–20. *See also* Web standards

white hat SEO techniques, 9, 20
white papers, 94–95
Word documents, indexing, 169, 172
WordPress, 134–149
- archiving options, 140
- caching features, 142, 149
- creating themes in, 135–136
- default installation, 134
- defining update services in, 136–137
- displaying most popular posts in, 141–142
- displaying most recent posts in, 143–144
- displaying post tags in, 148–149
- displaying related posts in, 145
- documentation, 134
- encouraging social exchanges in, 144–145
- and findability, 134
- forums, 134
- improving findability in, 136–149
- installing plugins for, 135
- and OpenSearch, 178
- popularity of, 134
- recommended book on, 134
- remapping permalink URLs in, 138–139
- and RSS feeds, 144
- SEO plugins, 146–147
- setting up, 134
- summarizing posts in, 140–141
- tagging posts in, 147–149

Wordtracker, 101–103
World Wide Web. *See* Web
World Wide Web Consortium. *See* W3C
WP-Cache, 149
WrenSoft, 171
WSFTP Pro, 138

X

Xenu, 61
xFolk, 44
XHR, 65
XHTML
- and `alt` attributes, 30
- for hiding content, 184
- *vs.* HTML, 14
- and image replacement, 33
- and keyword placement, 21
- for microformat content, 46
- and scripted style problems, 184
- for showing microformat icons/links, 45–46
- and Web standards, 13
- and WordPress, 136

XML
- and Ajax, 159
- compressing, 71–73
- and Flash, 204, 205, 206
- meaning of acronym, 13
- for setting up OpenSearch, 177
- sitemap format, 146
- and Web standards, 13

XMLHttpRequests, 65

Y

Yahoo!
- keyword research tool, 105
- and microformats, 46
- Search Builder, 168–169
- selective cloaking standard, 27
- Upcoming.org site, 116
- YSlow program, 75–76
- YUI, 180, 189

YouTube, 207
YSlow, 75–76
YUI, 180, 189

Z

Zeldman, Jeffrey, 5, 12
Zoom Search Engine, 171–172

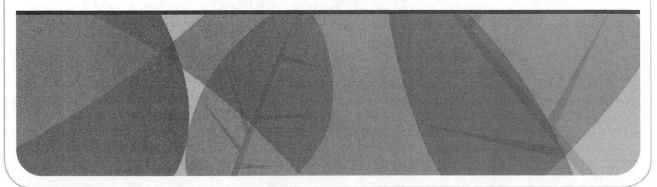

Safari
Books Online

Get free online access to this book!

And sign up for a free trial to Safari Books Online to get access to thousands more!

With the purchase of this book you have instant online, searchable access to it on Safari Books Online (for a limited time). And while you're there, be sure to check out the Safari on-demand digital library and its Free Trial Offer (a separate sign-up process)—where you can access thousands of technical and inspirational books, instructional videos, and articles from the world's leading creative professionals with a Safari Books Online subscription.

Simply visit www.peachpit.com/safarienabled and enter code GRHRYCB to try it today.